Com

Tomasz Wiśniewski

Complicite, Theatre and Aesthetics

From Scraps of Leather

Tomasz Wiśniewski
University of Gdańsk, Poland

ISBN 978-3-319-33442-4   ISBN 978-3-319-33443-1   (eBook)
DOI 10.1007/978-3-319-33443-1

Library of Congress Control Number: 2016955057

Printed on acid-free paper

This Palgrave Macmillan imprint is published by Springer Nature
The registered company is Springer International Publishing AG Switzerland

for Magda

'*And from all of this chaos, we pull out the bits of information that suit us and weave them into a story that we think makes sense.*' *(The Encounter)*[1]

[1] As spoken at *The Encounter*, Edinburgh International Festival, 10 August 2015. Quotations from Complicite with the permission of the Company.

ACKNOWLEDGEMENTS

I would like to emphasise that the book presents my own assessments and does not necessarily express the views of Complicite. The thesis proposed represents my response to the work of the Company and any shortcomings in the study are solely my responsibility.

I also wish to acknowledge the generous support I have received from members of the Company during the writing of the book. Not only have they patiently supported this research, providing indispensable archival resources, but they have also accommodated my visits to their Kentish Town office even at the most hectic of times. I owe particular gratitude to Judith Dimant for her guidance and the trust she has placed in my research. I would also like to acknowledge the invaluable help of Poppy Keeling, Claire Gilbert and other members of the office team. The book would not have been possible without consultations with long-time associates of the Company, including its co-founder Marcello Magni, as well as Clive Mendus, Jos Houben, Eric Mallett and Douglas Rintoul. I thank them all for the time they have generously given in talking with me.

***

On the academic plane, I would like to express my gratitude to Professor Andrzej Zgorzelski for the years of his scholarly guidance, for long hours of inspiring discussions, and for his critical and penetrating response to my ideas. Earlier versions of the manuscript have been read by, and discussed with, Professor Jerzy Limon, Professor Artur Blaim and Professor S.E. Gontarski: their remarks directed the argument into regions I could not initially have foreseen. I am profoundly indebted to Professor Kenneth

Pickering for his continuous advice concerning the writing process, and his extensive linguistic expertise in the final stages of writing the book. For consultations on various aspects of this book, I owe my gratitude to Professor Derek Attridge, Professor Enoch Brater, Professor Paul Allain, Professor H. Porter Abbott, Professor Bogusław Żyłko, Professor Olga Kubińska, Professor Jean Ward, Dr Stanisław Modrzewski, Jon McKenna, John Calder, David Gothard and Krzysztof Miklaszewski.

I would like to thank Professor David Malcolm, Dr Monika Szuba and the team for developing the Between.Pomiędzy Festival, which since its founding has included seminars on Complicite as well as workshops by Marcello Magni and Douglas Rintoul, and so many other inspiring events.

I am immensely grateful to Professor Andrzej Ceynowa, the Dean of the Faculty of Languages at the University of Gdańsk, who has placed great trust in my scholarship and provided generous institutional and financial support for my work. Izabela Żochowska, Hanna Niżnik and Dr Katarzyna Świerk have provided indispensable administrative support at the University of Gdańsk as did Jenny McCall, Paula Kennedy, April James and others at Palgrave Macmillan.

On a more practical plane my thanks go to Jon McKenna, Debby Mulholland, Rob Newman and Krzysztof Łoś for offering accommodation during my numerous visits to London and Amsterdam. It is impossible to enumerate all those whose professional assistance has made my research effective at institutions such as the National Theatre Archive, the V&A Theatre and Performance Archive, the British Library and the University of Gdańsk Library. Their help cannot be overestimated.

On a more personal note, this book would not have come into being without the overall help of Joanna Wiśniewska-Pickering and Simon Pickering. I would like to thank Aśka and Gavin for introducing me to the work of Complicite.

Finally, I owe so much to Magdalena Urban-Wiśniewska for her infinite patience and continuous support, and for showing me what really matters in life. Each word in this book is dedicated to her.

CONTENTS

CHAPTER 1

Introduction

This book is about a London-based company founded in 1983 as Théâtre de Complicité by Simon McBurney, Annabel Arden and Marcello Magni, following their graduation from École Internationale de Théâtre Jacques Lecoq in Paris.[1] Ever since then the company has cultivated its international character, collaborative spirit and sensitivity to aesthetic shifts and creative experimentations, but there are few other features that appear to be constant. On the contrary, Simon McBurney, who has not only been the artistic director but also 'the first among the equals' (Gross 1999), insists that there is 'no pattern, no reason' in anything he does (McCabe 2005: 20). Neither is there, he claims, a particular 'style', a single 'school' (Morris interview 36:20–36:40) nor exact 'method' (Rintoul and Freedman: 3) that determines his artistic output. Symptomatically, when asked whether he could describe his company in just one sentence, he answered: 'No, I can't' (Dickson interview 2010). It is no accident, then, that the company's materials stress that 'Complicite is a constantly evolving ensemble of performers and collaborators'. Needless to say, such a 'promotional' strategy[2] causes considerable confusion among critics and scholars who, by definition, are supposed to approach the work of a company that makes special efforts to elude definitions, classifications and typologies. As Lyn Gardner has put it, 'critics have tried and failed to define the essence of Complicite' (2002).

© The Author(s) 2016
T. Wiśniewski, *Complicite, Theatre and Aesthetics,*
DOI 10.1007/978-3-319-33443-1_1

THE NAME OF THE COMPANY

The fluctuating nature of the company's work is epitomised by its changing name.[3] Initially, a debt to the tradition of theatre in the mode of Jacques Lecoq was reflected in the use of the French language. In the early years, the company was called Théâtre de la Complicité,[4] but it was quickly shortened to Théâtre de Complicité. Marcello Magni insists Théâtre de la Complicité was an optional name in the 1980s (email correspondence), and Judith Dimant hints at archived early posters which use the name Théâtre de la Complicité (in conversation).

The name declared exposure to continental inspirations: in itself a somewhat subversive assertion for a British company. In essence, British mainstream theatre of the 1980s tended to pursue commercial entertainment that ignored continental experiments exploring the artistic autonomy of theatre. As Michael Billington observes:

> Where British theatre in previous decades had been famed for its writers, actors and directors, in the 1980s it became identified with its musicals— *Cats, Starlight Express, Les Miserables, The Phantom of the Opera, Miss Saigon.* Even the big national companies were seduced into believing that a popular musical was a passport to survival. (2013)

The founders of Théâtre de Complicité aimed to challenge the model of theatre that had been predominant in previous decades as well as the one that prevailed in the era of Margaret Thatcher. Their ethos was derived from street theatre, *commedia dell'arte* and physical improvisation rather than from the spirit of 'mainstream popular musical'. Dissatisfied with the current situation, they contested both models of theatre in Billington's description and intended to challenge the medium by non-commercial, non-institutional and experimental means. In an interview with Stephen Knapper, McBurney says: 'I began making theatre with a small group of people in the 1980s and the intention was simply to make the kind of theatre that I didn't see: a theatre which was largely a place that combined several different disciplines.' He later adds, 'since the arrival of television, theatre had become more and more an upper-middle-class activity, there was that tradition of theatre—very class-determined, literary, intellectual—and we didn't feel part of that' (2010: 235, 239). Significantly, after 30 years McBurney still perceives 'all theatre [as] an act of resistance' (São Paulo interview 2014) and lays much emphasis on the links between aesthetic and political views (see his essay 'Touching History').

In the 1990s there was a graphic simplification of the name. By omitting the French diacritics, the company turned into Theatre de Complicite, which symbolically marked its increasing assimilation into British culture. Roughly at the same time, text-based performances, including Friedrich Dürrenmatt's *The Visit* and Shakespeare's *The Tempest*, substantially upgraded the company's reputation among British critics. Symptomatically, the leading role of Simon McBurney at that time increased, and that of Annabel Arden and Marcello Magni diminished. Arden appears to have been more active within the company within the first ten years of its development than in the subsequent years.[5] Magni, being Italian, had to face some problems caused by his expressive—i.e. unmistakeably imported—style of acting and foreign accent. This turned out to be particularly problematic when playing Shakespeare for British audiences, especially those at the National Theatre in London (Magni 2015: 140). In addition to this, in 1993 Judith Dimant joined the company as 'administrator with responsibility for touring, press and marketing', becoming producer in 1996 (www.complicite.org/peopleproduction/JudithDimant). Ever since then she has been increasingly responsible for grasping 'the "organised chaos"' typical of Complicite's style of work. Dimant says: 'We all have to be very reactive. We have to build in so many contingencies. Preparing something when you don't know if it's going to have eight people or 18, is a good one' (Frizzell 2013). In the interview with Jeffreys the producer shares an anecdote about how, when she applied for the job, no one turned out to interview her at the appointed time, which made her aware of how much she was needed by the company. In the same conversation, McBurney stresses that Dimant's role in Complicite has been far more prominent than that of a usual producer. McBurney is also reported to have said: 'Working with Judith [Dimant] is one of the most critical experiences of my life. … Simply put, without Judith, there is a great deal that I have made which I could never have made had she not been there to bring some light in the darkness. She is my torch' (in Nathan 2008).

Early in the new millennium the name was shortened to Complicité, which was, perhaps, meant to underscore the fact that the company collaborated with a variety of artists who were not always rooted in theatre. At that time, the status of what had developed into an internationally recognised company that explored theatre and other forms of art was consolidated so it was no longer necessary to repeatedly define the medium in which it worked. Around the year 2008, the previously restored final French diacritic disappeared, which led to the juxtaposition of the graphic and the sonic constituents. Since then the group has used the name Complicite—pronounced by the company members in the English (as 'complicity'), rather than French ('complicité'), manner. Even this condensation was not the final shift, as in recent productions—such as *The Magic Flute* and *The Master and Margarita*—the name of director follows that of the company so that these productions are credited to 'Complicite/ Simon McBurney'. This, however, does not apply to *Lionboy* as it was not directed by Simon McBurney.[6] The production of *The Encounter*, for a change, was announced as a one-man show featuring and directed by the artistic director of Complicite (it premiered at the Edinburgh International Festival on 8 August 2015).

Declared inconsistencies in methods of creative work are paired with shifts in the company's name: for Complicite, the signified is firmly integrated with the signifier. When interviewed by Morris, McBurney stresses that, for him, 'form' and 'content' are inseparable notions. Accordingly, a general discussion of the changing name reveals many features that are key to an appreciation of the company. For example, the intriguing juxtaposition of the French origins and the context of British language/theatre/ culture suggests:

- the international (continental) character of the company,
- awareness of cognitive discrepancies imposed by various languages,
- tensions between the written and the spoken,
- complementariness of the world visions that are fostered by divergent systems of meaning creation (in this case the two natural languages).

In addition to this, the very direction of the shifts in the semantics of the name seems meaningful. The fact that it is the English language that displaces French is, perhaps, significant in the age of globalisation and digital mass communication. One may wonder whether or not the evolution of the name has been dictated by the irresistible demand for all-engrossing simplification and/or the commercial requirements of the 'artistic market'. As Dan Rebellato's book *Theatre and Globalisation* illustrates, similar doubts emerge also from other grounds, for example, when Complicite assumes the universal dimension of the Eurocentric story presented in *Mnemonic* (2009: 64–6, 74, compare Harvie 2005: 139–43).

Since the descriptive part ('Theatre de') was dropped, the company ceased to be defined solely in terms of this medium. In other words, the range of artistic activities undertaken by the ensemble broadened.

However, even though this fact is no longer declared verbally by the name, the concept of theatre remains central for Complicite. Again, the shift brings to the fore the ambiguous consequences of the strategy of simplification. On the one hand, such condensation facilitates communication of the prominent idea in the most unequivocal way, and on the other hand idiosyncratic nuances such as the legacy of the theatre pedagogy of Jacques Lecoq are less explicitly marked.

Moreover, the recent inclusion of the director's name in performances credited to 'Complicite/Simon McBurney' indicates the usual theatrical tension between collective and individual authorship. This marks an ongoing conceptual shift that has occurred in the long history of Complicite. Over the years, the pronounced collaborative nature of the creative process has shifted towards a more individualised one. Thus, the meanings suggested by 'Théâtre de Complicité' differ from those implied by 'Complicite/Simon McBurney'.

Together with the principle of inconsistency/indecisiveness/indeterminacy, we shall revisit many of these topics throughout this book. We shall consider, for example, the chronological sequence that has been established by the shifts in the name of the company (i.e. Théâtre de la Complicité → Théâtre de Complicité → Theatre de Complicite → Complicité → Complicite → Complicite/Simon McBurney) so as to reflect particular phases in its history. Even though these names are not always treated in a dogmatic way—especially when it comes to precise dating—they seem to serve well in sequencing particular phases in the evolution of the company.[7]

It is equally important to stress that the evolution of the name highlights a mechanism frequently employed by Complicite when creating meanings. The ensemble aims at immediate, direct and straightforward communication in which carefully selected fragments condense in themselves complicated networks of associations. At present it is enough to use the name 'Complicite' to refer to one particular theatre company and, simultaneously, to evoke associations that epitomise the principles of the work of the ensemble directed by Simon McBurney. In this sense, the principle of equivalent[8] is capable of inducing previously conceived—and frequently long-forgotten—meanings from the history of the company and/or from the history of the natural language (like the name of the company, the word 'complicity'—according to *OED*—came to the English language from French). For anyone aware of the derivation of 'Complicite', the very name—and its possible conflict with the name of Simon McBurney—not only enlivens connotations established by the names used in the past (i.e. the company's history) but also testifies to partial accommodation of the French tradition by the English theatre. In short, what we are dealing with here is a classic example of the intermingling of Roman Jakobson's 'projection of diachrony into synchrony' with Jacques Derrida's concept of 'différance'.

Derrida's name has been mentioned deliberately. It is striking that the company's name as it is used today is neither fully French nor exactly English. Whereas there is no final diacritic that would make it a French word, the rules of the English language are violated on the graphic plane, even when 'Complicite' is pronounced as 'complicity'.[9] By disobeying the linguistic standards of the two languages, and enlivening confrontation of the written with the spoken, the company's name echoes the prominence of the term 'complicité' for Lecoq's pedagogy and confronts it with a strong sense of its assimilation with the artistic practice of the company that is based in London. In other words, the word 'Complicite' itself makes extensive use of linguistic aporia.[10]

In his public statements, McBurney insists that the name is meant to reflect at least two issues. On the one hand, it is evidence that actors develop a strong sense of ensemble whose intensive creative engrossment guarantees the alertness of individual performers to the collaborative nature of their onstage presence. On the other hand, the name of the company hints at an unremitting bond between the ensemble (the stage) and the audience. The latter indicates that Complicite pays due respect to the 'liveness'[11] of a performance, since the performers explore the potential of the live physical presence of those involved in theatre communication.

It is striking that both of these meanings creatively develop Lecoq's understanding of 'complicité'. To illustrate this legacy, we might consider the conclusions Lecoq draws from his explorations of the strategies used by clowns:

> It is not possible to be a clown *for* an audience; you play *with* your audience. As the clown comes on stage, he establishes contact with all the people making up his audience and their reactions influence his playing. (2009: 157) [12]

By juxtaposing the prepositions 'for' and 'with', Lecoq lays emphasis on the special status of a performance as a collective process of communication that aims not only at the collaboration of those immediately involved in the onstage *semiosis* (i.e. actors)[13] but also at cultivating intimacy between two groups of interlocutors (i.e. actors and audience).[14] Unmistakeably, the sense of total theatre emerges in which liveness of theatrical communication becomes the decisive factor for the creation of meanings and aesthetic/artistic effects.[15]

Artistic Masters

Simon McBurney compares actors and directors to magpies as they steal from all possible sources (in Jeffreys' interview 2013). Indeed, throughout the years, Complicite has incorporated, either temporarily or permanently, achievements and solutions from theatre practitioners and conventions. The company has also assimilated elements derived from other artistic disciplines, such as film, visual arts, music and literature. Although in many cases this has meant internalisation of conventions whose origins cannot be ascribed to particular individuals, there are examples—such as Jacques Lecoq and John Berger—of clearly personalised influences.

While the impact of Lecoq was more explicit in the early stages of the company's evolution (from *Put It On Your Head* to *The Street of Crocodiles*), the collaboration with John Berger was particularly influential as regards the epical, narrative, visual and political dimensions of the company from *The Three Lives of Lucie Cabrol* to *Mnemonic*. This is not to imply that, in the later phase of the company's evolution, Lecoq's and Berger's influences ceased to be relevant. On the contrary, they both remain important points of reference for Complicite.

Many of their artistic solutions have been profoundly internalised, endowed with new meanings, and function within the repertoire of the company's own methods of meaning creation. Such assimilation of techniques and devices has substantially contributed to establishing the foundations for Complicite's ever-fluctuating artistic explorations. Jos Houben—one of the prominent associates of Théâtre de Complicité—describes this process when saying: 'To speak in Lecoqian terms you need something that can work as foundations—you cannot question your foundations all the time. The foundations are solid and then if you never evolve, you die very quickly' (2013: 100).

Jacques Lecoq

Complicite's direct personal involvement with Lecoq has been well documented (e.g. Lecoq 2009: ix–x, *Les deux voyages de Jacques Lecoq*, Fay Lecoq 2013, Jos Houben 2013, Murray 2013, Harvie 2005: 136) and it is generally assumed that the company's early shows are rooted in his training. Clive Mendus—a long-time associate of Complicite and graduate of Lecoq training—suggests that

> Lecoq's work is important insofar as Simon [McBurney] will use aspects of it with every company for every show, to a greater or lesser degree as seems necessary, and as it has been mediated over time by him and other practitioners who have worked with Complicite, to establish a Common Language between the company. (email correspondence)

Then, Simon Murray observes in his study that 'For Lecoq and McBurney, the business of transposing reality for theatrical purposes is a celebration of "collective imagining" and a process of harnessing some very elemental human desires and needs' (2003: 108). It is particularly fascinating to notice the way in which the pedagogy of Jacques Lecoq participates in establishing the fundamentals of the 'stage language' of Théâtre de Complicité. In terms of historical evolution, the 'stage language' was fully developed as early as 1984 with the piece *A Minute Too Late* (see Chap. 4).

Interestingly, the relationship between Lecoq and Complicite cannot be restricted to this. Certain aspects of the training re-emerge at various phases of the company's evolution, at times in most unexpected conditions. The relationship took a startling turn after the death of Lecoq. As very successful disciples of the master, associates of the company cultivated the achievements of his pedagogy. Whereas Simon McBurney actively participated in promoting it in the English-speaking world, Marcello Magni and Jos Houben became teachers in his Paris school.[16] Relations between Lecoq and Complicite represent a most noble tradition of balanced and life-long affiliation between a master and his disciples.

The issue is broadly and accurately analysed by Simon Murray in his book *Jacques Lecoq*, especially in a chapter entitled 'Traces of Jacques Lecoq: Théâtre de Complicité's *Street of Crocodiles* and the work of Mumenschanz' (2003: 95–126). Of the features recognised by Murray as crucial, the following seem to be particularly relevant for my argument:

- the formal approach to the craftsmanship of theatre artists,
- the incessant alertness to the perspective of an audience,
- the attentiveness to the processes of selection and combination of the material,
- the preoccupation with the singularity of theatrical communication,
- the attentiveness to the concept of total theatre,

- the mastery of verbal and non-verbal codes enabling precision and lucidity of theatre communication,
- the exploration of metaphoric/symbolic/poetic meanings that derive from individual and collective improvisation,
- the multiplication of codes, channels and levels of communication that are involved in creation of the stage language,
- the attention given to the verbal language as a code that emerges from silence,
- the recognition of the dichotomy juxtaposing the collective and the individual derivation of onstage communication,
- the adaptation of the carnival conventions (particularly *commedia dell'arte*) to the needs of modern theatre,
- the predilection for the irrational, archetypal and pre-linguistic modes of communication,
- investigating the sense of forgetting (i.e. the mechanisms of cultural oblivion).

The last point demands further attention. Lecoq, and in turn Complicite, examine the consequences of the rudimentary feature of theatre communication: its one-time, unrepeatable, ephemeral and transient nature. For them, the momentariness of the conceived meanings has no negative connotations, nor is it treated as an obstacle imposed on communication. On the contrary, it is the intrinsic and central feature of Lecoq's legacy to appreciate this. Even towards the end of his life, Lecoq was unwilling to allow for a more systemic record of his achievements in theatrical pedagogy.[17]

This is reflected in the ephemeral quality of the 'stage language' of Théâtre de Complicité. The systemic recording of the creative process and artistic achievements, even if somehow visible in the present enterprise of the company, was certainly not considered important in its early shows. Given the fluctuations characterising improvised performances, we may allow ourselves some frustration about the number of meanings that passed and will remain forever inaccessible.

JOHN BERGER

Complicite's associations with John Berger, although later than those with Lecoq, are equally dynamic. Their cooperation has resulted in:

- the theatrical adaptation of the long-short story *The Three Lives of Lucie Cabrol,*
- the radio adaptation of the novel *To the Wedding,*
- the conception of two devised pieces—*A Vertical Line* and *Mnemonic,*
- consultancy on numerous other projects.[18]

As the British Library archives demonstrate, over the years the correspondence between Berger and McBurney contributed to the elucidation of the aesthetic and socio-political views of the latter (Overton 2012). It is also worth remembering that certain episodes in the writings of Berger refer to Simon McBurney. At times these are rather personal passages. For example, in 'Le Pont d'Arc'—the sixth story of *Here Is Where We Meet*—Berger writes:

> I watch the birds upstream as they dive across the silver surface. Earlier this morning I went to pray for Anne in the church under the limestone cliffs. She is the mother of my friend Simon and is dying in her house with a garden in Cambridge. If I could, I would have sent her the sound of the Ardèche with its unwavering yet imprecise promise. (Berger 2005: 129)

In fact, the narrative is about the Chauvet cave where 'the oldest known rock painting in the world' was rediscovered and which in 1994 inspired *A Vertical Line*, an installation in which Berger collaborated with Complicite.

QUESTIONING LOGO-CENTRISM

Distinct as they are, Lecoq and Berger have epitomised the radical restlessness and unpredictability of adventurous lifestyles. They met but never worked together (Fay Lecoq in conversation), yet they shared not only an appreciation of radical independence but also a subversive disrespect for mainstream institutional authorities and the fossilised cultural establishment, which may be best illustrated by Berger's donation to the Black Panthers from the funds provided by the Booker Prize in 1972.[19] In addition to this, each of them collaborated in a number of styles, genres and media with a variety of artists from several parts of the globe, and this reveals their liberal, cosmopolitan and collaborative nature. They settled in France: Lecoq in metropolitan Paris and Berger in a small village in Provence. For the former, the choice seems rather straightforward as it reflects the cosmopolitan and artistic aspirations of the Frenchman.

For the English-born Berger, the decision to live in rural France meant assuming the role of an outsider. This is reflected, for example, in his English-language narratives on life in rural France, which aspire to be European in scope (e.g. *Pig Earth*).

These parallels are reflected in the worldview of Simon McBurney and the aesthetics of Complicite. Furthermore, Lecoq and Berger—and McBurney/Complicite—reveal a similar attitude to the tradition of Western (Judeo-Christian) logo-centrism. They all question, in their own ways, the primacy of the natural language[20] over non-verbal codes of communication, and are apprehensive about written discourse. Theirs is an artistic pursuit of the issue verbalised in *Lessons of the Masters* by George Steiner:

> Before writing, during the history of writing and in challenge to it, the spoken word is integral to the act of teaching. The Master *speaks* to the disciple. From Plato to Wittgenstein, the ideal of lived truth is one of orality, of face-to-face address and response. To many eminent teachers and thinkers, the setting down of their lessons in the mute immobility of a script is an inevitable falsification and betrayal. (2003: 8)

Throughout his professional career, Lecoq explored the semantic capacities of 'movement and gesture', and the artistic potential of 'the poetic body' in theatre. The fact that he was a man of theatrical pedagogy, with no literary aspirations, led to his anecdotal refusal to put his concepts in a published form. His reluctance to allow publication resulted from Lecoq's axiomatic belief that written communication deprives theatrical practice of its rudimental features. In 'Translator's Preface' to *Theatre of Movement and Gesture*, David Bradby formulates the matter in the following way:

> Lecoq was always acutely conscious of the limitations of language: in his writing one can sense the impatience of a man who had a marvellous physical expressivity at his command, and who feels constrained by the limitations of print. His style is elliptical, poetic, and occasionally difficult to follow, but not because of indulgence in technical jargon: his hallmark is the flash of imaginative insight. He enjoys raising a wealth of interesting ideas, and rather than exhausting any one of them, he leaves it to his readers to pursue them at will. (in Lecoq 2006: x)

Berger approaches the issue from a different angle. Paradoxically for a writer, he assumes the primacy of the visual mode of communication over

the verbal one, and this, in practice, leads him to be responsive to painting, film and various forms of visual arts. Besides, he has frequently collaborated with those whose expertise in these fields has made him trust them. The opening of his *The Ways of Seeing* concisely summarises Berger's views on the constrictions of the available means of communication:

> **Seeing comes before words.** The child looks and recognizes before it can speak. ... But there is also another sense in which seeing comes before words. It is seeing which establishes our place in the surrounding world; we explain that world with words, but words can never undo the fact that we are surrounded by it. The relation between what we see and what we know is never settled. (2008: 7, emphasis added)

Not only are the visual and the verbal associated in this passage with the developing perspective of an infant, but it also underlines the prominence of the cognitive discrepancy between the sense of seeing, means of perception and the surrounding world.

The impact of Berger's scepticism regarding dogmatic logo-centrism on McBurney may be best illustrated by a comparison between the imagery used by Berger with that which appears in a short essay, 'Here', which was published by McBurney in the programme to *Endgame*. The quotation below comprises the compositional framework of the essay (i.e. its beginning and its ending):

> My daughter is in the bath. She is a few months old. She has no language yet. When she looks at her octopus she smiles. She does not know what it is, she has no name for it but she recognises it. She does not have a name for me either, but she roars with laughter when she sees me. **Seeing comes before words.** I look at her. I watch her looking. There is only the present in her eyes. No past and no future. And I wonder as I look at her if somehow the meaning we gain in language is the beginning of a constriction in what we see.
>
> ...
>
> My daughter splashes water on to me. I am not paying attention. I am thinking of tomorrow's rehearsals. But she is here. Now. And that is what I need to be tomorrow. For in *Endgame* the only answer to 'Where are we?' is... here. ((McBurney 2009: 14, 15—unnumbered, emphasis added)[21]

In 'Here', McBurney assumes the role of a father. His unnamed infant daughter offers him a natural way of overcoming the constrictions imposed by the schemes of natural/verbal language. The narrator assumes she experiences the world solely through her senses. As we will see in Chap. 2, in adult life similar states are seen as rare moments of epiphany and such moments frequently happen to interlocutors of theatre communication. Typically, McBurney not only intermingles internalised concepts of Berger with autobiographical observations but also combines concrete and personal imagery with abstract meanings that are endowed with universal (archetypal present time) or meta-theatrical (infancy as a desired perspective for a theatre-maker) connotations.

We can see then that the anti-logocentric tendency, which may initially seem a mere appropriation of the most fashionable features of contemporary theatre, conveys original meanings that are deeply rooted in Lecoq and Berger. These are intricate diachronic (Lecoq) and inter-media (Berger) processes, rather than purely synchronic pursuits of fashion, which are decisive for the specificity of the ways in which McBurney and his company challenge assumptions of logo-centrism.[22] Thus, a discussion of many typical features of (contemporary) theatre frequently turns into an analysis of how a convention is rendered less automatic through the peculiarities of Complicite's aesthetics.

The Mind and the Body

There is one more general point that needs to be mentioned when speaking about the influence of Lecoq and Berger on Complicite. McBurney's insistent preoccupation with the cognitive discrepancy between various kinds of perception of the surrounding world (e.g. verbal and non-verbal) derives from the common-sense practice of his masters rather than from erudite intellectual debate fostered by all sorts of philosophers, linguists and philologists. The authority of Lecoq and Berger takes priority over Kant, Quine, Ingarden, Derrida and the like. According to McCabe, 'When [Simon McBurney] is working on a show, he never brings a theoretical apparatus along with him' (2005: 18). This is another lesson McBurney takes from Lecoq and Berger: personal contact, real-life experience and common sense—rather than institutionally (academically) approved elucidations—are decisive for gathering knowledge.

Simon Murray finds reasons for the rejection of Lecoq's practice by contemporary French intellectuals in his uncompromising insistence on what were habitually seen as 'anti-intellectual' attitudes. Murray writes:

Perhaps the most interesting element of this debate is that it reveals a way of thinking about the intellect which is predicated upon an assumption that separates mind from body, thinking from doing and feeling from movement. If Lecoq enjoined his students to learn through action, the senses and somatic experiences, rather than through talk and reading books, this does not make him 'anti-intellectual.' Rather, it suggests a perspective which proposes that learning can only ever be successful if it works on the assumption of an integrated mind-body, or indeed a human species where mind and body are but one. (2003: 57)

There certainly is a parallel 'anti-intellectual' tendency in Complicite. In *Mnemonic*, the prestige of scientific knowledge is subverted with a parody of an academic conference (scene 34), and *A Disappearing Number* mocks academic stereotypes when an Indian cleaner corrects Ramanujan's equation (scene 4). One may perhaps go even further and postulate that the attitude is rooted in the Doctore from *commedia dell'arte*. As for Lecoq, for Complicite, knowledge is not necessarily the preserve of either institutional authorisation or professional appointment.

Other Influences

If Lecoq and Berger are unquestionably the main points of reference for the aesthetics of Complicite, there is a whole range of individuals and conventions that should be mentioned, when placing the company in a broader context. Concise and incomplete as it is, the following enumeration attempts to indicate at least some directions that deserve further scrutiny.

To begin with, Peter Brook's concept of the devised theatre and the primacy given to 'the empty space' over all other means of theatre communication have obviously been influential in developing Complicite's style of creative work. The company cultivates—in its original ways—the very idea and techniques that were developed by Brook. For example, Brook's international aspirations and his merging of English-speaking theatre with continental and global stage practice are certainly reflected in Complicite's output. The relation is reciprocal as, in his recent productions (e.g. *The Magic Flute*, *Fragments* and *The Valley of Astonishment*), Brook involves long-time collaborators of Complicite such as Marcello Magni, Kathryn Hunter and Jos Houben. Moreover, certain parallels in the selection of material for performances by Brook and Complicite may be observed (e.g. *The Magic Flute* and Samuel Beckett).[23] Finally, McBurney's comments in Kustow's biography of Peter Brook are very informative.

Next, Bertolt Brecht's epic theatre has been referred to, not only in the stage adaptation of his *The Caucasian Chalk Circle*, but also in the 'Prologue' to the 2005 production of *A Minute Too Late*. Jos Houben mentions the role of the alienation effect in the piece. The features of 'epic theatre' are substantial in many of Complicite's performances, as are echoes of Brecht's ideological and political views. Apart from *The Caucasian Chalk Circle*, this is most visible in *The Three Lives of Lucie Cabrol* and *Light*. Besides, a very clear visual allusion to Brecht occurs whenever a specific lighting effect is used, as happens, for example, in *The Chairs* (3:20–3:36).

Additionally, Tadeusz Kantor's 'theatre of the dead' provides particular theatre devices, such as the image of the dead class, and that of books as flying birds, the procession of the dead, mannequins, the chorus of the dead, and the props such as a picture frame and an umbrella. Although Kantor's solutions were most explicitly hinted at in *The Street of Crocodiles*,[24] some of them were assimilated and further developed in later plays. In *The Three Lives of Lucie Cabrol* there appears the chorus of the dead, and in Part Two the theatrical communication reflects Kantor's confrontation of the stage of the dead with the living audience. In *Mnemonic*, Simon/Director/Virgil remotely reflects Kantor's stage presence in spectacles he directed.[25]

Finally, David Gothard, who directed the Riverside Studios in London in the early 1980s and observed some the early work of Théâtre de Complicité, suggests that, at the time, one could recognise McBurney's interest in Shuji Terayama (email correspondence). Indeed, McBurney comments on this fascination in the short essay 'Edge of the Seat': 'At the end of the 1970s a very influential production for me was directed by a Japanese man called Shuji Terayama. ... This play [Jonathan Swift's *Directions to Servants*] metamorphosed at the end of the show in one incredible moment when they were no longer able to be either masters or servants, and all hierarchy broke down; they were changing roles so fast it was impossible to tell who was being who.' McBurney then contemplates the incredible visual power of the ending, when a single light source depicted 'bodies moving' beneath as one mass (2011).

The broad range of texts that inspired the productions of Complicite proves the eclectic interests of the company. They include plays, poems, narratives, essays and memoirs originally written in English, Italian, German, French, Russian, Polish, Swedish and Japanese. Their authors range from the Renaissance (Ruzzante, William Shakespeare) and modernist playwrights (Bertolt Brecht, Samuel Beckett, Eugene Ionesco,

Friedrich Dürrenmatt) through the futurist poet (Daniil Kharms), to modernist (Mikhail Bulgakov, Bruno Schulz, Jun'ichiro Tanizaki) and contemporary (Haruki Murakami, J.M. Coetzee, Torgny Lindgren, John Berger and Zizou Corder) fiction writers. Other texts include essays by Jun'ichiro Tanizaki, a book by Petru Popescu, letters by Bruno Schulz and memoirs by Konrad Spindler, Rebecca West and G.H. Hardy. In addition to this, books frequently appear as significant props (e.g. *The Street of Crocodiles*, *The Elephant Vanishes* and *A Disappearing Number*) and/or large-scale visual projections (e.g. *A Dog's Heart* and *The Master and Margarita*), and the action of reading is one of frequently repeated onstage events (e.g. *The Street of Crocodiles*, *The Elephant Vanishes* and *Shun-kin*).

The scope of inspirations is accurately summarised by David Williams in his entry on Simon McBurney in *Fifty Key Theatre Directors*. Williams observes that Complicite '[s]uccessfully navigat[es] the apparent divide between avant-garde experiment and a popular mainstream' (2005: 247) and mentions the importance of street theatre, stand-up, choreographic and physical theatre practices as well as the impact of Monika Pagueux and Gesamtkunstwerk.[26] He then concludes that

> [a]esthetically and dramaturgically, McBurney is no less catholic in his sources for stimulus, drawing on aspects of Brook, Meyerhold, Brecht and Kantor, as well as the neo-expressionist dance-theatre of Pina Bausch and Josef Nadj, the transformative manipulations of object-theatre and puppetry, the spatio-temporal polyrhythms and mobilities of film languages, and the critical intelligence of John Berger's fiction, to create something unique in contemporary popular theatre. (249)

THE COMMUNAL AND THE PERSONAL

The above should not, however, lead us to the conclusion that Complicite prioritises the collective aspect of theatrical *semiosis* over the 'singularity' of profoundly personal involvement. On the contrary, the paradox of integrating the communal with the individual seems to be at the core of most of the activities that have been undertaken by the company. McBurney's debt to the concept of total theatre is paired with his obsessive insistence on the particular and the individual. A sense of integration of these seemingly contradictory views may be well illustrated by two quotations from his interview with Tom Morris. At one point McBurney reveals his awareness of the dangers of generalisation ('Because everything is significant, nothing can be generalised' [18:30]) so as to explicitly pronounce—at another point—his fascination with the concept of total theatre ('Everything you see, every single moment is significant. What we often forget about the theatre [is that] the audience sees everything, all the time' [19:35]). Contradictory as these two statements are, they configure the main preoccupation of McBurney's artistic work: universality that coincides with the particular.

In spite of its paradoxical nature, the combination of the collective and the individual is decisive for the 'singularity of theatre communication' as modelled by Complicite. The simultaneity of the experience of being an individual (an actor/spectator) and the experience of being a member of a group (ensemble/audience) is meant to be accompanied—it seems to me—by an awareness of this dichotomy. Analysis of the aesthetic consequences of this rudimentary observation is one of important aspects of my further argument.

The Sense of Unknowing

The metaphor of 'scraps of leather', which appears in the subtitle of this book, reveals an important aspect of the aesthetics of Complicite. Rooted in *Mnemonic*, 'scraps of leather' depict random, marginal and fragmented items that were found near the body of the 'Iceman' found in the Ötztaler Alps, and later became a significant part of the investigation that aimed to model a picture of the life of the Neolithic man. The very phrase 'scraps of leather' was adapted by the company from the English translation of Konrad Spindler's *The Man in the Ice*, a written account by the Austrian scholar who investigated the corpse immediately after its recovery from a glacier. Published in English in 1994, the book was the main textual inspiration for the performance.

As the subject of numerous archaeological procedures, 'scraps of leather' serve well to describe processes that are similar to those involved in theatre studies. What is analysed is not the 'living body' of a performance itself but remnants that survived and have been preserved afterwards. These may include memories, recordings, photographs, rehearsal notes, diaries, production materials, interviews and other such sources. The range and quality of such 'scraps of leather' are as pivotal for theatre investigation as the awareness of the vastness of the material which has not survived. Both in archaeology and in theatre studies, the sense of unknowing cannot be underestimated.[27]

Such a perspective substantially enhances the role of the investigator—the one who proposes the model of relations that are reconstructed from 'scraps of leather'—and the tools that are used for this purpose. Thus, the human component of modelling procedures increases and strengthens its singular character: when following an argument, it is equally vital to be aware of the material which is analysed, the research perspective which is proposed, and the tools which are used. Interestingly, *Mnemonic* seems to reveal Complicite's awareness of all these, otherwise strictly scholarly, issues.

SINGULARITY OF THEATRE COMMUNICATION

The notion of 'singularity of theatre communication' has been developed from Derek Attridge, whose 'singularity of literature' is meant to contrast 'mechanical/instrumental' and 'creative/responsible' types of reading.[28] Attridge concentrates on 'response to singularity' of an artistic work, a response that is 'open to otherness', vulnerable to 'alterity' and exposed to 'the unknown' (2004: 80–2). Making it clear that his proposal—deprived of any psychological ambitions—operates in the domain of structural relations, Attridge insists that he is speaking about 'a disposition, a habit, a way of being into the world of words' (130) rather than anything else.

These final words reveal the dangers of transposing a concept originating in one discipline to the domain of another.[29] In theatre studies we should speak about 'a way of being into the world of multigeneous signs' rather than 'words', since 'words' are just one kind of sign functioning among others (i.e. the verbal vs the visual/aural and so on). In fact, Attridge takes into consideration a more general context of his proposal when he writes: 'I hope [the book] will be read with profit by some whose particular interest is in an art form other than literature' (3).

Throughout *The Singularity of Literature*, Attridge defines the concept of 'singularity' in several ways out of which the following seem the most relevant to our consideration:

> The event of singularity ... takes place in reception: it does not occur outside the responses of those who encounter and thereby constitute it. (64)
>
> [The] singularity [of the literary work], each time it is read, lies in its performance (in performing and being performed), and although, as we have seen, that singularity can only be apprehended as it turns into, and by virtue of, generality, it is reborn as a new singularity with each new performance. (106)

The experience of singularity involves an apprehension of *otherness*, registered in the event of its apprehension, that is to say, in the mental and emotional opening that it produces. Singularity is ... also inseparable from *inventiveness*: the experience that I am describing involves an appreciation, a living-through, of the invention that makes the work not just different but a creative re-imagination of cultural materials. ... Singularity arises from the work's constitution *as a set of active relations*, put in play in the reading, that never settle into a fixed configuration. (67–8)

For obvious reasons, Attridge's metaphor of reading-as-performance ceases to be valid in the context of theatre studies. Unlike in Attridge's literature-based model, singularity in theatre comprises physical material presence (liveness) of all subjects that are involved in the communicative process, at a given place and time of theatre communication. This is to say that innovative creation on the part of an ensemble is simultaneous with the creative response of an audience. By definition, the internal relations within the triad (inventive creation → the event of performance → creative response) vary from one night to another. Moreover, unlike the solitary experience of otherness while reading, the experience of theatrical singularity not only involves material, if transient, encounter with the 'otherness', but also encompasses the paradoxical experience of being in the company—and lonely—at the very same time.

Bearing in mind the introductory discussion emerging from the analysis of the name of the company, I suggest that features that appear to be decisive for the particularity of the theatre medium in general have been at the centre of Complicite's artistic explorations. This is to say that the aesthetics of the company are constructed in accordance with the rules that are intrinsic to the medium of theatre. To make matters even more complicated, by employing a host of theatrical conventions, the singularity of the aesthetics of Complicite is grounded in the company's innovative response to the theatre medium and other materials used in their creative work. All in all, the *oeuvre* of Complicite explores auto-referential meanings that aim at defining the company's understanding of theatre. Therefore, when analysing the singularity of Complicite's aesthetics, I will be frequently pursuing their understanding of the theatre medium as such.

The main parallel between the model of communication proposed by Attridge and that operative in Complicite emerges from their 'ethically responsible' treatment of all those who are involved in artistic communication (again I [mis-]employ Attridge's terminology). Diverse as they are, the meanings of the word 'complicite' and that of the term 'singularity' lay equal emphasis on a profoundly personal contact between individuals and/or collectives that are involved in communicative processes. Artistic, aesthetic and ethical risks are undertaken both by those who create and those who creatively respond to the event of their 'performance'.

Attridge's model is additionally attractive because it introduces the concept of 'idioculture' understood as 'a complex matrix of habits, cognitive models, representations, beliefs, expectations, prejudices, and preferences that operate intellectually, emotionally, and physically' as 'a changing array of interlocking, overlapping, and often contradictory cultural systems' (21). Obviously the response to the singularity of the aesthetics of Complicite proposed in this book is to a large extent determined by *my* scholarly experience and *my* academic background. A degree of cultural distance (50–3) between the research material (i.e. the *oeuvre* of Complicite) and the researcher (i.e. myself) enhances the singularity of the aesthetic experience described in this book. My analysis of some aspects of the company's aesthetics (e.g. traces of Beckett, Schulz, the textual tissue) and avoidance of others (e.g. the verbal tissue of the Japanese plays) has been conditioned by my academic standpoint, or—in other words—my 'idioculture'.

The implications of Attridge's conclusion to his chapter entitled 'Singularity' seem particularly valid at this point:

> The experience of intimacy that we sometimes have in reading a work for the first time … is not a sign that it lacks singularity, inventiveness, and alterity. On the contrary, a sense that the work speaks to my inmost, perhaps secret, being, that it utters thoughts I have long nurtured but never had the power to express, is likely to be an effect not so much of its confirming already distinct and fully configured ideas and preferences but rather of its tapping into deeply rooted elements of my idioculture, precipitating and crystallising them, bringing some obscured perceptions out of the shadows while discarding others. The singularity of the work thus speaks to my own singularity. (78)

According to Attridge, 'authorial signature' necessitates 'reader's countersignature'[30] so as to accentuate the unrepeatable and irreducible specificity of the intimate encounter of two individuals involved in artistic communication. By 'countersigning'—i.e. creatively responding to the authorial proposal—the addressee completes the process that was initiated by the writer and thus confirms its artistic status. The degree of responsibility given to the addressee in such a model endows his/her proceedings with an ethical dimension. Unlike many scholars today, Attridge insists on the necessity of the 'responsible response' to a piece of art and thus cultivates, in innovative and original ways, the tradition of humanistic approach to communication.[31]

SCRAPS OF LEATHER, OR THE RESEARCH MATERIAL

My approach is grounded in an 'archaeological' effort to reconstruct the aesthetics of the company 'from scraps of leather', such as recordings, recollections, archives, texts and other available sources. I propose to divide them into four groups.

The first group consists of the performances I have attended (*The Elephant Vanishes, A Disappearing Number, Shun-kin, Endgame, A Dog's Heart, The Magic Flute, The Master and Margarita, Lionboy* and *The Encounter*), together with available archival materials on these and other performances. I am fully aware of the limitations the latter sources impose: transience of theatre experience and exclusion of liveness in recordings being the most obvious. For this reason, it is important to take into consideration the archival and/or documentary—rather than artistic—status of materials such as DVD/video recordings, unpublished manuscripts, research and development materials, notes, stills, photographs and so on. Notwithstanding their importance, they cannot be mistaken for the 'real thing', which is a theatre performance itself.

The second group of sources consists of the six printed plays and three radio plays that have been published by the company.[32] It is noteworthy that the print publications include some textual variants, as is the case with *The Three Lives of Lucie Cabrol* (1995, 2003), *The Street of Crocodiles* (1999, 2003) and *Mnemonic* (1999, 2001, 2003). Still, *Light* (2000), *A Disappearing Number* (2008) and *Lionboy* (2014) were published just in one version (though unpublished variants of the scripts of *A Disappearing Number* abound). The radio plays produced by Complicite—*To the Wedding* (1997), *Mnemonic* (2001) and *A Disappearing Number* (2008)—constitute a significant point of reference, as do visual (e.g. photographs and recordings) and textual (e.g. notes, essays and manuscripts) sources available in libraries and archives.

The third group of research materials consists of the whole range of public statements by artists associated with Complicite. For obvious reasons, those credited to Simon McBurney play a central role. These sources include filmed and printed interviews, published theatre programmes, the album *Complicite. Twenty One Years*, the visual essay *Complicite. Rehearsal Notes*, educational packs, film trailers, showreels, social media, the website and others. Directed at those who are interested in the company, they shape its authorised public image and will be considered primarily in this role. This group of sources is complemented by interviews conducted by me with the associates of the company (Marcello Magni, Judith Dimant, Poppy Keeling, Douglas Rintoul, Eric Mallett, Clive Mendus and Jos Houben), and theatre laboratories/workshops by Magni and Rintoul.

Finally, the collection of Simon McBurney's essays *Who You Hear It from* is given a slightly different status. As we shall see in Chap. 2, the collection is as autobiographical as it is auto-referential. While it reveals strong features of a literary work, the volume provides important themes and motifs, and suggests artistic principles employed by the company. Treated as an incidental 'manifesto', *Who You Hear It from* provides technical and thematic hints that represent Simon McBurney's artistic signature.

THE TOOLS

When analysing the aesthetics of Complicite, I have made extensive use of interpretative devices that originate in the Tartu-Moscow School of semiotics and the tradition of Eastern European scholarship that is grounded in formal and structural studies. Particular attention is given to theoretical proposals offered by Yuri Loman in books such as *The Universe of the Mind*, *Culture and Explosion*, *Analysis of the Poetic Text* and various articles on culture and art. Moreover, coined in 1982—notably a year before Théâtre de Complicité was founded—Lotman's concept of the 'semiosphere' is in many ways fundamental for the composition of my book, and its central role should become more explicit in Chaps. 6 and 7.[33]

My intention is to approach the aesthetics of the company with all available means of analysis and interpretation. The tools offered by Lotman are particularly useful in the context of theatre studies—and hence Complicite—even if they have not been frequently applied. As is the case with other theories and methodological suggestions, I do not use Lotman's semiotics dogmatically but adapt its most stimulating elements to the purposes of my discussions. This is to say that it is analytical and interpretative practice—in terms of Attridge's 'creative response' to artistic work—and not theoretical purity which is seen as central to my work.

NOTES

1. At times McBurney refers to Fiona Gordon as the fourth founder of the company (Trueman 2013). Yet, as a rule, official materials and other sources (e.g. *Oxford Companion to Theatre and Performance*, Kennedy 2011: 133) speak of three founders of Théâtre de Complicité. According to Marcello Magni, after joining the company and performing in *Put It On Your Head*, Gordon decided to pursue her artistic career independently in Belgium (in conversation). The entry in *The Cambridge Guide to Theatre* inaccurately suggests Kathryn Hunter as one of 'the founder members' of Théâtre de Complicité (Banham 1995: 1085).
2. In his Sao Paulo interview, McBurney (2015) explicitly shows his aversion to treating his company in mercantile terms. When speaking about 'promotion' I mean artistic rather than commercial purposes that aim at defining the authorial concept of Complicite.
3. The importance of shifts in the name of the company was suggested by Poppy Keeling during her presentation of Complicite before Douglas Rintoul's workshop in Sopot, Poland (21 May 2011).
4. In the 'Glossary' to Lecoq's *The Moving Body*, Bradby provides the following definition of 'complicity': 'A term used by Lecoq to mean shared understanding between two actors… or between actors and audience. It was seen as a key term by Simon McBurney and the founders of Theatre de Complicite (all former pupils of Lecoq), the company originally called itself Théâtre de Complicité' (in Lecoq 2009: 174). For a more theoretical analysis of shifts in the role of spectator/audience in the twentieth century, see Fischer-Lichte 1997: 41–60.
5. When answering a question concerning the 'big breakthrough' of her theatre career Arden says: '[It was] being part of Théâtre de Complicité. We started the company in 1983; I worked with it exclusively for 10 years, and I'm still an associate artist' (Barnett 2007). On her return to Complicite after 14 years as the director of *Lionboy*, see Trueman 2013.
6. Having said all that, I need to stress that the argument presents a model situation that in theatrical practice was far more complicated as the name of the company was spelled with—and without—French diacritics even in promotional materials.
7. Dimant stresses that, in the administrative sense, the original name (i.e. Theatre de Complicite) invariably serves as the proper one (in conversation).
8. Henceforth, the term 'equivalent' is used—after Tynianow 1978 and Zgorzelski 1999—to describe the artistic device in which one sign hints at the meanings conveyed by a developed network of associations from which it originates.

9. This is most frequently done by Simon McBurney and other associates of the company.

10. Interestingly, the very word 'complicity' is not infrequent in the English-language translations of Derrida's writings.

11. For a general application of Peggy Phelan's term in theatre and performance studies, see Allain and Harvie 2006: 59–61, 168–9. See also Jackson 2004.

12. For a more detailed description of Lecoq's clowns, see Lecoq 2006: 115–16 and Lecoq 2009: 152–63.

13. As McBurney notes in his 'Foreword' to Lecoq's *The Moving Body*, 'theatre is the most extreme artistic representation… of the art of collaboration' (2009: ix).

14. It is true that, in addition to the above meanings of the company's name, McBurney furthers its semantic capacity. At times he does so in a rather provocative way, as, for example, in the conversation cited by McCabe: 'Complicité in French doesn't have quite the pejorative meaning it does in English though I like the idea that it's a partnership in an illegal action, that there is something wicked about it. It's meant in the sense that when the audience watch the actors the sense of relationship between the actors on stage might be so intimate that with a bit of luck the audience might whisper to one another in the middle of the show: "I bet they're fucking each other"' (McCabe 2005: 18).

15. My understanding of the terms 'aesthetic' and 'artistic' follows the theoretical assumptions of Ossowski 1958. For a slightly different approach to this distinction see Iser 2000 and 2006: esp. 57–69.

16. 'After my husband's death Marcello came and taught the *commedia dell arte*. That was either in 1999 or 2000' (Fay Lecoq 2013: 90).

17. Whereas Allain and Harvie accurately speak of Lecoq as 'a reluctant author' (2006: 50), Jos Houben states that 'It is probably more accurate to say that Lecoq was not against literature but that he just did not treat theatre as literature' (2013:108).

18. For more details, see Knapper 2010: 234.

19. Certain ambiguities of this image are discussed in Hertel and Malcolm 2015. Their 'Introduction: Telling stories—About John Berger' begins: 'Although John Berger has often been regarded as—and has rather successfully fashioned himself into—an outsider of the literary establishment, it comes as a surprise that so far no collection of essays has been published on his work' (2016: 11).

20. By natural languages I mean verbal languages used in everyday situations (i.e. Lotman's 'primary modelling systems').

21. A slightly different version of the essay appeared in the *Guardian* as 'My Week: Simon McBurney'.

22. This somehow echoes George Steiner's observation from his 1961 essay 'The Retreat from the Word': 'Language can only deal meaningfully with a special, restricted segment of reality. The rest, and it is presumably the much larger part, is silence' (in Steiner 1970: 21).

23. Fay Lecoq claims that Peter Brook decided to invite Complicite to his Parisian theatre, Bouffes du Nord, after watching *The Three Lives of Lucie Cabrol* (2013: 90).

24. 'Théâtre de Complicité's *Street of Crocodiles* (1992, UK), directed by Simon McBurney and based on another story by Schulz, was visually and thematically inspired by *The Dead Class* and Kantor's work, a testament to the long-lasting impact Kantor has had' (Allain and Harvie 2006: 92). See also: Billington 1992, Miklaszewski 1992 (film), 2009 and 2014, Ojrzyńska 2012a, b.

25. In *The Dead Class*, Kantor's 'participatory presence clearly framed the *mise en scène* as a representation of his own experience, and made the audience aware of his ongoing role as director and creator of that experience—a practice common to all Cricot 2 productions' (Allain and Harvie 2006: 91).

26. Jen Harvie adds to this list the name of Gaulier (2005: 136).

27. Compare: H. Porter Abbott's discussion on 'the experience of unknowing' in narrative forms (Abbott 2013).

28. There is an obvious echo of Iser's statement that '… successful communication must ultimately depend on the reader's creative activity' (1978: 112).

29. For a similar reason, I avoid the metaphor of 'reading a performance' and the metaphor of 'theatre-text'. Even though they are commonly employed in theatre semiotics, they blur intrinsic differences between the textual (materially recorded) and the performative (transient, unrecorded) modes of communication that characterise—respectively—literature and theatre.

30. When using the metaphor based on legal terms, Attridge refers to Derrida.

31. I discuss Attridge's concept in the context of the role of dramaturg in theatre in 'Intermingling Literary and Theatrical Conventions', where I support my argument with examples taken from the work of Complicite (Wiśniewski 2015).

32. In February 2016, Nick Hern Books announced the forthcoming publication of *The Encounter*.

33. My understanding of Lotman's semiotics owes a lot to numerous discussions with Andrzej Zgorzelski over the past several years and with the Polish translator of Lotman's work—Bogusław Żyłko. See Zgorzelski 1999 and Żyłko 2009 and 2011.

CHAPTER 2

The Artistic Signature of Simon McBurney

INDIVIDUAL SIGNATURE AND ARCHETYPAL GENERALISATION

We begin our detailed exploration of the work of the theatre company Complicite by considering the distinctive approach and qualities of its principal founder/director, Simon McBurney. In his book *Culture and Explosion* Yuri Lotman recognises the domain of 'the proper names' (i.e. specific features defining an individual) as a quality that defines humanity. He argues that the paradoxical combination of confronting and integrating the concepts of 'myself' with 'the other' enables individuals to function within the network of 'proper names'. The position within this semiotic domain is defined by a decision as to how to structure one's internal world in relation to the external world. It is as much about giving 'the name' to oneself as it is about being named by others, and additionally about naming elements belonging to the surrounding world. For Lotman, the question of the 'proper name' is immediately related to the profoundly human distinction between the sphere of words/signs and the non-semiotic sphere (the natural world). A human being—as part of both—is capable of fulfilling roles which may be contradictory in character. For example, one is aware of the singularity of his/her individual existence, while also remaining a representative of a group (e.g. mankind).

Lotman claims that the dialectics of 'the proper' names (where 'I' embodies an individual) and 'the common' names (where 'I' represents one of many) is particularly complicated in the domain of art. In this 'testing ground for mental experiment', the individual ambitions of the

© The Author(s) 2016
T. Wiśniewski, *Complicite, Theatre and Aesthetics*,
DOI 10.1007/978-3-319-33443-1_2

storyteller are constantly intermingled with the objectives of the generalising ('third' person) narrative. In artistic communication, an 'I' reveals individual meaning that simultaneously conveys the sense of 'everyone else assuming the situation of an "I"'. Owing to the selection and combination of the material, artistic communication is the process in which the domain of 'proper' names (i.e. singular/idiosyncratic/autobiographical notions) is intrinsically linked with the 'common' names (i.e. universal/archetypal notions) in an exceptionally organised way (Lotman 1999: 63–72).

The poetics of McBurney's essays in *Who You Hear It from* is much in line with the observations of Lotman. Whereas autobiographical recollections sketch the life of an artist, McBurney's interpretation of the narrated episodes suggests their more universal relevance. The dialectics of an individual experience and its archetypal generalisation is certainly one of the central features of the authorial signature of Simon McBurney (i.e. specific features defining his artistic style).[1] This and other features of the collection of essays are echoed in the aesthetics of Complicite. Yet, the dialectics of the individual signature and the archetypal generalisation is far more complicated in the case of theatre as it raises the question of the collective intentionality of theatrical communication.

Autobiography as Communicated Self-Identification

According to Małgorzata Czermińska, autobiography is primarily an attempt at answering the question 'who am I?' and originates in the need to recognise individual features of oneself at a given moment of one's life.[2] It emerges from existential aspiration to recognise—or impose—order in what otherwise may seem a chaotic course of life. Yet, Czermińska stresses that the status of autobiography changes a lot after its publication, when its primary objective is no longer to communicate with oneself but to reveal to the readers an act of recognising one's identity. What was initiated as an internal psychological process enters the public domain so as to reveal one's understanding of individual features of personality and one's perception of the world (see Czermińska 1987, 2000 and 2015).

When analysing similar issues in his book *Circles of Initiation* (*Kręgi wtajemniczenia*), Edward Balcerzan argues that even the most refined artistic communication '*potentially* replicates the mechanism of competing for initiation' ['gry o wtajemniczenie'] (1982: 13). What Balcerzan means is that artistic communication involves the public desire for increased access to the personality of an author. Seen as a continuous and, by definition, infinite process, the 'competing for initiation' imposes various roles on the part of the addressee: it is one thing to decode a work by an unknown author, in which case the text is the sole determiner of meanings, and another to be a member of the artist's circle. In the latter case, personal contact makes interpretation not only less universal but also influenced by biographical detail. Balcerzan argues that authors are part of the mechanism of literary communication and, willingly or not, shape the reception of their work as much as the aspirations of unprofessional readers, scholarly expertise and the skills of translators do. Needless to say, autobiographical writing serves an important role in such 'competing for initiation'.

The processes that Lotman, Czermińska and Balcerzan describe resonate in any interpretation of *Who You Hear It from*, and in much of Complicite's work. There are several reasons for this. To begin with, McBurney's essays are shaped as personal notes that were published separately at first, and then as a collection. They provide access to the private views of the artistic director of Complicite and thus reveal the specificity of his perception of the world. All this hints at the possibility of recognising a more personal subtext in the body of the company's work. In particular essays, McBurney presents himself in different situations and roles; his creative self is evolving, so it soon becomes clear that his perception of the self is not of an essentialist (substantial) but a narrative (accumulative) type.[3]

In spite of his sense of an ever-changing identity, McBurney repeatedly presents himself in three roles. He is a cosmopolitan nomad. He is sensitive to family bonds. He is, above all, a creative artist. The autobiographical dimension of *Who You Hear It from* does not culminate in a simple recognition of these roles. The question 'who am I?' is followed by others: 'what does it mean to be a nomad?', 'what are the implications of being a son?', 'of having an older brother?', 'how to find a home?', 'what does it mean to be a theatre artist?' As may be expected, these formative questions are never fully answered, but the mere fact of considering them is certainly seminal for the rite of passage into the more personal dimensions of McBurney's work. In this sense, Czermińska's approach to autobiographical writing and Balcerzan's 'competing for initiation' delineate artistic strategies that are used by McBurney in setting what Lotman perceives as the dialectics of the 'proper' and the 'common' names.

A COSMOPOLITAN NOMAD

The notion of existential homesickness is extensively explored in McBurney's opening essay: 'To kill a caribou (and feast on its guts)'. A quotation from the German romantic thinker Novalis—'*Philosophy is really home sickness. It is the desire to be at home everywhere*'—is set as a motto and corresponds well with the first paragraph of the narrative: 'I have just moved. But I have rarely felt "home" anywhere.' It is of some relevance that the former was popularised by Georg Lukács in his 1914 essay and then by John Berger, and the latter is additionally used in *Who You Hear It from* as the motto to 'part one' in the table of contents (2012: 6) and the title page of 'part one' (9).

Although Novalis's quotation discloses philosophical universality and McBurney's words describe more personal matters, the two statements have one thing in common: they refer to the situation in which homesickness is an existential condition. An interesting interplay of 'the desire to be at home everywhere' and 'I have rarely felt "home" anywhere' makes the condition disturbing: what is desired on the philosophical plane is hardly attainable in personal life. This unsolvable conflict of the desire and the being is developed into more elaborate explorations of a contemporary topos based on the metaphor stating that 'life is a nomadic journey'. This reveals one of the narrative strategies used in *Who You Hear It from*: basic mimetic statements are frequently endowed with additional, more universal, meanings. This is, in fact, to say that, despite their clearly autobiographical provenance, McBurney's essays are to be read not only as a personal narrative but also, on a more general plane, as literary writings. Echoes of Lotman's dialectics of the individual and the general are striking.

In *Who You Hear It from*, McBurney travels around the globe, using all accessible means of transport. As a cosmopolitan traveller, he is in London, Paris, New York, Tokyo, Moscow, Kyoto, Chennai, Srebrenica, Thessaloniki, Munich, Helsinki, Warsaw and Strasbourg. We find him also in less metropolitan destinations such as an Arctic island in the polar circle, Zenica in Bosnia, Alma Ata in Kazakhstan and Tashkent in Uzbekistan. The means of transport vary from a transcontinental plane journey from London to Chennai to a hazardously overloaded Yak-40 with dilapidated seats, holes in the floor and goats on board. There is also a minivan in which he travels from post-Soviet Kazakhstan to Uzbekistan in the early 1990s, and an ultra-modern bullet train from Tokyo to Kyoto. As in proper travel literature, his adventures vary. When on the Arctic island, he participates in hunting caribou with native Inuit. In Paris, he leads a bohemian life as a student actor. In the Namakkal temple in India, he experiences mysterious awareness of the unknown. On another, much later, visit to Paris, he is sitting in a café, reflecting on the European tour of his now-famous theatre company and the death of his close friend, the actress Katrin Cartlidge.

Constant motion results in a sense of homelessness. The cosmopolitan nomad 'desires to be at home everywhere' but he 'rarely feels at home anywhere'. He is in one place for a short time and then moves somewhere else, so there is no possibility of putting down roots.

In *Who You Hear It from*, constant motion is reflected not only on the thematic plane but also in the episodic construction of the collection. Individual essays present separate narratives. Except for the person of the narrator and the style of his writing, the stories do not have much in common. They are not linked in any immediately obvious way. One journey/narrative/essay ends and another begins. Generically, the collection constantly combines conventions—for example, autobiographical writing and travel essay—and thus succeeds in depicting McBurney's personal condition ('who am I?') within the topos 'life is a nomadic journey', not only through the stories told but also in the construction.

The above observations are reflected in the artistic output of Complicite, which suggests that, collective as it is, the theatrical and dramatic work of the company bears the strong signature of Simon McBurney. From this perspective, the monological character of theatre communication dictates univocal semantics which are subject to the artistic decisions of just one person: the artistic director of Complicite.

First, the sense of homesickness accompanies numerous characters and is explored in the entire complexity of its manifestations. Lucie Cabrol, for instance, becomes a restless, crippled recluse after the death of her parents. Expelled from the home village by her brothers, she is forever searching for a place in the world. Jean, the narrator of *The Three Lives of Lucie Cabrol*, leaves the village for the wide world but feels at home neither in Argentine nor in Canada and, after a dissatisfying life spent abroad, feels the urge to come back to his mother's house.

In *Mnemonic*, the action involves Simonides' never-ending economic migration, the trans-European journey of Alice, who is desperately following traces of her unknown father, and allusions to the tradition of the wanderings of Jews. The condition of a man is best epitomised here by the desperate and fatal flight of the Neolithic Iceman through the glacial Alps. His body is only found over five thousand years after his death.

Still other types of homesickness are presented in *A Disappearing Number* where, in his search for knowledge, Srinivasa Ramanujan decides to break all the social and cultural rules of his cast so as to leave India for Cambridge. In the same play, there appear contemporary cosmopolitan nomads named Ruth, Al and Aninda. Their professional obligations involve incessant transcontinental motion. These examples are sufficient to illustrate a broad field of associations based on the motif of 'homesickness', which is explored in a variety of plays. As for McBurney in his essays, life for Complicite characters certainly is a nomadic journey.

Second, individual plays are set in different places around the globe and, at times, these are the same places as those mentioned in *Who You Hear It from*. Theatrical performances by Complicite are set in metropolitan cities such as Moscow (*A Dog's Heart, The Master and Margarita*), Tokyo (*An Elephant Vanishes*), Chennai (*A Disappearing Number*) and— in *Mnemonic*—London, Paris and Berlin. There are also less cosmopolitan settings such as pre-modern Japan (*Shun-kin*), a French village (*The Three Lives of Lucie Cabrol*), Kadis—a legendary village in Northern Sweden (*Light*)—and Drohobycz, a provincial town in Poland before the Second World War (*The Street of Crocodiles*). Numerous other towns and villages, placed in different parts of Europe and the world, are evoked in the spatial setting of these and other plays, and this demonstrates the cosmopolitan aspirations of Complicite. In the printed versions of the plays, the multinational dimension of the company is further documented by international casts and long lists of theatres, towns and countries where they were performed. McBurney is as voracious a traveller in life as he is in his art.

Finally, travelling and various means of transport gradually become more and more substantial elements of the onstage action. In such plays as *The Three Lives of Lucie Cabrol* and *The Street of Crocodiles* exotic peregrinations are narrated verbally (Jean's migration to South and North America in the former) or sporadically referred to (Emil's Madagascar in the latter) so that their role is supplementary. The journeys motivate the narration (Jean) or mark the specificity of the character (Emil). In more recent plays, especially *Mnemonic* and *A Disappearing Number*, travelling is not only one of the constructional dominants but also becomes part of the onstage action. On the one hand, journeys structure stories told by the characters, which is the case with Alice's story in *Mnemonic* and Ruth's in *A Disappearing Number*. On the other hand, various means of transport are repeatedly implied verbally (a plane, a ship, a train, a taxi, a helicopter and so on), visually (a plane, a ship, a train and a taxi) and aurally (a plane, a helicopter, a train and so on). In these two plays incessant motion becomes the central activity performed by nearly all the characters. Life is presented as a 'nomadic' journey in a very literal way.

THE CONCEPT OF A 'HOME' IN ESSAYS

Attractive as it may be, the life of an existential nomad is strongly related to the feeling of alienation on the one hand and the strong desire to establish a casual home that will satisfy the basic urge for belonging on the other. Everlasting homesickness involves removing the concept of home from physical space and placing it in the mentalscape of the traveller. All these issues are addressed in 'To kill a caribou (and feast on its guts)'. Set four hundred miles from the North Pole on a polar day in June, the narrative places 18-year-old McBurney in a world totally incompatible with his earlier life experience. Left by a Vietnamese pilot in, as he describes, 'pebble-strewn', 'silent', 'overwhelming' and 'inhospitable' tundra where he unexpectedly feels 'agoraphobic' (11), McBurney and his companions (Chuck and Diane) are soon joined by trappers and a group of native Inuit teenagers (all male peers of McBurney). In this new situation, the narrator goes through unusual experiences. Not only does he go fishing and hunting—right after midnight, when the sun is shining from a narrow angle—but also swallows a raw trout eye and hesitantly consumes warm caribou liver provided directly from the freshly shot beast. He is spared, however, full engagement in the subsequent ceremony of eating 'fresh half-digested grass', which is 'cut after first stomach'. As he briskly remarks, its 'sickly sweet' smell resembles that of 'shit' (17). Given the circumstances, the narrator's earlier comment that he was then as far from home as he had ever been is entirely justified, not only in geographical but also cultural ways.

In this naturalistic narrative, McBurney presents his 18-year-old self in the position of a complete outsider, thrilled with what goes on around him. The success of the caribou hunting (Roger, the one who actually shoots the animal, unambiguously appreciates 'Simon's' help in front of the less successful hunters) converts his extraordinary adventure into a rite of passage to the nomadic lifestyle. From now on, it is clear that, even in the most awkward circumstances, McBurney is capable of overcoming the all-pervading sense of alienation and homesickness. The concluding image of the exhausted hunters going back, westward, up and down Arctic hills, to the remote camp, carrying their prey, in the middle of the night, with the sun shining at its lowest point, encapsulates McBurney's revelation concisely. Remaining a complete outsider in the Arctic world, he unexpectedly recognises the archetypal conditioning of his present experience. The passage reads as follows:

> I suddenly wondered what time it was. Two, three, four in the morning? The thought disappeared as fast as it had come. There was no time. It had dissolved. What I was looking at was the same as it had always been. Roger stopped and looked back at me.
>
> – I feel at home, I told him.
> – Of course you are, he said, it is you and me. Here. Now.
>
> And we walked down the hill. Back home. Home. To the ice-scattered sea. (18)

Here we can observe the succinct way in which the above, rather concrete, autobiographical recollection conveys McBurney's understanding of the existential topos. In what seems a moment of epiphany (i.e. a sudden manifestation of essential meaning), McBurney experiences the crux of the nomadic lifestyle and identifies the concept of home with an internal state rather than a physical place. Notwithstanding the unusual scenery, the intense bond with Roger confirms, if only for a moment, the possibility of overcoming the alienation of an individual self. The hunting adventure enables him to commune with Roger and the 'overwhelming' and 'inhospitable' world around him.

The decision to choose such a conclusion to the opening essay (i.e. the life journey includes moments of epiphany) results in a productive interpretation of the nomadic life. In 'To kill a caribou (and feast on its guts)', McBurney communicates his belief in the possibility of overcoming the boundaries of the individual self: on the personal, cultural and archetypal levels. As a human being he feels, at times, interrelated with other human beings. The situation presented is of a universal character so that the 18-year-old self of McBurney is shaped to represent the experience of an everyman. What emerges is a strong hint of the dialectics of individual and collective types of experience.

Other essays prove the validity of this observation and this is illustrated by the following passage from the essay titled '*A Disappearing Number*'.

After a long flight to India, followed by a troublesome drive in an old van, McBurney gets some rest in a temple:

> The heat is stifling. Perhaps hotter than outside where it is still thirty-five degrees though night. ... I find a corner of the temple where it is calm. Everything here is mysterious, but not mystical. The mysterious is part of the everyday. The unknown feels familiar.
>
> My hands touch the rock. I put my back against it, squat and feel reassured. I have been travelling for nearly thirty hours. I gaze up at the night sky. No answer comes to me, no vision, no sign. But it is warm. And I feel more at home than I have done for ages. (74)

As was the case with the caribou hunting, the narrator reveals a strong sense of detachment from the surrounding world (exhaustion, heat). Yet, there comes a moment when he feels communion with the mysterious and the unknown. This is neither a religious nor mystical experience. But it enables the cosmopolitan nomad to constitute his casual home in the otherwise overwhelming heat of India.

A recollection of another similar situation—shaped in a more meta-theatrical manner—is presented in the opening paragraphs of 'You must remember this'. McBurney recalls himself fumbling across the dark stage towards the end of his introductory monologue in *Mnemonic*, performed during the annual theatre festival held in the Bosnian city of Zenica. Unequivocal historical connotations of the place (the narrator mentions that it was '[w]here the first refugees arrived from Srebrenica' [49]) put the actor again in the position of an outsider. Even though he initially seems to control the theatrical situation—as ever at this phase of the performance, he is amused by the trick the show has just played on the audience—it soon turns out that the audience's memories of recent atrocities interrupt the purely theatrical communication and give this particular performance an unrepeatable singular character. In the darkness of the crowded Bosnian theatre, McBurney/actor achieves an unexpected transformation from an onstage director to an onstage spectator, when his recorded voice poses the question of where the members of the audience were ten years earlier. At this point, conventional rules of theatre are broken as someone shouts hoarsely, if emotionally, that he was in a cellar with his 'fucking family'. The performance takes an unpredictable course, breaking the usual barrier between the theatrical and the real. The narrator comments that when he asks the same question in London 'few remember', whereas in Zenica 'memories of ten years ago are all too clear'

(49). For a moment, McBurney/actor becomes an 'outsider' in his own performance, since the world of the stage transcends its preconceived nature when the actor communes with the audience in a reciprocal act of communication. (Henceforth, this situation will be referred to as the Zenica case.)

The retrospective description of this event is chosen as the opening image of 'part two' of *Who You Hear It from*. The reader is informed that the Bosnian performance was the first evening of 'Complicite's European tour of ... *Mnemonic*' (49) and that the essay presents McBurney's thoughts on the tour's final night in Paris. The narrative of the nomadic journey of the company shapes subsequent theatres as 'casual homes' to be accommodated by actors with their performance. The memory of Zenica proves that, even during a performance, the stage is not immune from the unknown or the unpredictable. 'You must remember this' contemplates the unexpected twist in this particular presentation of *Mnemonic*, which astonishes its main creator.

The discussion so far reveals certain features that characterise the signature of McBurney. They may be summarised as follows:

- The essays combine dynamic mechanisms with static ones. The omnipresent topos of 'life as a nomadic journey' on the one hand, and the incessant search for a 'home' on the other, are two contradictory mechanisms that shape the life of one individual. In the emerging poetics, the semantic potential of complementary oppositions is vividly explored.
- The narrator interprets idiosyncratic autobiographical recollections in the context of archetypal universalisation. Seen in such a perspective, McBurney's individual experience (killing a caribou) exemplifies the principles that govern the lives of all people (a rite of passage). The artist assumes the role of an everyman. It is striking that the similarity between the combination of the dynamic and static and the juxtaposition of the idiosyncratic with the universal acquires a complementary character.
- In *Who You Hear It from*, juxtaposed notions enrich, rather than annihilate, each other. The principle is reflected in the narrator's attitude to the surrounding world. He is repeatedly put in the position of an 'outsider'. Clearly aware of the discrepancy between the internal and external ways of perceiving the world (his 18-year-old self as

opposed to the Inuit peers), McBurney is invariably fascinated by the unusual, the unknown and the other (see Gardner 2002). This attitude enables him to recognise and pursue the positive implications of the sense of detachment.

- McBurney's world vision assumes a possibility of transcending the limitations of the self, which has practical consequences for his understanding of communication. Notwithstanding all sorts of obstacles, human beings are capable of conveying their varied visions of the world. Verbal and non-verbal communication establishes grounds for overcoming the sense of detachment and alienation. This is true as much on the individual plane (Roger—'Simon') as it is on the cultural one (the Inuit—the British). In this context, it is remarkable that the examples discussed here are set in such distinct locations as an Arctic island, a temple in India and a stage in Bosnia.

- On the auto-referential plane, the principle of juxtaposition establishes the relations between the encoder and the decoder. Their perspectives are confronted so as to make artistic communication dynamic. The process is well illustrated by the recollection of a moment of theatrical unpredictability (the Zenica case). Because it provides access to the onstage thoughts of McBurney-the-actor, the scene reveals a sense of confessional intimacy. The reader is made aware of the profoundly personal character of communication, and in this way we get through another layer in what Balcerzan defines as 'competing for initiation'.

THE CONCEPT OF A 'HOME' IN PLAYS

As was the case with the topos of 'life is a nomadic journey', the notions of 'homesickness', alienation and the possibility of overcoming them are not only presented in *Who You Hear It from* as recurrent facets of McBurney's life but are also manifested in Complicite's plays. Fields of associations constructed upon these motifs are pivotal for the creation of theatre meanings.

In *A Disappearing Number*, for instance, Ramanujan—a natural-born mathematical genius—decides to leave his Indian home behind so as to settle in Cambridge. As a provincial Brahmin, vegetarian and man of fixed principles, Ramanujan finds Britain at the outbreak of the Great War a hostile place. Even influential academics tend to perceive him as an unwanted recluse whose mathematical achievements are downgraded by his underprivileged origins and non-institutional education. This situation may be well illustrated by an episode in scene 12, when Professor Hardy, after proposing Ramanujan for a fellowship in his college, is challenged by intimidating, if embarrassing, comments from his colleagues:

> FELLOW 1: ...Master, I have to say this, I'm not having a black man as a fellow of Trinity...
>
> ...
>
> FELLOW 3: ... Can we talk a little of your doubts over his lack of use of proofs...
> FELLOW 1: ...We thought that was a dirty trick...
> FELLOW 3: ...Some of his methods are quite unorthodox. Nobody knows how he has arrived at his...
> FELLOW 1: ...There's actually a rumour that he tried to top himself...
> (2008: 77)

Perceived by many as an academic outsider, Ramanujan manages to transcend his intellectual alienation thanks to Professor Hardy, who recognises the exceptional potential of his rare mathematical qualities. In spite of the divergence of their social and cultural backgrounds, Ramanujan and Hardy manage to overcome such practicalities in their exceptional pursuit of a purely abstract mathematical reality. Transient as it is, their academic collaboration transcends the everyday course of institutional practice and fosters a casual sense of intellectual accommodation in an otherwise hostile world. The personal attachment of the two mathematicians bridges the gap between two divergent cultures: the world of a Brahmin and that of a Cambridge professor.

Quotations from *A Mathematician's Apology*—Hardy's memories of Ramanujan's life—articulate an internal conflict between Ramanujan's aspirations and his sense of existential homesickness. As an intellectual outsider, he finds a sense of belonging and life-purpose in the abstract world of mathematics. Simultaneously, he feels detached from the aggressive madness of the external world where his role is reduced to a powerless item by restrictions imposed by institutional scholarship, martial politics and the predestined fatalism of his Brahmin lot. Alienated both in Britain and in India, Ramanujan epitomises an existential outsider: 'a homesick recluse'. Yet, his passion allows him to experience transient moments of finding 'a casual home' in the world of mathematics.

The sense of detachment from the merciless brutality of the surrounding world carries slightly different implications in *The Street of Crocodiles*. By intermingling Bruno Schulz's short stories with his biography, Complicite establishes an independent theatre narrative structured upon the opposition between the world of Schulz's omnipotent imagination and the cruel inhumanness of the Second World War. The compositional framework is fixed by the 'Prologue' and 'Epilogue', which are set in Schulz's hometown, Drohobycz, on 19 November 1942, the day Schulz was killed. The framework reveals that, notwithstanding his first name, the protagonist of the play (called Joseph, not Bruno) incorporates features of the narrator of Schulz's short stories as well as those of the author.

The 'Prologue' already sanctions the rudimentary opposition between the disastrous hostility of the external world and the internal world of imagination. It is achieved non-verbally, by arranging the stage in a specific way. Packed with '*piles of discarded books*' which are '*highlighted by spotlights*' a '*half dark*' '*warehouse on the outskirts of Drohobycz, Poland*' is filled with '*the sound of dripping water as the audience enter the mist-filled auditorium*' (2003: 9). Despite the conventional tribute paid to the rudimentary requirements of verisimilitude (fixed place, fixed date), the opening stage directions inaugurate a disturbing otherworldliness of the presented image on the one hand ('*half dark*', '*mist-filled auditorium*') and its meta-theatrical connotations ('*spotlights*' focus attention, '*the audience enter*' the theatre) on the other.

In the subsequent mime, Joseph is completely engrossed in '*sorting and cataloguing books*', and treats individual volumes with visible admiration and intimacy. One of them appeals to him so much that he cannot help but open it, smell its pages and begin to read. This silent, if most human, onstage action is alarmingly contrasted with harsh external sounds, such as piercing commands given in German, or a most frightening '*sound of marching feet*' (9–10). After a while, towards the end of the 'Prologue', the onstage reading takes Joseph to a different dimension where music, not 'the marching feet', dominate his soundscape.

The play presents a moment of epiphany in which reading enables Joseph to recognise—for the last time—his place in this world. He transcends the boundaries of the hostile world of the Second World War by immersing himself in the internal world of his imagination. 'Part One: Act of Remembrance' begins with the following stage directions:

The cast gradually appear on stage as if called up by **Joseph***'s imagination. One of* **Father***'s assistants,* **Theodore,** *walks down the wall perpendicular to the audience, pauses to take his hat and looks up as, out of the bucket, his twin assistant,* **Leon,** *appears—wet and dripping. Having struggled out of the small bucket, he picks it up. There is no trace of where he has come from.* **Maria** *emerges from the packing case of books.* **Charles, Emil** *and* **Agatha** *emerge from behind bookcases.* **Mother,** *swathed in cloth, shuffles forward on her knees with a book covered in a shawl. At a signal, they all produce books in their hands and look at* **Joseph.** (11)

The group mime is nothing like a realistic one. In spite of its surreal, non-verbal eccentricity, the image quite clearly introduces the notion of an internal 'home', where a meeting with the absent and the dead is possible. While reading alone in a Drohobycz warehouse in 1942, Joseph is meeting with his Mother, Father and all those who in the past constituted his home. His life is certainly not one of a cosmopolitan nomad. Still, the strong notion of existential homesickness is well justified by the entrapment of a peripheral warehouse in Drohobycz during the Second World War.

The theme of alienation is explored in yet another way in *A Minute Too Late*[4] where the sense of despair after the death of the beloved one is soothed by the employment of carnival elements. This is to say that the tremendous shock caused by the death of a wife—the feeling of existential estrangement—is alleviated in the course of the performance by the onstage treatment of social conventions accompanying a death.

The performance explores the consequences of finding oneself dejected and dispossessed in the midst of what previously seemed to constitute a sense of life. Simple domestic activities ('Scene 7: Martin Webster's flat') prove, for example, that 'a home' is not what it used to be. Carnival treatment of despair results in surreal imagery that originates in the tradition of '"*bouffonesque*" mockery' (Lecoq 2009: 124 –34), and the uncompromising parody of social rites connected with funeral procedures. After the death of the beloved, Martin Webster (the protagonist) not only finds himself in an inexplicable world of mourning but is also made to deal with overpowering institutions. It is mockery which helps him to get through. Hence, for example, the exaggerated travesty of the absurd futility of his hopes for Janet's recovery ('Scene 8: The Doctor'), the tragicomedy of registering the corpse ('Scene 5: The Registrar's Office'), the farce of the undertaker's wide ride through the city with a body in the boot of the hearse ('Scene 6: The Hearse')[5] and startling gags on the funeral ceremony and offering condolences ('Scene 4: The Church'). Extended exploration of gags, tragicomedy, situational and verbal black humour, and funeral farce defamiliarise the nihilistic tradition in the manner of Joe Orton.[6]

We soon learn that the carnival dimension of *A Minute Too Late* is counterbalanced by its human foundations. In spite of extensive parody of petrified social and institutional funeral formalities, the feeling of grief and despair is presented primarily as an intensely emotional—lyrical—experience. In the final scene of the performance ('Scene 10: The Cemetery 3'), when the protagonist is left alone at the grave of Janette (his wife), social and institutional matters are put aside and the audience is confronted with the universally human feeling of inexplicable loss. After a long hesitation Martin finally manages to utter his simple farewell. In *A Minute Too Late* carnival exaggeration, parody, '"*bouffonesque*" mockery', tragicomedy and black humour—all of them revolving around the themes of death, grief and loss—aim at accommodating the feeling of detachment from the world in which those whom one loves die.

The figure of an individual who experiences the hardships of life imposed by the inhospitable external world becomes one of the pivotal images in McBurney's essays and in his theatre.[7] However, unlike in many literary and artistic traditions, the aesthetics of Complicite respect neither the classical restrictions of artistic decorum nor the constraints of bitter irony imposed by (post-)modernism. When confronting existential matters, the company refers to invigorating powers of 'human comedy' and allows for much carnival mockery. Complicite's vision of the world seems to suggest that, in the course of cosmopolitan life journeys, the contemporary nomad experiences moments of transcendence that soothe the usual sense of detachment, alienation and 'homesickness'. And this is achieved on the personal, existential and archetypal planes.

INTIMACY OF DEATH

The theme of the death of a close relative—be it a partner, or a parent—is frequently presented as a turning point in one's life, by both McBurney and Complicite. It is related to the multidimensional understanding of searching for personal roots ('a home') on the one hand, and to an investigation into the relevance of family bonds in the world today on the other. It is striking that in *Who You Hear It from* parents and siblings appear in nearly all of the essays, and Complicite's performances frequently refer to the theme of family relations. Again, biographic experience exerts a strong impact on artistic practice.

As has been stressed a number of times, *A Minute Too Late* is deeply rooted in McBurney's reaction to the death of his father (e.g. *AMTL* programme 2005, Houben 2013). Although this is reflected in 'Fragmentary thoughts on remounting of *A Minute Too Late*'—an appendix to *Who You Hear It from*—the title of the essay is somehow misleading as the narrative is less obviously about the revival of the performance than about thoughts revolving around the death of McBurney's parents.

Retrospective descriptions of the narrator's state of mind and his feelings place an emphasis on unpredictability and inconsistency. Solemnity and grief result in such diverse recollections as those of:

- the inexplicability of sorrow ('There were no words to describe what it would be like' [2012: 107]),
- the physicality of a dead body ('A dead body is very cold. Much colder than you can possibly imagine until you have had your hand on it. It is a shock' [107]),
- the moment of actual death ('My father died as if he was climbing a mountain. ... My mother was the opposite. She became quieter and quieter' [111]),
- puzzling paradoxes of social taboos surrounding the death ('Nobody must see the plastic bag being loaded in the trunk. No one must see the body. Not even a plastic bag. No one in fact should know that anyone has died at all' [109]).

But typically of McBurney, grave as they are, the reminiscences also foster hilarious images. Faced with the ultimate and the unavoidable, the family is tightly closed together. As ever, the narrator expresses much curiosity concerning what is going on—be it the smell left by the corpse or the strange behaviour of those who avoid the bereaved. The company of his sister and unpredictability of reactions are seen at their best during the conduct at the funeral as they approach the crematorium, impulsively erupting with laughter on seeing the absurdity of unsuitable 'drop handles' rhythmically hitting an undertaker's ear. In the following passage McBurney/narrator implies that *risus purus*, the laughter laughing at itself,[8] and an anarchic blend of grief and the ridiculous, is as much part of life as it is of theatre:

The inappropriate has always been funny. As has the inevitable. The repetition of all our bodily functions is a rhythmic source of human comedy. We show what will happen. She will fall in love. He will two time her. Death will come. It is our future. The question is not whether it will happen but when and how. And it will happen alone. We, the living, can only witness and imagine. (111)

In 'Fragmentary thoughts on remounting of *A Minute Too Late*', McBurney consistently reminds us about basic truths connected with human existence. One of them says that when someone close dies, it substantially changes your life.

This is true not only of the narrator but also of his mother. As we learn in 'To kill a caribou (and feast on its guts)', after her husband's death, McBurney's mother feels increasingly 'homesick'. Six years later, completely engrossed in loneliness, she announces to the bewildered son her wish to sell the family house. She intends to find a new home in which she can die comfortably. Revealing a nomadic spirit at this late stage of life, the mother succeeds in her aspirations:

When she moved into her new house, her new home, she said: 'I feel I can die here.' She died in her bedroom. In her bed. Facing a particular direction. She wanted to look at the walnut tree. Concentrate on it. That was when she felt at home. (17–18)

Once again, a home turns out to be an internal state rather than a physical notion. The death of her husband—so prominent to her son[9]—necessitates also her redefinition of the self and compels her to pursue a new place in the world. It is also relevant that, when dying, McBurney's mother wants to concentrate on the walnut tree, which symbolises 'following a unique path and easing transitions' (Kerrigan). In this way the intimate recollection of her death is inscribed in the universal domain of symbols.[10]

FAMILY BONDS

In 'To kill a caribou (and feast on its guts)' the story of hunting is tightly interwoven with dispersed recollections of time spent by the narrator with parents and siblings. Some of them refer to his early childhood, others to the time when he was in his late twenties and his parents were already dead or dying. The essay reveals no distressing, psychoanalytically loaded attitudes. Instead, it concentrates on productive facets of family bonds and relates them to a very literal way of understanding the word 'home'.

It is quite early in the text—after his short comment on 'homesickness' (paragraph one) and the description of being deposited on the Arctic island (paragraph two)—that McBurney introduces memories of his family home (paragraph three) and confronts them with his thoughts when visiting Cambridge in the present (paragraph four).

Paragraph three begins with a syntactic emphasis laid on the word 'home', which—together with the opening motif of 'homesickness/homelessness' and the final image of communion with the universal ('archetypal home')—firmly sanctions the pivotal role of the notion for the narrative. From the perspective of a six-year-old boy, the 'home' appears as a big dark house with a garden, deprived of simple facilities ('no central heating, no television'). Given the 'Arctic' context of the memory, one observes elements underlying dimmed shades of light, openness to outdoor nature (windows), and freezing nights. Notwithstanding the obvious opposition between a polar island (wide nature/remoteness/the unknown/alienation) and the parental home (security/familiarity/the recognisable/the sense of belonging), the narrative suggests a disturbing correspondence between the two images. The paragraph reads as follows:

> Home. **That was then**. When I was six. That house. It was dark. Big. Forty watt bulbs, no central heating, no television, a garden that had apples, plums and pears in the autumn, a bedroom where all us children would sleep with windows always open at night. Once, my parents woke to find something hard lying on them. It was their quilt, which had frozen solid in the night and had a covering of white hoar frost on it. (2012: 11–12, emphasis added)

Interestingly, when mentioned for the first time, his parents are waking at night covered by 'a solidly frozen quilt' and 'white hoar frost' as if waking from the dead. It is striking that the association of the cold and the dead is also emphasised in the appendix. Again, archetypal grounds of a simple, apparently strictly mimetic, description are irresistible. As was the case in *The Street of Crocodiles*, the telling of a story of the dead by a son brings parents back to life (the parallel will re-emerge in Chap. 5). We already know that such a two-dimensional arrangement of the narrative is a characteristic feature of the poetics of McBurney.

The structure of paragraph four depends on the complexity of its dispersed temporal references. Its anaphoric beginning refers us back to the previous paragraph as both of them are mutually interconnected, not only thematically but also stylistically:

> **But that was then**. Now when I go back to Cambridge, I can only remember my father's description of going back to America. He was born in Massachusetts. His home there took on a mythical dimension when I was a child. I knew every room. And every story my father told me about every room. His home. But I can still see the despair on his face when he came back from seeing it again, 'It is not what I remember,' he said. (12, emphasis added)

Begun as if it fostered the time of storytelling, the narrative sharply shifts from McBurney's present visits to Cambridge to his father's idealised memories of his family home in Massachusetts, and the disappointment caused by visiting it in his adult life. The Chinese box convention (the memories of his father's home brought to the present through the recollections of the narrator's home town) establishes one of the principal features of the semantics of 'home'. This is an abstract construct, an unachievable, idealised notion shaped by memory. 'Home' is something that both McBurney in the present, and his father all those years ago, created in their imagination. The non-literal meanings of the concept are functional within the abstract domain of archetypal universalisation.

All in all, 'To kill a caribou (and feast on its guts)' firmly associates the nomadic journey with the nostalgic sense of 'homesickness' that may be overcome either in moments of profound internal experience of epiphany or through idealised memories of the family home. Transient as they are, the rare moments of feeling 'at home' provide the speaker with images which enable him to define and communicate an existential position in the otherwise chaotic course of a nomadic journey. The inhospitality of the external world is soothed by the internal power to create, or recognise, visions of 'a home'.

The domestic dimension of the narrative provides patterns for the evolution of the self. The past worries of his father, which were incomprehensible for the boy, have now become the narrator's personal experience ('At six that worried me. So where is his home if it is not there or not here? I wondered' [12]). Among other queries from his six-year-old self, we get to know his self-scrutinising dilemma of being an East Anglian born of an American father and Irish mother (13), which is treated with sentimental wit by his present self. In spite of all the differences, the speaker follows the steps of his father so that he recognises it is still worthwhile to look back at where he comes from.

McBurney recurrently alludes to eating and food sharing, the motif of a feast already appearing in the title of the opening essay. After killing caribou, the young hunters follow the rituals of their Inuit fathers. When they share the prey, they follow patterns set by their ancestors. Now, it is immediately relevant that the narrator recollects his father—an archaeologist—stressing that the sharing of food is a rudimentary condition of all cultures and associating eating with the concept of 'home'. His father says, 'Human beings and wild dogs are the only creatures that will share their food with those beyond their immediate family. Where we eat, that is our home' (14–15). These words are clearly echoed in the feast on the caribou guts. This is a vision of the world in which people may transcend constrictions of their own cultures and habits of their own generations, because in spite of all cultural differences, human beings are—and have been—internally all the same.

Personal Relations

Although in the work of Complicite personal relations are frequently the basis for the construction of a plot, they are usually presented in a less affirmative way. Still, in *The Street of Crocodiles* the recollection of Father, Mother and the family home is opposed to the ominous oppression of the Second World War and fulfils a reconciliatory function. Then, *The Magic Flute* depicts an idealised love story which overcomes all obstacles, even those imposed by faery creatures. But in the majority of the plays, melodramatic overtones aim at exploring the ambiguities of personal relations in the contemporary world.

A Minute Too Late is a special case as it explicitly reveals the shift which occurs in the process of the artistic arrangement of autobiographical material. As we learn from the essay 'Fragmentary thoughts on remounting of *A Minute Too Late*' and other sources, the piece originates in McBurney's experience of his father's death. Yet, the plot of the performance is built upon the motif of mourning the death of a beloved wife. The fact that the father is replaced by Janet and Simon McBurney takes the role of Martin Webster stresses the ontological discrepancy between the autobiographical material (personal experience) and the fictional world (semiotic reality). Notwithstanding the declarations of the author concerning the origins of the play, *A Minute Too Late* is constructed as a theatrical performance, which is decisive for the primacy of artistic means of creating meanings. On the one hand, the depths of despair are intensified: the shock of bereavement is less natural in the case of the death of a young wife. On the other hand, the autobiographical experience is universalised: the episodic composition of the performance puts the protagonist in the role of an everyman. For us it is crucial that the autobiographical context does not determine theatrical communication in any significant way. It is not necessary to be familiar with the origins of the performance in order to fully participate in theatre communication. On the contrary, in numerous episodes it ceases to be relevant whose death is being mourned as the action concentrates on the given situation (e.g. registering a body) and not on the particularities of individual experience. As we have already seen, the emotional intimacy of Martin Webster's mourning is sharply highlighted in the final scene, where the protagonist is left alone in despair at Janette's grave.

If, in his autobiographical recollections, McBurney evades various damaging facets of human relations, some of Complicite's plays explore such ambiguities. The motif of miscarriage appears in *A Disappearing Number*, an obsessively sleepless housewife detests the routine of her daily life in *The Elephant Vanishes*, vicious siblings ruin the reputation of Lucie in *The Three Lives of Lucie Cabrol*, and a mother rejects her child in *The Caucasian Chalk Circle*. In *Mnemonic* the action revolves around the problematic intimacy of Alice and Virgil and their attempt to rebuild mutual trust. But it is *Shun-kin* which examines the most intricate sado-masochistic bond between Sasuke and Shunkin. The complexities of their affair may be epitomised by the former's decision to blind himself so as to immerse completely in the world of his beloved. Onstage, the act of Sasuke's blinding is presented by a powerful image utilising the convention of unrolling red ribbons.[11] This is a kind of intimacy that leads to the complete annihilation of individual needs and desires.

A MODEL OF COMMUNICATION

The authorial signature encompasses those features of the aesthetics of Complicite which testify to the authorship of Simon McBurney. Among these features, the ones echoed in the poetics emerging from his essays are particularly prominent. In one way or another, McBurney's worldview, the singularity of his style and particularities of his biography result in a well-established subtext for the interpretation of the work of his company.

The publication of *Who You Hear It from* made this more evident than ever.

The spectrum of personal relations appears to be more complex in the performances by Complicite than in the essays by Simon McBurney where positive (idealised) recollections of family relations take priority. Yet, it is quite clear that, for the poetics of McBurney, and for the aesthetics of Complicite, the matter of effective communication invariably remains of crucial importance. Different as they are, the 18-year-old self of McBurney communes with Roger thanks to the shared experience of the caribou hunting. The same seems to be achieved by Sasuke and Shunkin when the former commits the act of self-sacrificial blinding. In both cases the act of communication is completed not only by verbal means. Approaching the unknown engages suitable actions.

This leads us back to *Explosion and Culture* by Lotman. In Chap. 3—entitled 'The System With One Language'—the scholar revises Roman Jakobson's model of communication by underlining the informative potential of the interlocutors' difference. Unlike for Jakobson, for Lotman what matters most is not the initial identity of speakers but the sphere that differentiates them and seems to obstruct, or in extreme cases block, their communication. The otherness of the Inuit lifestyle for McBurney and the blindness of Shunkin for Sasuke exemplify the sphere of the unknown. Lotman proposes the model in which he distinguishes:

- the individual sphere of interlocutor A, which is the unknown for interlocutor B,
- the individual sphere of interlocutor B, which is the unknown for interlocutor A,
- the semiotic sphere which is shared by both of them.

According to Lotman, the effectiveness of communication depends on the capability of establishing numerous (more than one) 'languages' that are functional within the sphere shared by the involved parties.

It is probably more accurate to speak of semiotic codes than 'languages' so as to avoid the risk of reducing them solely to implying the natural language (such as English, Spanish, German, Japanese and others). Among the codes in question there are heterogeneous systems of signs that are endowed with their own rules of organisation ('grammar'). Conveniently enough, natural languages fit well under this category.

In the work of Complicite, Simon McBurney's signature enlivens structures that encourage a biographical mode of interpretation. Yet, when arranging the material in an artistic way, his personal experience is made universal (father's death → Janette's death → everyman's experience of the death of a close relative), which is in tune with the dialectics of what Lotman labels as 'proper' and 'common' names. The contrasting, if complementary, juxtaposition of the autobiographic mode of interpretation with the one of generalising, at times archetypal, universalisation is actively involved in communication. The dialectics of the autobiographic and the universal formulates a code that, in the process of artistic communication, functions within the semiotic sphere shared by all interlocutors (sphere 3 in Lotman's model).

CREATIVE ARTIST

McBurney's artistic signature derives from *Who You Hear It from* and turns out to be applicable to Complicite's theatrical work. Yet, even in the collection of essays, the dialectics of the autobiographical and the universalising generalisation cannot be treated as the sole key to interpretation. There appears to be at least one more dimension that needs to be taken into consideration. As the narrator of the collected essays, Simon McBurney also takes the role of a creative artist. His meta-theatrical statements emerge from personal recollections and are usually not involved in archetypal generalisations. In this way, the discussed code fluctuates between three dimensions (1. autobiographic, 2. universalising, 3. meta-theatrical), but only the first one is constant, the remaining two being optional.

Generally speaking, the five essays constituting 'part two' of *Who You Hear It from* differ from those gathered in 'part one', as they present journeys motivated by the profession of the author/narrator: the role he assumes is primarily that of a creative artist. To begin with, in 'You must remember this', the recollections of the European tour of *Mnemonic* take us from Zenica in Bosnia—through Thessaloniki, Munich, Warsaw, Helsinki and Strasbourg—to Paris. The narrative is finished by the narrator's indication of future performances in London. Here, as elsewhere in *Who You Hear It from*, London acquires the status of the centre of McBurney's world.

Both the play and the essay are focused on Europe, which in itself promotes a cosmopolitan and, as some critics complain, Eurocentric[12] vision of the world. The correspondence between the company's tour and spatial context of Alice's search for identity is even more intriguing when we take into consideration commentaries on the recent death of Katrin Cartlidge, the actress who originally created and played the role of Alice. In the essay, the European tour of *Mnemonic* resembles a pursuit of spectres: the narrative finishes in a Parisian café where the vision of his dead friend makes McBurney order lunch ('I stand in the cafe for a moment of indecision. I see her sitting at the table looking at me as the waiter is also looking at me. "Why are you turning down the possibility of a fantastic lunch?" her look is saying. I sit down' [2012: 54]). What is more, the course of the tour (from Southern Europe, through Eastern Europe and Paris, to London) mirrors the fictional journey of Alice/Cartlidge (from London, through Paris and Eastern Europe, to the South) and thus endows the geographical verisimilitude of the essay with some non-literal generalisation.[13] One may say that the European tour of *Mnemonic* is shaped as a return home (i.e. London) from the internal world of imagination (i.e. the continent) and observes an interesting dichotomy of the spatial imagery in which Londoners undertake a trans-European quest for identity.

'*The Elephant Vanishes*', which is the second essay in 'part two', fosters the global dimension of Complicite's work and takes us to Japan, more specifically to an ultra-fast bullet train rushing from Tokyo to Kyoto and all the way back. What motivates this outlandish journey is a revival of the performance based on Haruki Murakami's short stories. Assuming, once again, the role of a complete outsider, McBurney presents himself not only as a creative artist who is hesitant about the aesthetic effect of what he is doing, but also as a Westerner lost in the exotic world that surrounds him.

As elsewhere, the description of personal experience acquires generalised meanings. It is, for instance, visible in the passage in which an ultra-fast train journey out of Tokyo is shaped to parallel the economic determination of progress in contemporary life. As the following passage—subtracted from paragraphs five and six—illustrates, the current mania of incessant searching for novelty is rhetorically embodied by horizontal movement in space:

> …We live in an age obsessed by the new. An age where progress is measured by the sheer number of novelties achieved, delivered, sold. The more we produce and the quicker we do it the more successful we are. One product after another, one project after another. An endless speeding horizontal line. Like the one I am on now.

> We are now travelling at huge speed. But after an hour we are still only passing through the suburbs; Tokyo is immense. ... (58)

Interestingly, the ambiguity of 'travelling at huge speed' (social/economic senses overlap with a strictly geographical reference) is embedded in the meta-theatrical context. The issue of assessing the value of progress addresses the work conditions of a theatre director in a very straightforward way and seeks to explain why theatre artists should move from one project to another rather than rely on the achievements of the past.

The beginning of paragraph five challenges such a perception of the creative process:

> The question about reviving a production most often asked is... why do it again? That question supposes that once a production is up and running after press night it is finished. The director leaves and the piece is merely repeated with more or less success until it ends. ... (58)

The paradox of the explored image—in which social, commercial and meta-theatrical associations are interwoven with the tangibility of the bullet train journey across Japan—is that it juxtaposes the narrator's declaration with his actual condition. As with all the others, he is involved in the world in which life is 'travelling at huge speed', and the art of theatre is invariably competitive.

In the sixth paragraph of '*The Elephant Vanishes*', McBurney diminishes social/economic generalisations and replaces them with more personal deliberations. Their meta-theatrical appeal raises concrete dilemmas based on the varied reactions of the European and Japanese audiences to the performance. At this point, the speed of the bullet train ceases to epitomise the mad rat race dictated by economics and begins to illustrate the impulsiveness of creative thinking:

> We are now travelling at huge speed. But after an hour we are still only passing through the suburbs; Tokyo is immense. And I am wondering over and over why this piece provoked so much laughter in London and so little in Tokyo last year. A whole host of questions shoot through my mind as fast as the images of the countryside flash before me from the bullet train, and I realise gradually that I am pushing away the single thought I do not want to entertain. That quite simply last year, here in Japan, I got it wrong. Well not entirely wrong. But certainly I did not get it entirely right. And who knows if I will find answers this time. I can't even seem to master the language with any more ease. (58)

After a reluctant admittance that there was some misconception when presenting *The Elephant Vanishes* to the Japanese audience the previous year, McBurney decides to examine linguistic, artistic and cultural discrepancies between himself (a director) and his Japanese cast in an attempt to overcome the separateness of Western and Japanese aesthetics. He explores nuances of Japanese syntax and grammar and studies the patterned rigidity of detailed gestures during a traditionally conducted tea ceremony. When in Kyoto, he stays in a nineteenth-century ex-Buddhist temple—turned into the house of his hosts—and sleeps there so well that he is overtaken by the feeling that he has found yet another 'casual home'. But of course, a sensation of detachment from the surrounding world remains the predominant feeling.

The exploration of the unknown in Japan finally leads McBurney to a discovery of what attracts him to the country so much. In summary, he discovers anew the notions which are rudimentary for his own aesthetic sense, such as:

- the search for a correct order ('The sequence is the thing. The order is all' [62]),
- the attraction of the uncertain,
- the recognition of cosmopolitan relevance in what is local,
- the mixed admiration for the traditional (epitomised by the tea ceremony) and the unconditional pursuit of the ultra-modern (the bullet train).

The exploration of Japan seems crucial for McBurney's self-identity as it enables him to redefine both his personal vision of the world and his concept of aesthetics.

In this essay, McBurney assumes primarily the role of a creative artist. This is not to say that the notion of a contemporary nomad or one who is cultivating family bonds ceases to be of relevance. On the contrary, both these roles remain vital for the narrator's understanding of his creative self. It may be well exemplified by the overwhelming sense of estrangement ('I stand on the platform, the humid heat of Tokyo in June is like an oppressive blanket, and I feel an outsider more than ever before' [58]) and the casual home he finds in Kyoto.

'*A Disappearing Number*'—the third essay in 'part two'—is constructed in a similar way. The narrative begins with McBurney making his intercontinental flight from (presumably) London to India. He reaches Chennai airport at four in the morning where he is collected by Rugu—'a man ... waiting with a sign' (70)—and taken out of town in an old van in what turns out to be a prolonged, ten-hour-long expedition to Trichy. Here, after 'a few hours of sleep', he meets Michael Levine (the designer for the production) and Polly Stokes (the assistant producer), and together they 'cram into an ancient four-wheel drive to get to Namakkal' (72). They finally reach their destination, the temple where Srinivasa Ramanujan 'slept for three days and nights in 1913' (73) before taking the momentous decision to disobey the strict rules of his cast to pursue an academic career in Cambridge. Based on the research and development phase of creative work, the essay presents a journey to India. The escapade is organised to gather source materials for the forthcoming production of what is to develop into *A Disappearing Number*.

The narratives presented in the three essays from 'part two' reveal meta-theatrical motivations for travelling, and thus introduce interesting equivalences between the process of artistic creation and the topos of a journey. McBurney's narratives prove that artistic creation involves:

- the quest for inspiration (the Namakkal temple),
- revisiting of the unknown (reworking *The Elephant Vanishes* for the Japanese audience),
- theatrical tours that allow for creating unexpected meanings (as in the Zenica case).

The remaining two essays in 'part two' abound in further meta-theatrical and auto-referential comments. 'Between servant and mistress, over and over' presents another journey to Tokyo, this time motivated by *Shun-kin*, 'the project of bringing [Jun'ichiro] Tanizaki's words to life' (82). The narrative of conceiving *Shun-kin* proves McBurney's fascination with 'shadows', 'darkness', 'the obscure' and 'the ambiguous' as well as his interest in the corporeal (the motif of a Japanese toilet) and the aesthetic value of imperfection. As we read, in Japan: 'The beauty of an old pot ... is enhanced because age has darkened it and cracked its perfection. Its imperfection is an essential part of its beauty, suggesting a life lived rather than a goal achieved' (81). A notion of imperfection is later ascribed to the theatrical output of Complicite. For example, a sense of deficiency is echoed when problems of inter-linguistic (Japanese–English), inter-cultural (the Japanese–the European) and inter-semiotic (literature–film–contemporary media–theatre) modes of translation are mentioned by the narrator so as to underline that, when accommodating the unknown, something is always lost. Additionally, 'Between servant and mistress, over and over' contemplates the artistic value of well-devised repetition: its prominence for musical, rhythmic and ritualistic patterning, which aims at ennobling the everyday routine (see also Nightingale 2009).

'Learned by Heart', the last essay in 'part two', verbalises what seems implicit in all work by Complicite: intensity, profoundness and independence of artistic communication. The essay deals with the production of the Raskatov's opera *A Dog's Heart* and provides retrospection on the times of the Cold War. The narrative of McBurney's 1987 visit to Moscow gives an image of the declining USSR and is meant to explain the origins of his long-lasting fascination with Bulgakov. As a Westerner (outsider), McBurney discovers the overwhelming power of 'samizdat'—'another kind of "talks"', 'an essential ingredient of resistance' (100)—the kind of communication which facilitates a most profound reading by memorising and rewriting texts. The absurd stories by Daniil Kharms, the poems of Osip Mandelstam and fictions of Bulgakov epitomise the mode of reading that involves complete internalisation and probes the depths of communication. This is literature which requires full internalisation of the artistic vision:

> For a moment I close my eyes and think of Sasha Raskatov drinking vodka in my apartment. All I know is that he has imagined and nurtured and grown out of Bulgakov's novel, and made something no other composer today could. Because he knows this story, these words. They are in him. It is a novel he knows 'by heart.' First as fragments of talk in intoxicating hot apartments. To be remembered by heart before they were even published. Then as words on illegal pages. Then from a book on a shelf. And now in his score. From one heart to another. Something graphic, painful, ambiguous, funny, brutal, disturbing and utterly alive. (101–2)

In the aesthetics of Complicite, the process of reading—and by extension all reception of art—is at its best as a demanding, intense and profound procedure of artistic creation. Theatrical communication is an enduring journey that requires due care. McBurney insists we give priority to what George Steiner sees as the profound devouring of art over a superficial digesting of meanings. This attitude testifies to personal treatment of both interlocutors of artistic communication (encoder and decoder).

ARTISTIC SIGNATURE

In her book *Autobiography and the Novel, or the Writer and his Characters*, Małgorzata Czermińska comments on the interpretative power of auto-biographical writing. It is usual, she states, for the publication of an auto-biographic text to reshape any previous understanding of the *oeuvre* of an artist and focus interpretative attention on revealing more or less explicit autobiographical elements (1987: 24). Notably, Czermińska distinguishes between the 'private' and 'creative' selves of authors, insisting that while the former encompasses internal self-recognition, which frequently remains hidden from other people, the latter is primarily a construct that belongs to the sphere of cultural meanings and as such creates the public image of an author. The distinction is followed by recognising in auto-biographical writing the dominance of self-created meanings over factu-ally determined plausibility. It is typical of autobiography that it creates the public self of an author but does not necessarily provide an accurate account of his/her private life (10).

Czermińska's observation is in line with the notion of 'competing for initiation' that was coined by Balcerzan. Both scholars expose, in their own ways, a gradable nature of semiotic relations between the aesthetic and biographical dimensions of an artistic piece. Depending on the external knowledge of the reader, the semantic potential of one and the same text may range from abstract aesthetic/artistic meanings to those which illuminate the psychological and social experience of the author. It is certainly one thing to encounter a text by an unknown author, and another to reinterpret the same piece after getting acquainted with the artist's notes, diaries, essays, interviews, textual variants and (auto-)bio-graphical writings. What can be seen as increasing intimacy between inter-locutors of artistic communication depends as much on the self-exposing activities of an encoder (there are artists who reject being actively engaged in the creation of their public image[14]) as it does on the erudition of the decoder (some other aspects of *A Disappearing Number* will catch the attention of—say—a theatre-maker, a semiotician, a psychoanalyst and a mathematician).

This chapter, in which premises inspired by the studies of Lotman, Czermińska and Balcerzan have been applied to the analysis of the poetics of *Who You Hear It from*, leads to the following conclusions:

- In McBurney's collection of essays the multiplicity of simultaneously generated, if semantically incongruous, themes is of complementary—and not exclusive—character. In the case of the topos of a
journey, none of the three fields of reference takes priority over the
other—the autobiographical, the symbolical and the auto-referential
are equally prominent for the overall semantics of *Who You Hear It
from*. Although such a complexity of semiotic relations may undergo
substantial remodelling in particular plays of Complicite, one should
take their prominence into consideration when analysing the aesthetics of the company.
- Autobiographical explicitness in *Who You Hear It from* implies the
relevance of tracing biographical parallels in the theatrical output of
Complicite. Even though the interpretative potential of such analysis
is substantially weakened by the collective nature of the company's
work, the essays pronounce what may be seen as the artistic signature
of Simon McBurney. Because of its specific meta-theatrical features,
the collection highlights the aesthetic and artistic craftsmanship that
characterises McBurney and his company. Some of these features are
broadly discussed as themes in particular essays (e.g. repetitions and
sequentiality), while others are indirectly implied by the solutions
assumed in the presented narratives (e.g. the frame composition,
the fragmentation of spatio-temporal imagery). In addition, the aesthetics of Complicite makes use of the biographical key in some of
their productions (e.g. *The Street of Crocodiles, The Noise of Time, The
Master and Margarita*).
- Essays by McBurney illumine the work of a theatre company, which
reveals the challenging issue of juxtaposing individual and collective modes of creation. The relation between Simon McBurney and
Complicite is set on the trope of metonymy: the artistic director represents his personal self (and views) to a lesser extent than he epitomises the company he leads. Simultaneously, the company merges
his individual aspirations with those of other artists and facilitates the
transcending of his personal limitations. It is a curious example of an
individual who is a part of a collective he epitomises, and this furthers
the dialectics of 'proper' and 'common' names proposed by Lotman.
Further discussion on this matter will be offered in Chap. 3, but for
the time being, I need to stress that, by dispersing authorisation,
Complicite (McBurney) depersonalises its artistic communication.
And yet, by revealing autobiographical potential, *Who You Hear It*

from lays emphasis on the intimate, personal and profoundly singular potential of Complicite. It is crucial that what is thus revealed is the artistic signature of McBurney's poetics rather than the immediately autobiographic anecdote. We get to know more about the structures through which meanings are created than about the 'real life' facts.

- In the case of Complicite, a hermeneutic act is a rather dynamic process in which both interlocutors actively participate in establishing a highly personal contact. (So as to avoid involvement in a detailed discussion on nuances of relations between author/company and reader/spectator/audience, I refer to the very general and abstract notions of encoder and decoder.) Incessant evolution of particular productions results in exploration of the poetics of *the work in progress*, which is related to the strategy of stressing receptive limitations as the decoder gets access merely to a variant of a more developed structure. The issue will be discussed in more detail in Chap. 7, but it seems important now that such a strategy polarises artistic communication and thus encourages active reception.

- The aesthetics of Complicite emerge not only from the natural languages, the conventions characterising theatre and drama, but additionally involves the three-dimensional code (autobiographic–universal–meta-theatrical). Its autobiographical provenance fosters the intrusion of 'real life' verisimilitude and guarantees the mimetic credibility of all references to the contemporary world. For example, the account of the intercontinental flight to Chennai, and the description of the Japanese bullet train, give credence to the vagrant expertise of the cosmopolitan nomad. In this way, the semantics of the counterfactual (fictional/artistic) concurs with the sense of verisimilitude (autobiographic/referential).

- Among communicative strategies that shape the aesthetics of Complicite and the poetics of McBurney, the one which juxtaposes—within a single structure or image—an internal and deeply personal experience with archetypal generalisation, is endowed with much prominence. By intermingling the autobiographical with the archetypal, McBurney cultivates two extremes within one dichotomy. The device epitomises the dualistic world vision which is structured upon the dominance of the conciliatory principle of *coincidentia oppositorum* over the antagonistic opposition of the binary notions. It seems that the implementation of this vision is a key feature of the artistic signature of Simon McBurney and in effect of (Theatre de) Complicite.

NOTES

1. In many ways Chapter 1 has been inspired by H. Porter Abbott's excellent book *Beckett Writing Beckett. The Author in the Autograph* (1996).
2. In the interview with Knapper, Simon McBurney states: 'What I see now, in all the shows, is the constant question: what the fuck are we doing? Who are we and what does it mean to be who we are?' (2010: 237).
3. The distinction has been proposed by Czermińska (1987: 7).
4. This early performance does not have a published version; my analysis is based on a recording of the 2005 revival of the play and its unpublished scripts (1998, 2005).
5. The ride is presented in the 2005 version. In the 1998 manuscript, Martin is simply given a lift by the undertaker.
6. As McCabe puts it: 'McBurney has always occupied an ambiguous position in British theatre, somewhere between the iconoclast and the clown' (2005: 16).
7. This has been a seminal topos in British culture, ever since the Anglo-Saxon poem *The Wanderer*.
8. See Bakhtin's discussion on the carnival tradition in Rabelais (1984b). McBurney discusses his fascination with Rabelais and the carnival in 'French Passions: Simon McBurney on Rabelais'. For a more theoretical discussion on the notion of carnival in theatre, see Anthony Gash's article 'Carnival and the Poetics of Reversal' in Hilton (ed.) 1993: 87–119.
9. According to Jos Houben, *A Minute Too Late* was a formative performance for all who were involved in it (2013: 105).
10. From a tweet posted on 25 August 2012 we learn that McBurney's mother died in 2002, on his forty-fifth birthday.
11. The scene can be watched in the generally available 2011 and 2015 show-reels of Complicite: (www.complicite.org/resources.php) (accessed 14 January 2016).
12. For instance, Janelle Reinelt claims that 'Complicite may not be aware of the strong message of human homogeneity and inevitable violence that the production of [*Mnemonic*] carries—there is much tenderness, empathy, and beauty in the images as well—but finally, the world-view of the play is a return to universalism and even a kind of fatalism. Ironically, it repeats an 'old Europe' ideology that seems reactionary' (2001: 241). See also: Harvie 2005: 139–43.
13. There are some intriguing parallels between *Mnemonic* and the Macedonian film *Before the Rain*, directed by Milcho Manchevski (1994). In both of them Katrin Cartlidge takes a prominent role.
14. The case of Thomas Pynchon serves the best example. See Krafft 2012 (especially 12–14). I owe this observation to Dr Arkadiusz Misztal.

CHAPTER 3

The Logic of the Plot
in Théâtre de Complicité

SEMIOTIC INFILTRATION

According to Yuri Lotman, the figure of antinomy is at the core of the relationship between the 'language and/or culture' (i.e. the semiotic reality) and the surrounding/natural (i.e. the non-semiotic) world (1999: 27).[1] Simultaneously, the scholar maintains that incessant reciprocal infiltration of the two spheres accompanies all processes of conveying significant information (57). Lotman argues that artistic communication is neither an 'isolated immanent process' nor a 'passive sphere of external influences' (183), which means the antithetical spheres of semiotic reality and the surrounding world coexist as clashing, yet mutually enriching oppositions. Some of their unpredictable intersections are pivotal for what he labels 'explosions' of artistic meaning.

Lotman's statements on the semiotics of culture establish a broad and accurate perspective for theatre studies.[2] Moreover, his understanding of artistic processes frequently indicates concepts that seem perfectly suited to grasping the aesthetics of Complicite.[3] The following list enumerates those concepts proposed by Lotman in *Culture and Explosion* that are most relevant for our purposes. The proposed notions have been adjusted to the nomenclature that prevails in this book.

- A semiotic system does not function in complete isolation. When used in an act of artistic communication (e.g. a performance), the system formulates a complex structure of signs, in which the system

© The Author(s) 2016
T. Wiśniewski, *Complicite, Theatre and Aesthetics*,
DOI 10.1007/978-3-319-33443-1_3

interferes with the world outside. The spheres which are external to the given semiotic system are either other semiotic systems or the natural world. The semiotic studies aim at: 1. distinguishing the very nature of the analysed system (e.g. the aesthetics of Complicite), 2. analysing artistic applications of this system (e.g. particular productions of the company), and 3. detecting and recognising the spheres which infiltrate the analysed system most (examples below).

- Artistic systems are immersed in the external world. They absorb certain elements from the world outside, and simultaneously eject those which are no longer attractive for artistic purposes. These are dynamic and incessant processes leading to moments of 'semiotic explosions' whenever particularly stimulating structures and/or systems intersect (186).

- A semiotic explosion results in a sudden flourishing of artistic meanings and values. Their manifestations are usually unexpected and unpredictable, even though when analysed retrospectively they may seem inevitable. Because the semiotic explosion originates in a particularly abrupt intersection of structures and/or systems (183), one may assume that a multiplicity of notions interfering with the given system is likely to provoke such eruptions.

- A semiotic explosion creates variants of structures that may initially seem synonymic but are gradually revealing their semantic autonomy. Although an external observer may see it otherwise, it is the difference of such structures which is decisive for their artistic value (186). For this reason, the most potent artistic innovations are not necessarily immediately recognised by the systems of cultural evaluation.

- The absorption of external structures and/or codes leads to renaming ('re-nominating') of the structures and/or codes functioning already within the given semiotic system. Such an act of defamiliarisation involves the re-evaluation of the internalised meanings. In consequence, semiotic explosions tend to generate singular meanings that cannot be reduced to the sum of their elements (183).

- A semiotic explosion may be manifested as an artistic inspiration. In this case it is patterned either in accordance with the logic of a scientific discovery or takes the artist from the sphere of logic to that of unpredictable creativity. In both cases the semiotic eruption appears as a process in which the incomprehensible becomes obvious, incongruous turns into adequate, untranslatable is translated and notions which previously seemed contradictory are now seen as coherent. In other words, artistic explosion allows for an ignition of new senses, especially those which are intrinsically paradoxical (53).

EVOLUTION OF (THEATRE DE) COMPLICITE

In theatre studies the type of semiotic infiltration we have discussed occurs on a number of levels. Permanent tensions between the *oeuvre* of Complicite (i.e. an internal semiotic system) on the one hand and, on the other, external artistic structures, cultural systems and related elements of the surrounding world may well illustrate the relevance of Lotman's proposals for describing this process. The *oeuvre* is understood here as the system encompassing all manifestations of the artistically valued activities of the company and it delineates the basis for formulating the aesthetics of Complicite.

In accordance with Lotman's observations concerning the history of culture, the semiotic infiltration is dynamic. The diachronic dimension of the *oeuvre* encompasses the history of inclusions and exclusions of certain structures and systems. As in Lotman's model, the semiotic interference comprises sluggish periods of accumulative evolution and moments of radical explosions/eruptions. This chapter aims at defining major shifts in the demarcation line between the aesthetics of Complicite and the world outside. As we will see, the latter includes elements deriving from both the theatrical/artistic/cultural phenomena and the non-semiotic world.

Since 1983 the aesthetics of Complicite has evolved from one directed towards the maximum exchange with the world outside to one promoting the artistic autonomy of a theatre production. Initially, the company accentuated the unpredictability of largely improvised shows that absorbed conventions coming from street theatre, *commedia dell'arte*, stand-up comedy, devised theatre[4] and other similar traditions. The shift which occurred in the late 1980s and early 1990s testified to the increasing prominence of the codified 'stage language' of the company. The impact of more classically structured formulas, such as dramatic plays, multi/inter-media theatre, large-scale opera productions and theatrical adaptations of narrative texts, has become more evident since the production of Friedrich Dürrenmatt's *The Visit* (1989). It is noteworthy that the process has been paralleled by the increasing explicitness of Simon McBurney's signature in the aesthetics of Complicite.

FLUIDITY OF STRUCTURES

Sparse as they are, recollections of early shows indicate their peculiar fluidity, which means that performances were vastly exposed to interaction with the surrounding world. Actors frequently played in a non-theatrical environment and assumed performative tasks emerging from street theatre such as:

- determining the playing area and establishing its proxemics,
- reacting to the improvised actions of other actors,
- responding to the reactions of spectators, and those who happened to be passing by.

The dynamics of such interaction led to unpredictable artistic and non-artistic consequences.

Jon McKenna, one of the original street performers at Covent Garden, recalls in a short memoir, 'How I Met Simon McBurney', an unconventional treatment of the market space in a street performance proposed by McBurney and his companions in the early 1980s. Initially, the clumsy figure of McBurney did not stand out much from the market crowd. Dressed in 'a dirty raincoat', with 'protruding teeth' and 'wearing National Health spectacles', he was heading slowly, and generally unnoticed, from 'the south end of the piazza' to the litter bin left on purpose in the middle of the playing area by the earlier performer. Public awareness of the ongoing show was caught when 'this crumby, myopic, dishevelled little man' loudly collided with the bin. The farce of the struggle to get out of the bin was followed by equally hilarious 'wiping ketchup off his spectacles'. The attention of the gathered audience focused on the pitiable man until the playing area was abruptly enlarged by a simple gesture. When he could finally see through the lenses, McBurney pointed at 'a beautiful woman in Victorian attire [who] was leaning precipitously from a balcony some twenty metres above street. [She was] attached to the balcony only by the handle of her umbrella hooked into the wrought-iron railings. She was looking directly at the man in spectacles. And he at her. And us at the unfolding of the greatest love story ever to hit the streets' (2013: 117–19).

McKenna's recollection reveals that, since their earliest street shows, Théâtre de Complicité have been fully aware of the vast semiotic potential of the proxemics of a performance. In the show he describes, three major shifts in spatial relations are marked by:

- McBurney's emergence from the crowd,
- his announcement of the ongoing performance by colliding with the litter bin,
- the sudden enlarging of the playing area with the accompanying introduction of the love story convention.

Thus, the performers aimed at unexpected shifts in perspectives, which created the impression of blurring the borderline between prepared actions (internal structures) and accidental events (the surrounding world). From the perspective of the spectators, the playing area appeared to be a fluctuating structure.

Put It On Your Head

Covent Garden was certainly not the only non-theatrical space where Théâtre de Complicité performed. They did shows and drama workshops in arts centres, schools and prisons (Lane 2005). Marcello Magni mentions the Battersea Arts Centre, the Angel and Camden. On one such occasion, Magni claims, they did not stop performing even when arrested by the police (Magni 2013: 114).[5] Throughout the summer of 1983 the company improvised on the beach ('the seafront') and thus developed material for their first production, which opened in September 1983 at the Almeida Theatre in London. *Put It On Your Head* was 'a very simple show' that revolved around the Italian motif of 'pudori', which is 'the embarrassment of being with people on the beach'. Magni stresses that it was supposed to be very funny and somehow echoed Jacques Tati's film *Les vacances de Monsieur Hulot*. The general idea was to confront the 'idiosyncratic habits [and] mannerisms' of 'uptight British' characters (Fiona Gordon, Annabel Arden and Simon McBurney) with the confidence of a Mediterranean one (Magni). The action resulted from observing interactions between people spending their time on a beach. The summer improvisations lasted for one and a half months and they were changing from one day to another. Magni could not find the role which would suit him, so for a long time he moved from one character to another. He was, for example, 'an embarrassed cousin' and 'a muscular athletic swimmer' dressed in a swimming suit. When McBurney's mother came to watch the show, Magni improvised a character that imitated her (Magni 2013: 113–14).

In the Almeida production, the characters were called Frank, Alice, Mary and Giorgio. The production leaflet describes the performance concisely as 'A flight of fantasy about the English seaside and the social agonies of Englishness on the beach'. The leaflet sketchily summarises the action as confronting the characters' attempt at finishing lunch with its surreal, if 'hilariously funny' consequences. Vague statements such as 'For this is a tale which begins in the ordinary and ridiculous and moves rapidly towards the ordinary and ridiculous' and 'The main thing is to keep going, somehow hold it, balance it, in the last resort just put it on your head' reflect verbally the irrational/surreal/absurd character of the onstage action. Photographic documentation confirms this impression. In promotional photographs Arden is tied by the rope and pulled by the other members of the company, Magni exposes his body as the athletic swimmer, Gordon is jumping by the deckchair with her knickers down and McBurney is jumping, dressed like a girl. The images abound in a mixture of everyday objects (e.g. a deckchair, a sunbathing towel, a portable stereo) and hilarious exaggeration (facial expressions and gestures). To avoid the audience's mistaking the nature of the show, the leaflet accurately explains that 'Underneath it all there are the rigorous techniques of Pantomime Blanche, Melodrama, Clowning, and Commedia dell'Arte, which inspire the company's explosive visual style and the disconcerting characters they create'.

It seems paradoxical that the vast semiotic potential of fluid variants that constituted the overall structure of *Put It On Your Head* is now being reconstructed from fragmentary recollections and sparse archival documentation. Such is the lot of improvised acting. Still, the procedure allows us to illustrate some effects of the semiotic exposition to the surrounding world on the aesthetics of Théâtre de Complicité in its nascence.

First, the performance originates primarily from observation of 'real-life situations'. This highlights the four-stage mechanism for creating meanings that shape the performance:

1) the leisure interactions between the sunbathers ("pudori")

↓

2) the observations of these actions

↓

3) the improvisations based on performatively codified idiosyncrasies and habits

(summer shows)

↓

4) the arrangement of the material in the theatrical context (the Almeida production).

Diagram 3.1

Second, the shift in spatial relations between the two final stages of the process I have described embeds the beach situation within the framework of theatre communication. This necessitates the use of theatrical means to signal the proxemics of the presented world (e.g. the prop of a deckchair to indicate the beach), and thus hints at the artistic arrangement of the material.

Third, similarly to spatial relations, presented actions increase their semiotic potential in each stage of the process. What is more, the parody of personal and collective habits related to 'pudori' [the parody] is coupled with the stereotypes that result from the nationality of the performers and the style of their acting ('the uptight British' vs 'the robust Italian'). The onstage communication confronts the structures adapted from the code of English sunbathers with the exploitation of structures emerging from the code of national stereotypes. Although in both cases we observe intrusions of the surrounding world, they vary in character. Whereas the former is based on the behaviour of random people (adaptation of the code of behaviour), the latter explores the intrinsic potential of the involved actors (exploration of their artistic potential).

Finally, these observations illustrate the complex nature of the semiotic explosion that occurs in the case of *Put It On Your Head*. Spatial relations, onstage actions, styles of acting, the juxtaposition of the surreal/absurd/improvised with the mundane/habitual/arranged—all these factors participate in the sequence of unpredictable, unrepeatable, fluid and transient arrangements of signs, structures and systems/codes that marked the formulation of the 'stage language' of Théâtre de Complicité.

A Minute Too Late

A Minute Too Late, the second performance devised by Théâtre de Complicité, furthered some of the above principles and introduced others. The change between the shows was substantial but the semiotic core remained the same. Premiered in 1984, the piece was produced several times and its final production in January 2005 was meant to celebrate the twenty-first anniversary of the company ('coming out of age').[6] The history of performing *A Minute Too Late* illustrates some of the major shifts in the aesthetics of the company as it encompasses earlier and later phases of the company's evolution. There is, for example, an important difference between the status of the early presentations of the piece (the English tour → the Pegasus Theatre → the world tour) and its later 'retrospective' realisations.

Whereas the 1984–5 performances illustrated the actor-based, collective, improvised and fluctuating style of Théâtre de Complicité, the

2005 production was credited to the directorial supervision of Simon McBurney. Moreover, unlike in the original version, it now included a lighting designer and sound operator. The shift marked the need for the already famous theatre company to complement its original ambition to entertain an audience in the most vivid way possible with an attempt to satisfy the refined tastes of regular theatregoers searching for an insight into the past of the company. In 2005, the company members must have been aware that these are two completely different communicative objectives that require diverse artistic strategies. Notwithstanding the professionalism of the production, British reviewers of the 2005 version noted what they perceived as shortcomings resulting from the less standardised style of the company's work in the early years. This was the case with Mark Billington in the *Guardian* ('One vignette … where Houben's madcap undertaker drives a hearse … is simply there to demonstrate the trio's mimetic expertise. Even the adagio-like ending … seems structurally awkward' [2005]), Paul Taylor in the *Independent* ('Watching it … is a bit like seeing, say, the Monty Python team reunite to dust down the Dead Parrot sketch … for an Amnesty International benefit. … *A Minute Too Late* feels comparatively sophomoric and self-conscious' [2005]), Mark Shenton in *What's on Stage* ('there are a few moments when it sometimes seems a little too pleased with itself and the effects it pulls off …' [2005]) and others.

The fact that *A Minute Too Late* is an exceptional case of a performance that was changing, along with the company's aesthetics, for more than 20 years is central to my argument. I use the verb 'change' rather than 'evolve' deliberately so as to stress that I do not regard the company's earlier methods as better or worse, but as artistic solutions that conceived slightly different meanings. The factors Billington, Taylor and Shenton criticise (i.e. the self-referential style of the performance, its 'inappropriate' ending, and the unsettled coherence of the onstage action) were decisive in terms of the emerging 'stage language' of a company that was yet to become famous.

THE CREATIVE PROCESS

A Minute Too Late makes extensive use of Simon McBurney's personal experience of his father's death (see Chap. 2).[7] The mechanism of adapting autobiographical material for theatrical purposes parallels that used in *Put It On Your Head*. Jos Houben, a Flemish performer, who after graduating from Lecoq's school in 1983 joined McBurney, Arden and Magni in

London, distinguishes four stages in the creative process that resulted in the performance of *A Minute Too Late*.

First, having established 'the powerful theme … of loss and grief', the performers made observations in the surrounding world. They 'went to a cemetery', attended a funeral and gathered material from everyday situations. Besides this they made extensive use of the description of codified social behaviour after the death of someone close, which they found in the pamphlet *What to do after a death in England and Wales*. Second, personal experience and observations of social habits (codes) surrounding death were confronted with the ensemble's professional skills during a series of improvisations. Working collaboratively and exchanging their roles (actor/director),[8] the ensemble arrived at some sketches that codified the material in the language of the stage. Needless to say, the sketches were funny as they explored the carnival potential of the theme.

The third stage encompassed the selection of the material and the process of its construction. Further improvisations were conducted (then and later) but the central questions were of the following type: how 'to find out the links between these sketches', how to '[put] these situations together', how to begin, how to end and how to arrive at the 'conclusion that is resonant like in music' (Houben 2013: 103). This was the pivotal stage in the creative process because, as Houben stresses, 'it is when you are trying to find connections between distant thoughts that you find your language' (102).

Then, after four weeks spent rehearsing, the ensemble performed the fluctuating initial version of *A Minute Too Late* in 'community theatres all around England', 'learning the audience' before the London premiere at the Pegasus Theatre (103). The results of intense interaction between the ensemble confronted the world outside. Houben describes the type of changes introduced at this stage in the following way: 'When playing for an audience, we soon realized that certain sketches do not work. … After the show, little by little we reconstructed the reaction of the audience so as to get some help from outside' (103). The performers' self-evaluation was supported by the work of Annabel Arden who, while watching particular shows, would take notes on the audience's reactions. These were discussed by the ensemble and some of them motivated further improvements, while others were disregarded as marginal observations.

Houben stresses that, for one and a half years, *A Minute Too Late* evolved considerably (104). As the opening of the performance was burdened with the special role of setting up 'complicity with the audience', it changed frequently, especially during international tours in non-English-speaking countries. When performing in South America, for example, the actors experimented with beginning the show in broken Spanish before they skipped into English. Houben concludes: 'Big shifts, major adjustments were made at the beginning and then we made finer adjustments and then we made minute adjustments and that is the way the show grew and in a certain moment we arrived at its final shape' (104–5).

THE MECHANISM OF INTERFERENCE

In the case of *A Minute Too Late* the mechanism of interference between theatre communication (internal *semiosis*) and structures/codes emerging from the world outside formulated the sequence consisting of three stages:

1) initial research in the non-artistic world,

↓

2) theatrical adaptation of the gathered material,

↓

3) further adaptation of the artistic concept

to the practice of theatrical communication.

Diagram 3.2

This model undergoes more detailed specification:

1.1 Autobiographical experience of personal grief and the sensation of loss caused by the death of Simon McBurney's father determines the main theme of *A Minute Too Late*. Yet, the onstage action focuses on the death of a wife, not a father, which marks the process of universal generalisation of personal matters.

1.2 Observations of the 'real-life situations' concerning personal grief and social habits that accompany the death of a beloved are conducted by all members of the company. This is further investigated by reading the pamphlet presenting codified description of social behaviour.

2.1 Ensemble improvisations confront the collected material (personal experience, social observations and the pamphlet) with the theatrical tradition of carnival mockery. The adaptation is filtered through the Lecoq style of work that characterised all involved performers and was enriched by their international background (McBurney is British, Magni Italian and Houben Flemish). Although they mainly use the English language, theatrical styles that emerge onstage originate in various traditions. These ensemble improvisations result in a number of autonomous episodes.

2.2 The establishment of the 'language of the performance' (its 'super-code') involves the selection and arrangement of the artistic material. The initial sequence is established but its structure is tentative. The theatrical adaptation of the previously collected structures/ codes of social behaviour has thus been completed. (Yet, further investigations in the subject matter and ensemble improvisations certainly continue when the show is performed.[9])

3.1 The confrontation between the ensemble's theatrical proposal and the expectations and reactions of the English audience inaugurates interference with the new aspect of the surrounding world. Further improvisation, additional selection of the material and continuous rearrangement of the overall structure of the performance multiply its variants. One may perhaps conclude that whereas stages 2.1 and 2.2 explore the consequences of idiosyncratic tensions between individuals involved in the creative process (i.e. intra-stage *semiosis*), from now on reciprocal interactions between the stage and audience prevail in the process of artistic communication (i.e. intra-theatrical *semiosis*).

3.2 International tours,[10] which included non-English-speaking countries, necessitate the intrusion of new languages (e.g. Spanish) and strengthening of the non-verbal aspects of theatre communication.[11] The international status of the ensemble is now reflected by the increasingly international character of the theatrical communication (i.e. stage → audience).

3.3 Increasing codification of the performance is accompanied by the ongoing professionalism of the non-verbal aspects of communication (e.g. lighting and sound design) and growing directorial role of Simon McBurney. For these reasons, the 2005 production is endowed with a completely new function.[12] Even if its rather rigid structure allows much ground for improvisation in the style of *commedia dell'arte*, the performance is confronted this time with the expectations of a new type of audience. At the risk of oversimplifying the matter, I would suggest that, for a group of spectators, *A Minute Too Late* was no longer an episodic show improvised spontaneously by an ensemble of friends who wanted to spend holidays together,[13] but a canonical and formative production of a world famous theatre institution. The National Theatre programme for January–April 2005 announces the show in a very illustrative way: 'the National has invited Simon McBurney and Complicite to mark their survival by bringing this legendary piece of vaudeville back to life for a limited season' (4).

THE CONSTRUCTION

One of the side effects of the 1998 and 2005 revivals of *A Minute Too Late* was a relatively detailed archival documentation of the final variants of the performance. The following analysis is based on two manuscripts: the 'unedited version as @ Old Vic 1998' and the prompt script 'as at 27ᵗʰ January 2005'. An audiovisual recording provides additional research material. Fragmentary as it is, the material provides sufficient grounds for the recognition of how innovative employment of the conventions originating in *commedia dell'arte* shaped the logic of the plot.[14]

The episodic construction encourages structural and semantic juxtapositions between particular scenes and the whole performance. In addition to that, the comparison of the two scripts reveals that particular scenes function as variants of the depicted situation. As it is in the tradition of *commedia dell'arte*, the general scheme of the action and the roles of actors are rigidly prescribed, but each performance allows considerable scope for improvised variations in realising verbal and visual patterns.

The highly auto-referential Prologue is followed by ten scenes (the very word is used in the secondary text) that present a number of fictional episodes. The segmentation is well motivated by changes in spatio-temporal imagery and the variety of situations created by the actors.[15] Although the storyline does not follow exactly the principles of a well-made action in which one episode leads to another in accordance with the logic of cause and effect, the main onstage action focuses on establishing the field of carnival associations around the theme of death and social habits accompanying bereavement.

As we will see, the construction of *A Minute Too Late* rearranges the spheres of structural indeterminacy and internal incoherence. Although such an artistic strategy might seem idiosyncratic in the context of modern British theatre (hence the reservations of Billington, Taylor and Shenton), these are certainly standard features of attention-grasping, improvisation-based spectacles following traditions of popular entertainment, such as street theatre, melodrama, circus, *commedia dell'arte* and improvisation.[16]

INTERNAL FEATURES OF THE PROLOGUE

In the 1998 script, the fact that the Prologue is not yet 'the proper show' is stressed not only verbally but also visually. When J[os] notices the audience, he simply says that the show has not yet started. At this point M[arcello] and J are simply preparing for the forthcoming performance by arranging stones, a bucket of gravel, and rubbish (including a Coke can) as part of the stage design. They also put on their costumes. Finally, when S[imon] arrives and the trio state they are ready to begin, J announces—somewhat unexpectedly—the main theme by stating that the show is about death.

In the Prologue J explains to the audience their reasons for remounting the show for this particular occasion (to benefit the Kosovo Red Cross). He adds that the performance was created in 1983 and that it has not been done for the previous ten years. He talks about its simple character (no money, cheap objects and things) and indicates the sources of inspiration, such as melodrama, 70s B-movies, naturalism, bio-mechanics, Brechtian alienation techniques and physical theatre. M adds proudly that the show was created by themselves. There is much situational humour resulting from the performers' actions (e.g. the gag of misunderstanding each other) and verbal exchanges (apologies of McBurney). The poetics of evasiveness is much explored whenever J indicates a topic and then concludes that it is unimportant.

Most of this is repeated in the 2005 script but in this version some elements are added. For example, J introduces himself as Jos and M as Marcello, adding a couple of sentences on his Flemish origins and thus explaining his foreign accent. In addition, he indicates that the costumes they are about to put on are—with the agreement of those who contracted the production—20 years old and come from the original production. J is more explicit this time in indicating the communicative potential of the stage language. He not only stresses the possibilities of the language of gestures, illustrating this by drinking out of a cup created simply with his movements, and speaks about the language of movement, but also prepares the audience for the fact that actors are occasionally going to use their native languages, which he proves by saying 'something' in Flemish.

The Prologue, which in both manuscripts is a separate part of the script, confronts four spheres of theatre communication. It:

- anticipates the main onstage action,
- stresses auto-referential qualities of the ongoing communication,
- refers to the origins and history of the performance,
- blurs the boundaries between the onstage communication and the world outside.

There immediately emerges an explicit interrelation between verbal and non-verbal codes of communication. On the one hand, gestures, movements and actions establish the proxemics of the stage world and, on the other hand, the verbal dimension underscores the semantic potential of non-verbal signals. Interestingly, the 2005 script does not specify the exact wording of J's Flemish utterance, which indicates the primacy of the English language for theatre *semiosis*. The role of Flemish is that of an external intrusion. It functions more on an aesthetic than semantic level.

The semantic and structural autonomy of the Prologue is indisputable as no other scene is dominated by auto-referentiality and no other scene blurs the borderline between the *semiosis* and surrounding world to such a degree. Yet, the conventional character of theatre communication and its multidimensionality, once set in the Prologue, remain intrinsic features of the performance. Paradoxically, all this reveals that, in the case of *A Minute Too Late*, the principles responsible for artistic arrangement are to be found in the act of communication itself and not in the signs/structures/systems emerging from the surrounding world.

THE CARNIVAL AND THE LYRICAL

The spatial imagery of *A Minute Too Late* is grounded in the motif of the cemetery, which appears three times—in scenes 1, 3 and 10—and functions as the compositional framework for the main action. From the very beginning of scene 1, the place where the living come to meet the dead is confronted with the disturbing sounds of cars that are passing by on the adjacent road, which suggests a confrontation of two spatial points of reference (cemetery/onstage vs noisy road/offstage). In the course of the action, the contrast develops into a broad field of associations, in which **cemetery** (graves/flowers/internal experience of loss and despair) is confronted with the disturbing factors that come from the **world outside** (road noises/barking dogs/rubbish/Coke can/mobile phones).

The three cemetery scenes significantly differ in terms of their construction. Whereas 'Scene 1' develops a long sequence of episodes contrasting black humour with the cemetery routine, 'Scene 3' and 'Scene 10' are very short and rather univocal units. In 'Scene 1', the routine of visiting the grave with flowers, cleaning up, bringing water and searching for appropriate words embeds a sequence of baffling gags based on the motifs of a fresh grave, finding a corpse that turns into a zombie and the nightmare of being buried alive. Surreal and exaggerated as they are, the gags broaden the spectrum of associations by supplementing the sense of internal despair with the parody of cultural connotations such as the macabre, grotesque and gothic. The dualistic construction of 'Scene 1' [Webster's cemetery routine → the series of carnival gags → Webster's cemetery routine] allows for the presentation of incongruous emotions that accompany the bereavement.

'Scene 3' transposes carnival elements to the mourning routine of Martin Webster, and thus interweaves the two modes of experience. The protagonist reintroduces the mime of eating a sandwich on a grave that started at the end of 'Scene 1'. As it was suggested, he does so in an attempt to follow the advice of those with goodwill (eating is vital for keeping the body and soul together). At the opening of 'Scene 3', Webster is faced with what seems to be a rather absurd dilemma regarding whether it is margarine or butter that makes his sandwich too dry to eat. He then drops the sandwich on the grave and nearly manages to formulate his farewell speech before the intrusion of a barking dog acted by Magni, and then Houben. Now, Webster gets involved in cumbersome, if jovial, attempts to get rid of the dog, which provides substantial ground for improvised actions. The situational black humour arises, and the lyrical mode is suspended until the final episode.

'Scene 10' functions as the coda to the whole performance. Here, the personal way of experiencing the bereavement in accordance with Webster's feelings prevails over modes of behaviour that were imposed by despair, stereotypes, empty social habits and discomforting rituals. After so much reluctance, Webster manages to communicate verbally his rudimentary emotions and, thus, to come to terms with his new life situation. This is, perhaps, not a profoundly metaphysical kind of experience. But it epitomises the basic human need to come to terms with reality after the internal destabilisation caused by the death of someone close.

In terms of Lotman, the final scene sanctions the primacy of the world of 'proper' names over that of universal generalisations ('common' names). It turns out that it is Martin Webster's personal experience that retrospectively re-evaluates the meaning of an incongruous world vision that seemed to follow solely nihilistic principles of carnival mockery. The final scene is not, as Billington appeared to demand, a structural extravaganza of *A Minute Too Late*, but the factor which is decisive for setting the overall meaning. As we have known since Bakhtin, the carnival makes sense only when it is well demarcated (see Bakhtin 1984a). Re-establishing the world order in which a cemetery is the place where the living mourn the dead is precisely the role of 'Scene 10'.

THE MIMETIC AND THE COUNTERFACTUAL

The three cemetery scenes are strongly bound together and establish the core of *A Minute Too Late*. The story they sketch is further developed in two scenes entitled 'Martin Webster's Flat' (scenes 7 and 9) and the one which is embedded by them ('Scene 8: The Doctor'). When approached as a complex compositional unit, the three scenes formulate a sequence that echoes the episodic structuring of 'Scene 1' (Webster's mourning routine ('Scene 7') → hyperbolic recollection of a meeting with the doctor ('Scene 8') → Webster's mourning routine ('Scene 9').

Although scenes 7 and 9 depict Martin Webster's flat in accordance with the principles commonly ascribed to the convention of the fourth wall, spatial relations are established in the manner that exposes stage illusion. There are clear echoes of J's introductory comments from the Prologue on the specific nature of theatre communication. In the 2005 manuscript, Martin Webster's flat consists of a door (created by S's gestures), shelves (S's gestures), a chair (set by M), a table (set by J), a radio (created by J's voice), a kettle (J's voice), a cupboard (in this function J) and a lamp (a bulb in M's mouth). The action is rather static and dominated by Martin's home-routine mime. Having entered the room, he is mainly sitting, listening to the radio, unpacking bags, placing the purchased items on shelves, switching on the lamp, preparing and drinking tea, selecting and cutting Janette's photograph. Besides this, he reads aloud extracts from *What to do after a death in England and Wales* and delivers a soliloquy (these actions differ substantially in the two versions of the manuscript). It is quite clear that, in spite of advice from the pamphlet ('leaflet'), Martin is at a loss and in despair and cannot decide what to do in the new situation. The gags performed on stage (e.g. S's cutting of Janette's photograph) relieve the tension and endow the situation with humour.

In comparison, the recollection presented in Scene 8 is shaped in a rather different style. The scene presents one of Webster's numerous visits to the hospital. Janette is still undergoing treatment and Martin is meeting her doctor. The sketchy description of the action may seem quite mimetic, but its onstage presentation is distorted by the overall dominance of the overtly subjective perspective of Martin. The onstage account of his conversation with Dr Steward testifies to the counterfactual illusion of desperate hope-searching. For Martin, the matter-of-fact and sparse remarks of the doctor are magnified into sanguine signals.

As in the scenes set in Martin Webster's flat, in 'The Doctor' the device of soliloquy is used. But in scenes 7 and 9, the device serves to motivate a rather mimetic home routine. This time, however, the convention is used to underline the discrepancy between the actual state of affairs (the doctor's implication of the imminence of Janette's death) and counterfactual hope-searching on the part of Martin. In 'Scene 8', the incongruity of Martin's internal state and the world around him is the main source of disconcerting humour.

Uncompromising mockery of utter despair suggests a world vision in which the notion of human comedy prevails. When exposed to the imminence of death, a human being may act against reason in an attempt to resist the imminent course of events. Notwithstanding their efforts, human beings are part of nature and their existence is doomed from the very beginning: both the horror of inescapable death and the sense of inexplicable despair are part of the human lot.

AUTONOMY OF COMPOSITIONAL UNITS

My analysis of the six scenes may create the erroneous impression that in the case of *A Minute Too Late* structural incongruity results exclusively from the atomised fragmentation of the presented world (detachment of particular episodes), distorted verisimilitude of the onstage *semiosis* (meta-theatrical explicitness and misleadingly subjective delineation of the storyline) and disregard for chronological arrangement of the presented sequence. The temporal segmentation of the plot follows this pattern:

1) scene 8: the doctor

↓

2) scenes 7 and 9: Martin Webster's flat

↓

3) scenes 1, 3 and 10: the cemetery

Diagram 3.3

Yet, the matter turns out to be more complicated when we take into consideration the remaining part of the performance. Scenes 2, 4, 5 and 6 are deprived of deictic indicators that would unambiguously confirm their immediate links with the plot focused on Martin Webster. It is true that such connotations are encouraged visually by the unbroken succession of both the physical features of the three actors and the stability of their styles of performance.[17] Nonetheless, other stage signals imply that such equivalence is ill-founded. The world of the stage and the fictional reality belong to divergent modes of semiotic settlement. After all, in *A Minute Too Late* S[imon McBurney] plays chiefly the character of Martin Webster, whereas J[os Houben] takes a whole range of roles, including that of a performer, a mourner, an undertaker, a doctor, a kettle and a radio, and M[arcello Magni] may turn into a corpse, a zombie, a doctor, a lamp, a mourner or a dog.

Although the logic of the 'stage language' (where actors' words and actions are decisive for creating meanings, e.g. a lamp) does not coincide with the logic of the fictional world (in which a 'lamp' is a lamp, notwithstanding the means of its onstage representation), the performance is neither absurd nor incongruous. On the contrary, the discrepancy between the world of the stage and the world it depicts underscores one of the axioms of the emerging world model. There is an ontological abyss between semiotic systems as such and the natural world. For this reason, any kind of interaction between the two is of vital importance.

In other words, by constant confrontation of the singular logic of the company's 'stage language' with elements emerging from the surrounding world, Théâtre de Complicité reveals that the stage language is prone to fluctuation, transformations, juxtapositions and contrasts, and thus multiplies incongruous perspectives within itself. In this case, artistic eruptions result not only from the infiltration of the external into the internal (e.g. the parody of social stereotypes and assimilation of autobiographical material for artistic purposes) but also from enormous dispersion of atomised construction (e.g. the juxtaposition of the carnival and the lyrical modes).

Now the scenes in question develop their communicative autonomy, each in a very distinct way. Because the overt autonomy of individual scenes (i.e. 2, 4, 5 and 6) dominates in the first part of the performance, the audience is initially overwhelmed by the sense of complete incongruity of the overall construction. This impression is balanced by a contrary arrangement of the final part of the performance. Its more congruous arrangement results from the internal coherence of Martin Webster's plot.

In other words, the performance models a dynamic act of communication in which the ending retrospectively integrates the logic of the plot.

The onstage action presented in 'Scene 5: The Registrar's Office' and 'Scene 6: The Hearse' formulates a sequence that seems to be integrated with the story of Martin Webster. Yet, it does so in a rather superficial way. The impression is made by introducing certain motifs that are stressed at the opening of 'Scene 7' (e.g. Martin's appearance, coming back home, and mentioning the name of a neighbour: Mrs Green) as they echo those presented in scenes 5 and 6 (Martin's appearance has not changed, Mrs Green is the name of J's dead mother/sister, and S is on his way home in scene 6). However, the motifs do not formulate the cause-and-effect chain of events, or contribute to a more elaborate depiction of the protagonist. More than that, the motifs function as highly schematic indicators of compositional links between episodes that are not necessarily related in terms of the development of the plot. In other words, it is not the storyline but the field of associations developing around the theme of death that is crucial for the links between the scenes and the main plot.

Both episodes present hugely independent actions. In 'Scene 5: The Registrar's Office', the stage is divided in two parts: a waiting room and the office. Notably, the spatial dichotomy is achieved through the actors' actions and not physical objects, which becomes clear in the opening mime when J is knocking firmly three times on an invisible office door. At this point, there appear to be some differences between the two manuscripts. In the 2005 version S is hesitantly waiting for his turn and in the 1998 version he is about to leave the waiting room. In both cases, however, he allows the newcomer (J) to inquire whether the registrar is already in his office. As it turns out, M (the registrar) is asleep on his desk. J keeps this observation to himself and informs S that 'they' seem to be busy. From the perspective of the audience, it is quite clear at this stage that situational humour prevails.

Subsequent actions intensify the parody of administrative conduct. Taking advantage of S's indecisiveness, J sneaks in the queue so his case will be dealt with first, explaining that he is in a hurry as there is someone waiting for him in the car downstairs. J enters the office again so as to wake the registrar by banging the Bible on the desk. This is followed by other gags aimed at mercilessly elongating the registering process (e.g. squirting out orange juice, the stamping routine, and a desperate search for the right certificate on the floor). In scene 5, mimed slapstick gags are balanced with verbal and situational humour. At one point, for instance, ignoring J's matter-of-fact attitude, the registrar does his best to avoid the word 'die'. The humour results here from the contrast between the expectations of the petitioner (that the administrative procedure will be dealt with quickly) and the attitude of the registrar (to offer his professional pseudo-compassion). We encounter hyperbolic exploitation of stereotypes associated with the administrative treatment of bereavement. The professional code of behaviour of the clerk is confronted with the unexpectedly pragmatic attitude of the petitioner.

A similar kind of juxtaposition appears at the ending of the scene. After leaving the office, J asks S to hold the blue paper, and the latter realises it is a death certificate. He is immediately at a loss what to do. The situation develops into another compassion routine in which interlocutors misunderstand the conduct of one another.

Mise en abyme and Framing

Scene 5 is structured in accordance with the convention of frame composition, which may be best illustrated by the following diagram:

1) S and J in the waiting room,

↓

2) the registration procedure in the registrar's office,

↓

3) S and J in the waiting room.

Diagram 3.4

Such structuring establishes an intriguing parallel between scene 5 and the construction of the main performance. The analogy is striking when we compare diagrams 3.4 and 3.5, the latter presenting the frame composition of the main performance (scenes 1–10):

1) cemetery,

↓

2) action proper,

↓

3) cemetery.

Diagram 3.5

Such employment of the device of *mise en abyme* demonstrates the vivid functionality of framing. Firm delineation of the main action, and then similar segmentation of one episode, draws attention to the autonomy of various levels of construction. In both cases, internal structures, being opposed to external ones, pursue original rules of arrangement. Autonomy of meanings created within a concrete compositional unit (e.g. scene 5, or the main performance) necessitates recognition of various methods of segmentation and the individual treatment of each of them.[18]

Paradoxically, while stressing contrasts between internal and external structures, *A Minute Too Late* pronounces ongoing infiltration of these spheres. Whereas the Prologue anticipatorily embeds the main performance (scenes 1–10) in the world of theatre, scene 5 deals primarily with themes that dominate the main plot and in this way hints at the logic governing its arrangement. Even though it is J, and not Martin Webster, who registers a death, the type of event and its slapstick treatment is set within the field of associations we know from other scenes. It may not be clear what exactly the purpose of S's presence in the waiting room is, but the onstage treatment of administrative procedures clearly alludes to the inadequate reactions to bereavement. As elsewhere, the performance concentrates on the parody of stereotypical situations rather than on the psychological nuances of the protagonist's motivation. We observe here yet another way of employing the tradition of *commedia dell'arte*.

The relations we have seen are of a paradigmatic character, which means they pronounce abstract principles responsible for the general arrangement of the performance. Although scene 5 is less obviously inscribed in the main plot than those previously analysed, there also appear signals justifying its syntagmatic (i.e. sequential) positioning. This may, of course, be a good excuse for an actor to get some rest in this physically exhausting, 70–80-minute-long spectacle. As we discover towards the end of scene 5, the petitioner (J) is an undertaker. Persistent as he is, he manages to persuade S to act against his will and get in J's 'lovely black' limousine on his way back home (it now becomes clear who has been waiting for J in the car). In this way 'Scene 6: The Hearse' appears as a continuation of the previous episode. Those who accidentally met in the waiting room are now together on the slapstick hearse ride around the streets. Again, there are no firm indicators that S takes the role of Martin Webster, but—as we remember—the next scene supports this interpretative possibility (the appearance, Mrs Green and coming back home). In any case, scene 6 furthers the slapstick quality of the show in a series of events that are as detached from the main plot as those presented in scene 5.

Explicitly, the low-quality black humour that dominates scene 6 results mainly from visual and situational gags. The verbal dimension fulfils here a secondary role, as the characters' utterances merely support their actions. The boulevard dimension of the spectacle achieves its peak, and is particularly clear, in the 2005 version of the performance, as preserved in the video recording and the manuscript. When compared with the 1998 version of the script, scene 6 is much extended, and it includes the following series of gags: the company of a corpse and its falling forward (in this role, M), J's taking a sweetie from the urn, the routine of putting on and off the seatbelts, running over a pedestrian, a police chase, getting through a roadblock, Clint Eastwood-like shooting of a policeman (the recorded voice of Clint Eastwood is heard). One can hardly speak here of profound meanings. Neither is it appropriate to expect an explanation of issues that emerge in the remaining part of the performance (though the raid echoes the offstage 'street noises' that are heard from the cemetery). The vigorous series of gags aims at immediate carnival laughter on the part of the audience rather than at refining the logic of the performance. All in all, 'Scene 6: The Hearse' borders on boulevard farce, pursues slapstick black humour, and thus develops as a parody of the stereotypical treatment of death in popular entertainment. The carnival mode of *A Minute Too Late* achieves its climax at this point.

In spite of the considerable autonomy of the episodes (they function well as two independent stories), scene 5 and scene 6 establish an additional unit within the construction of *A Minute Too Late*. First, the events they present constitute a sequence (registering a death → the way back home). Second, the actors take the roles of the same characters. Whereas the self-confident petitioner acted by J turns out to be an undertaker and the insane driver, the indecisive supplicant acted by S becomes the irresolute passenger. Third, unlike in the majority of scenes, the role of S is marginalised. He is as passive and vulnerable in the waiting room of the registrar's office as during the insane ride in the hearse. Finally, just as in the case of the Prologue, the central role is given to J in both scenes (but in the Prologue he took the role of himself [i.e. actor] and not an undertaker).

The physicality of J's improvisation skills (i.e. Jos Houben's artistic signature) is crucial for delineating paradigmatic links between the Prologue and scenes 5 and 6. Indeed, the 1998 and 2005 manuscripts suggest that these are exactly the episodes which allow for most improvisation, as there are many textual variants. The changes range from auto-referential comments (e.g. in the 1998 Prologue, J explains the reason for reviving the show), through shifts in details concerning the fictional world (e.g. in the 1998 variant, Charlie Green dies at the age of sixty-seven, and in the 2005 manuscript at seventy-six), to the expansion of the course of the presented events (this change is most evident in the case of scene 6 since the sequence of gags is fully developed only in the 2005 version). All these fluctuations are signs of the improvised and non-institutional origins of the company's craftsmanship that were implemented in the stage language of *A Minute Too Late*. Seen as traces of 'genetic memory', episodes such as 'Scene 6: The Hearse' are crucial for the aesthetics of (Theatre de) Complicite, and not—as Billington claims—'simply ... to demonstrate the trio's mimic expertise', since they cultivate the complicity between the stage and the audience in the way that identified the company in the earliest stages of its development.[19] This is an emblematic example of assimilating structures derived from street shows and similar types of entertainment into theatre performance.

SEGMENTATION

The prominence of the undertaker's subplot is marked by its positioning within the sequence of the onstage action. It follows the church episode and precedes 'Scene 7: Martin Webster's Flat'. The shift is strong, as in both of the embedding episodes it is S—and not J—who is the leading actor. Yet, 'Scene 4: The Church' makes extensive use of black humour in which the profane challenges the sacred (see, for example, the uncompromising parody of the praying routines).[20] In this sense, scene 4 advances the carnival element of the performance and anticipates its climactic realisation in scenes 5 and 6. Compared with that, 'Scene 7: Martin Webster's Flat' is very different. Notwithstanding a certain degree of humour, scene 7 diminishes the carnival element and installs the lyrical mode that will dominate the ending of the performance. Certain motifs suggest an internal coherence between the undertaker's subplot and scene 7, but it is the contrast between the lyrical and carnival modes that is decisive for the semantics at this point. Between 'Scene 6: The Hearse' and 'Scene 7: Martin Webster's Flat' we go through the crucial compositional borderline that brings two contrasting fields of association into confrontation:

(**the carnival:** parody/gags/stereotypes/*risus purus*/the world of common names)

vs.

(**the lyrical:** internal/emotional/sense of despair/individual/ordinary/the world of proper names).

Diagram 3.6

The artistic potential of *A Minute Too Late* thrives on long-lasting and multifaceted semiotic explosions whenever the two modes of approaching the theme of death interact.

COMPOSITION AND CONSTRUCTION

We can see the following means of compositional and constructional arrangement in *A Minute Too Late*:

1. **Chronological structuring of the plot focused on Martin Webster:**

    1. (scene 8) → 2. (scenes 7 and 9) → 3. (scenes 1, 3 and 10)

    where 1. presents a highly subjective account of a meeting with a doctor when Janette is still alive; 2. struggles to redefine the sense of a home after Janette's death; and 3. attempts to formulate a basic farewell when visiting her grave.

2. **Episodes depicting highly autonomous actions that are incongruous with the main plot (i.e. with point 1.):**

    'Scene 2: The Wake' // 'Scene 4: The Church' // ['Scene 5: The Registrar's Office' and 'Scene 6: The Hearse']

    It should be added that scenes 5 and 6 form an optional unit as they coherently present the undertaker's subplot.

3. **The juxtaposition of scenes dominated by the carnival mode and those exploring the lyrical mode:**

    P vs [(1, 2, 3, 4, 5 and 6) vs (7, 8, 9 and 10)]

    The very juxtaposition is further contrasted with the Prologue, which results in the confrontation of explicit auto-referentiality with the fictional world.

4. **The notions ascribed to the stage reality differ between those indicating internal (subjective) states and those parodying stereotypical social behaviour (external world):**

    [8 (7 and 9) (1, 3 and 10)] vs [P, 2, 4, 5 and 6]

    In the first group the scenes range from an explicitly subjective account of counterfactual hope ('Scene 8: The Doctor') and depiction of Webster's deeply personal, if clearly confused, experience of bereavement, epitomised by the motifs of an empty home ('Scenes 7 and 9: Martin Webster's Flat') and fresh grave ('Scenes 1, 3 and 10: The Cemetery'). The second group contains those episodes that explicitly refer to structures and codes that were assimilated for artistic purposes from the surrounding world: the Prologue (relations between actors and audience), 'Scene 2: The Wake' (social codes of expressing condolences and formulating the farewell speech), 'Scene 4: The Church' (praying routines), 'Scene 5: The Registrar's Office' (administrative procedures) and 'Scene 6: The Hearse' (farce and slapstick humour).

5. **Finally, we arrive at the model of syntagmatic segmentation of the onstage action:**

$$P\,[(\text{scenes } 1\text{–}4)\ (\text{scenes } 5\text{–}6)\ //\ (\text{scenes } 7\text{–}10)]$$

where the initial impression of a complete fragmentation of unrelated episodes (scenes 1–4) is followed by the independently realised undertaker's subplot (scenes 5–6). The compositional shift that emerges between scenes 6 and 7 ('a pause') diverts the semantics and leads towards a retrogressive implication of the internal coherence. It is important to note here the compositional framework imposed by the cemetery scenes (1 and 10). Besides this, strong emphasis is laid on P, whose compositional detachment (its auto-referential status differs completely from the remaining part of the performance) is well justified by the anticipatory implication of internal coherence suggested by the Prologue.

THE LOGIC OF THE PLOT

Although it ignores nuances of artistic arrangement, the scheme of analysis employed here illustrates at least some of the general principles responsible for the semantics of *A Minute Too Late*. In the course of the performance, the initial impression of puzzling disintegration is replaced by the sense of the retrogressively imposed logic of the plot. Owing to the performative aspect of the show (one-time linear reception), the addressee may conclude that autonomous actions (i.e. point 2) are based on the recollections of Martin Webster, even though such interpretation does not find support in more scrupulous analysis. In addition to this, the syntagmatic arrangement of the spectacle leads us from the utterly carnival-like treatment of the theme of death that finds its climax in scene 6 to a subtler lyrical mode that culminates in Martin Webster's final formulation of his basic farewell 'speech'.

Here, we can observe the theatrical implementation of constructional and compositional principles that derive from spectacles such as *commedia dell'arte*, improvisation and street theatre. The consequences of this type of semiotic explosion invariably remain at the core of Complicite's aesthetics. This is not to say that the company treats them in a dogmatic way. On the contrary, only those aspects of the paradigm are employed that seem to be useful for the artistic objectives of the particular project.

FURTHER IMPLICATIONS

Materials documenting the early stages of Théâtre de Complicité have allowed us to put conclusions from Chap. 2 in a new context. It is true that the aesthetics of the company retrogressively reveals traces of Simon McBurney's signature. But it is equally true that improvised street shows, and performances such as *Put It On Your Head* and *A Minute Too Late*, establish aesthetic foundations for the company's 'stage language' by implementing external signs/structures/systems for artistic objectives that are pursued by the ensemble.

The aesthetics of Complicite promotes permutations resulting from the strongly developed improvisational skills of performers. As in the street and improvised shows, in which reactions of passers-by and unexpected events would shape the course of the action, more regular performances fluctuate from one night to another, and from one production to another. Such multiplication of variants, succinctly illustrated by the two versions of *A Minute Too Late*, escalates the sense of the fragmentariness of reception. Here, as elsewhere, the company explores the inherent transience of theatre communication. The unavoidable oblivion of much of such *semiosis* is not treated as derogative. Rather, in their artistic endeavours, members of Théâtre de Complicité continuously explore ambiguous mechanisms of remembering and forgetting. This is as true of McBurney (*Mnemonic*) as Magni (*The Valley of Astonishment, Tell Them That I Am Young and Beautiful, Marcel*) and Houben (*The Art of Laughter, Marcel*).

The construction of a fluctuating performance necessitates the creation of stable foundations that leave space for unpredictability and permutations. As Jos Houben insists, and our analysis of *A Minute Too Late* confirms, the strenuous processes of selection and combination of the improvised material leads to the establishment of clearly delineated segmentation. It is helpful to observe the explicit and multi-layered framing of the performance and abrupt shifts in the semantics of the spectacle (e.g. the role of the 'pause' between scenes 6 and 7). In addition to this, the course of the onstage action implies the unstable nature of the created meanings. For example, the initial confusion of the audience, caused by a sequence of unrelated episodes, is finally submerged by retrogressive suggestions of internal coherence. As we will see in Chap. 4, multi-layered framing, fluctuating meanings and clearly delineated segmentation are endowed with enormous semiotic capacity in much of the artistic output of the company.

It is intriguing that, contrary to the conclusions emerging from interpretations of the manuscript material, the video recording of *A Minute Too Late* diminishes the role of paradigmatic segmentation and brings to the fore syntagmatic coherence. This results from the increased prominence of the visual—highly physical—onstage action that characterises the recording and the performance itself. The extravagant characterisation of the three actors and their unmistakeably distinct styles of acting are decisive for the overall coherence of the visual dimension of the performance. From the perspective of the audience, M[arcello Magni] remains M[arcello Magni] even when he assumes the roles of a mourner, a speaker, a corpse, a policeman, a dog, a lamp and so on. This is to say that, in the 'stage language' of Théâtre de Complicité, the ontological discrepancy between the language of the stage and the fictional world it creates is particularly exposed. Together with the vast interest in composition and construction, the exploration of the semiotic consequences of the autonomy of the stage world testifies to the fascination with auto-referentiality. By exploring the autonomy of theatre communication, Théâtre de Complicité constitutes a singular 'language' that could be recreated solely from its employment in the given work. Thus, Théâtre de Complicité radically demarcates the logic of the onstage action from the logic of the fictional world.

The juxtaposition of the onstage action and the fictional world hints at the way in which Complicite adapted Brecht's alienation technique. From the perspective of the audience, the distance between performers and the characters they represent is fluctuating but nonetheless clear. The logic of the stage does not make us believe that barking M turns into a dog, but that the onstage signals (i.e. M's barking) communicate specificity of the theatre imagination and, thus, create a fictional world in which Martin Webster is chased by a dog when visiting the grave of his wife. Théâtre de Complicité demonstrates that the singularity of the theatre imagination emerges from the dichotomy between the stage signals and the fictional world that is communicated through the stage language by the theatre-makers. Simon McBurney consistently appreciates the role of the audience in theatre, as for example when saying that 'Without the audience theatre does not exist. ... [I]n fact, it only exists in the minds of the audience. It doesn't exist on stage because if you go up on the stage there's nothing there. It's complete illusion' (Knapper 2010: 243–4; see also Shevtsova and Innes 2009: 166 and the film recording 'Simon McBurney on the Theatre Audience').

In this chapter, the ways of assimilating theatrical traditions have been discussed. Certain principles deriving from *commedia dell'arte*, street performance and other forms of (popular) entertainment become integral elements of the 'stage language' of Théâtre de Complicité. Interestingly, assimilated structures are not necessarily taken with their diachronic semantic burden. Rather than treating them in a dogmatic way, Complicite tends to defamiliarise the functionality of such structures so as to integrate them into the artistic jargon of the ensemble. By assimilating the various devices, techniques and conventions discussed here, the company strengthens the performative aspect of its work and thus aims at achieving two objectives:

- enlivening the complicity between actors performing on the stage (intra-stage relations),
- reinforcing complicity between the stage and the audience in the course of theatre communication (intra-theatrical relations).

As we shall soon see, this early achievement of Théâtre de Complicité will be pursued in the subsequent stages of the evolution of the company.

NOTES

1. For other directions of the critical discussion on applying the tradition of Sapir-Whorf, Ferdinand de Saussure and Charles Peirce in the semiotic studies of theatre, see, for example, Aston and Savona 2005, Pfister 1991, Knowles 2004 and Limon 2002 and 2010.
2. Lotman tends to treat the terms of 'language', 'culture' and 'history' as synonymous, which may at times distort his argument. For this reason, I propose the following definitions: 'the semiotic reality' is a broad concept confronted with the surrounding (natural) world. Whereas 'the language' is equivalent to the natural verbal language, 'the code' is a broader concept

that encompasses semiotic systems of signs and the rules of their organisation. Unlike for Lotman, in this book 'the code' is not necessarily an artificial system and it may—but does not have to—reveal its history (diachrony). For a slightly different understanding of the functioning of signs in theatre, see Elam 1980.

3. There are some intriguing, if accidental, parallels between Yuri Lotman and Simon McBurney, the most indicative being their interest in Sergei Eisenstein and the historical importance of the early 1980s for their professional careers. In 1982 Lotman, who was at that time a widely recognised scholar, conceived his concept of the semiosphere. In 1983 McBurney finished at the Lecoq school and established his company in the UK.

4. 'The concept of 'devising' belongs to a more democratic and less hierarchical form of theatre than is common in the commercial world. It is a mode of creating plays and theatre pieces that do not emerge directly from a pre-existing text, and instead involves a company of actors in creating their own texts. The traditional roles of director and playwright are replaced by a collective although, finally, a work may become scripted and may even be subject to the direction of one particular member of the company' (Pickering 2010: 15). See also Allain and Harvie 2006: 146.

5. The event subverts Rozik's theoretical postulate: 'the extension of the principle of similarity to the imprinting matter is probably responsible for occasionally blurring the borderline between theatre and life. For example, street theatre may create the impression of a real social event, leaving people to wonder whether it is a real or an enacted situation. In street theatre, moreover, the stage, which should be seen as a domain marker of theatricality, is missing. Although bystanders may hesitate between these possible framings, once they are certain that they are observing an instance of theatre, their different attitude becomes evident: they allow themselves to apply the principle of acting or, rather, deflection of reference, and thus effectively read the event as a description of a fictional situation' (Rozik 2008: 87–8). Yet, the convention of street theatre allows for the unpredictability of the course of events and occasional annihilation of the separation of theatre and life. This was the case when Magni attempted to 'imprint' the rules of the fictional world upon the factual event of being arrested. His retrospective account of this event suggests that it should have been treated in terms of ongoing performative *semiosis* rather than as 'a social event'. This is, of course, a borderline phenomenon, but its treatment hints at the importance given to the unexpected.

6. Coming out of age was celebrated by the publication of a special brochure (visual essay) entitled *Complicite. Twenty-One Years 1983–2004.* In the introduction Simon McBurney writes: 'I cannot believe that 21 years has passed since four of us set out in a second hand yellow Commer Post

Office van and drove from arts centre to school attempting to make something out of nothing. It would be easy to say that this is what we intended. It would be easy to suggest that we planned in this way, the reality is that it simply happened. 21 years is a long time not to know what you are doing. It is not normal. It was not intended. It was only meant to fill a summer where there was nothing else to do' (Complicite 2004: 3).

7. In a conversation with Harriet Lane the origins of the show are described in the following way: '[...] the subject matter was shaped entirely by the death of McBurney's father, who taught architecture [sic!] at Cambridge. 'I watched him die of cancer when I was 19, 20. *A Minute Too Late* grew out of registering the death and everyone's reactions to me afterwards' (2005).

8. When asked about the way in which the piece was directed, Houben says: 'It was like in the Lecoq school, you never have a director. Annabel Arden would give us feedback on how the show was really constructed. So, you see the two of us, then a solo, then the three of us. The duos are the moments when Simon directed me and Marcello, and in the solos I or Marcello directed Simon, and there are shorter moments when the three of us play together' (Houben 2013: 103).

9. When asked by a member of the audience about the amount of improvisation in plays such as *Mnemonic*, McBurney answered: 'certain dialogues [are] improvised, but you need precision to preserve the musicality of the piece' (in Morris interview 31: 05). See also Frost and Yarrow 2007: 87.

10. According to Lane: 'Twenty-one years ago, the show was performed, with only a few tweaks, in Jamaica, America, Holland, France and Italy; it also played in Chilean shanty towns and British-run camps for Vietnamese refugees in Hong Kong' (2005).

11. Lane describes the situation in this way: 'Since they all spoke different languages, *A Minute Too Late*, as it took shape, was pretty text-light, relying much more on physicality. According to McBurney: "Any scene in which we didn't have to say anything was a marvellous excuse for us." Of the underlying pragmatism of the project, Houben said: "We needed to make a piece of theatre that would be accessible and entertaining at the same time. We wanted it to tour, to get an audience. That was important." This was counterbalanced by the trio's desire to experiment, as only 24-year-olds can, with the possibilities of theatre' (2005).

12. Lane observes one other important difference between the original version and its 2005 production: 'I ask how it feels, returning in your mid-forties to a project which you had created when very young. Houben says it's "familiar, but so distant. Every movement, every object, every walk is so familiar, and yet we've done so much in between." / McBurney says it reminds him of being a teenager, and having friends round, "and I'd show them my room and maybe there would be some toy in there from when I was six years old, and it would make me remember being given it when we

were on holiday in Iceland. It's an odd sensation. Not entirely comfortable."/ Houben is nodding in agreement. "Because you're rubbing up against your earlier selves"' (2005).

13. This is how the founding members of the company talked about the nature of their original collaboration. McCabe states that in early 1980s the company was 'a largely comic mime troupe' (2005: 16) and adds that 'even after five years, Complicite was less a theatre company than a functions collective of fellow travellers' (19).

14. I am aware of two earlier scripts of the performance.

15. I understand the question of segmentation in theatre studies differently to Rozik and the tradition he delineates (2008: 11–12). He concludes that: 'The basic structure of interaction is triadic: an action, a categorization of a previous action and a re-action, which in turn becomes an action, thus starting a new cycle again. For both verbal and non-verbal interaction, real segmentation applies to these three units' (39). Whereas for Rozik an analysis of theatrical segmentation reflects his theoretical presumptions (e.g. the elementary role of 'the iconic sentence' and the prominence of shifting speech-acts) (34–47), in my view it is the matter of unpredictable, multilayered, at times incongruous, yet simultaneously realised, shifts in the overall construction of the performance. In other words, the aesthetics of Complicite does not avoid divergent means of segmenting the signal material. For this reason, Rozik's proposal reveals one of several ways in which the performance may be functionally segmented. See also: Sinko 1982: 54–70, Serpieri 1989: 1–52.

16. For a more detailed discussion of these traditions see the following: street theatre (Pickering 2010: 191–2, Kennedy 2011: 578), melodrama (Lecoq 2009: 112–15), circus (Kennedy 2011: 119–20), *commedia dell'arte* (Lecoq 2009: 115–24, Rudlin 1994 and Kennedy 2011: 131–3) and improvisation (Lecoq 2006 and 2009, Frost and Yarrow 2007, Kennedy 2011: 288 and—in the context of Theatre de Complicite—Shvetsova's conversation with Mendus 2006).

17. For a theoretical discussion on the phenomenology of actors' physical presence on stage see: Rozik 2008: 174–187. In the context of *A Minute Too Late* his assumption that 'A performance-text does not aim at persuading spectators that they are witnessing a world and allowed to sneak a look at it, but rather at presenting a description of a world that is most meaningful to them' (178) seems somehow dubious. Spectators witness what is materially/physically happening on stage ('the world of the stage') and simultaneously pursue meanings created by the on-stage *semiosis*.

18. When discussing semiotic specificity of poetry, Lotman observes certain autonomy of intra- and inter-linear/stanzaic relations: meanings created within a stanza frequently differ from those created between stanzas. Similar arrangement may characterise the construction of a theatre performance:

meanings of individual episodes are not necessarily univocal with those suggested by the entire performance. This provides much ground for internal tensions.

19. For Rozik, this level of communication (stage → audience) is dominated by the mechanisms of rhetoric manipulation (persuasion) rather than those aiming at an aesthetic effect (2008: 133–145). Yet, I have pursued consequences of Jakobson's suggestion that in the domain of art the aesthetic function prevails.

20. As a similar episode in Rowan Atkinson's *Mr Bean* series illustrates, carnival treatment of the church routine was at the time conventional for British comedians. Jon McKenna suggests a broader context for the parody of church routine and mentions: Spike Milligan, Peter Sellers, Harry Secombe and their *The Goons Show*, *Father Ted*, Dave Allen and his religious jokes and sketches, and Monty Python. Besides, '[a]dventurous theatre companies who would parody and see the absurd side of anything were around even earlier from the late 1960s through to the early/mid 1980s. Companies like The Natural Theatre Company, Forkbeard Fantasy, The Incubus Theatre Company, Crystal Theatre, Cliffhanger and countless other small fringe companies' (email correspondence). See also Tony Dunn's article 'Sated, Starve or Satisfied: The Languages of Theatre in Britain Today' in Shank 1994: 19–40, esp. 24–25.

CHAPTER 4

The World of the Stage

FROM THE STAGE LANGUAGE OF THÉÂTRE DE COMPLICITÉ TO THE AESTHETICS OF COMPLICITE

The stage language of Théâtre de Complicité makes extensive use of the following juxtapositions:

1. the **fictional** vs. the **non-fictional** vs. the **auto-referential**,

2. the world of **proper names** vs. the world of **common names**,

3. the **correspondence** between the world of the stage and the fictional world

vs.

the **opposition** between the world of the stage and the fictional world.

Diagram 4.1

Even though they differ considerably, the juxtapositions set dynamic inter-relations, and for this reason should not be perceived in complete isolation. In particular performances they are mutually interwoven and enrich the meanings created by one another.

Treated as the starting point in the evolution, the stage language of Théâtre de Complicité has undergone significant—if unpredictable and inconsistent—transformations in the later phases of the development of the company's aesthetics. Among the ways in which particular features

© The Author(s) 2016
T. Wiśniewski, *Complicite, Theatre and Aesthetics,*
DOI 10.1007/978-3-319-33443-1_4

contributed to the shape of later performances, the following seem to be of greatest importance:

- the fluctuations within the 'open work',
- the frames within the construction,
- the communicative exploration of the spatio-temporal imagery,
- the confrontation of the world of the stage with the fictional world.

THE FLUCTUATIONS WITHIN THE 'OPEN WORK'

The principle of fluctuations resulting from the tradition of improvisation and constant improvements is preserved—in more or less obvious ways—in most of Complicite's work. As Simon McBurney puts it:

> The beginning is always now. I'm not being deliberately obscure when I say this, I'm always struck by how a piece of theatre varies from night to night and by how much it is made anew. The crucial percentage of difference has an enormous impact in the minds of the audience. (in Giannachi and Luckhurst 1999: 68)

For this reason, numerous collaborators have recognised the improvised spirit of rehearsals as one of the distinguishing features of the company and have felt much inspired by it. For example, Miranda Carter describes her interview with Kathryn Hunter—a prominent collaborator of Complicite in the 1990s:

> Meeting Complicite, a company with a 'language of movement,' was, [Hunter] says, 'a complete lightbulb.' But it was also bewildering. 'The improvisations were like nothing I'd encountered. There was this sense of play that didn't seem to exist in British theatre.' (1994)

A similar attitude is expressed by other theatre-makers who worked with Complicite (Magni workshop, Rintoul workshop, Houben 2013, Mendus email communication).[1]

The improvised nature of the creative process is specifically stressed in the visual essay that was published in book form in 2010 as *Complicite. Rehearsal Notes*. Designed by Russell Warren-Fisher, the book presents a collage of Sarah Ainslie's rehearsal photographs, archival material, quotes from reviews (e.g. Lyn Gardner, Benedict Nightingale, Michael Billington and Charles Spencer), opinions of widely recognised artists (e.g. Peter

Brook, Jude Kelly and David Farr), short notes from actors (e.g. Songha Cho, Tim McMullan and Shane Shambhu) and citations from those who have collaborated with the company through the years (e.g. John Berger, Michael Levine, Catherine Alexander and Douglas Rintoul).

There is also a one-page 'Foreword' written by Judith Dimant and a four-page-long 'Preface' by Simon McBurney, in which the artistic director of Complicite introduces the volume with these words:

> ... this book is not a record of Complicite rehearsals. You will not find any insight into the processes used in producing the work, or revelations about the results achieved on the stage as you turn these pages.
>
> What you will see are photographs.
>
> ... The moments are now fixed and belong to the past, but perhaps, when you look at the gestures, the feet, the faces, the hands of these theatre makers, you'll be about to imagine what may happen when they are performing in the fugitive but unceasing present of the stage. (2010b: 11–12)

Notwithstanding McBurney's reservations, *Complicite. Rehearsal Notes* does stress the prominence of rehearsals. Published by the company itself, the book provides an authorised image of what is important for Complicite. Both the visual essay and the collage of quotations hint at the significance of:

- games: 'In the beginning we played a lot of ball games. It's liberating, because you don't do what you are supposed to do.' (Stefan Metz, actor [in 2010: 60]; see also pages 62, 66, 88),
- images (see the photographs on pages 26/7, 29),
- movement: 'There are exercises and techniques which are given attention, the way a tennis player may practise his forehand. They underpin things on the level of the conscious and subconscious.' (Richard Katz, actor [in 2010: 84]; see the photographs on pages 24, 58, 83, 85, 88),
- playful spirit: 'In rehearsal there's a joyful mixture of work and play' (Angus Wright [in 2010: 65]; see also pages 16, 33, 92, 95),
- collaborative improvisation: 'The first time Simon asked me to come and work for him he said, "Do you want to come and play with us?," and although that play has often been very difficult in as many different ways as you can imagine, that first invitation has never lost its promise.' (Tim McMullan, actor [in 2010: 59]). Other members of the company say: 'The Complicite rehearsal is utterly collaborative,

shaped by the energies of the individuals present; and from this delicate balance of hearts and minds springs the work, unique, beautiful, precious' (Naomi Frederick, actor, [in 2010: 73]). 'What I enjoyed enormously in rehearsal was the freedom we had. We would investigate and try out things in groups and then show the results to each other. It was as if we were becoming scientists ourselves' (Stefan Metz, actor [in 2010: 23]). See also pages 35, 37, 43, 112.

It seems that the process of creating a performance is perceived by the theatre-makers as an integral part of conceiving the stage language rather than a preconceived concept that is imposed on the ensemble by the director.[2]

The improvised nature of Complicite's rehearsals is echoed in the fluctuating construction of the piece that is later presented to the general public. This reflects, of course, global trends in the twentieth century experimental theatre but seems something of a novelty on British ground. Particular performances leave more or less room for improvisation,[3] but all encourage fluctuations within productions. In *The Master and Margarita*, for example, Margarita was played by Sinéad Matthews in the original 2012 production, and by Susan Lynch since 2013. Not only do the two actresses present two different acting styles, but they are also put in slightly different stage situations, as is perhaps most explicit in Margarita's naked flight through the space. The Amsterdam and London productions of *The Magic Flute* go even further as they differ not only in cast but also in the language in which they are performed. Whereas the former was presented in the original German version, in the latter the libretto was an English translation. Additionally, in both cases the conductor and orchestra were different. The third case in point is *Mnemonic*. After the death of Katrin Cartlidge—the actress who originally created the female protagonist, i.e. Alice—the play was reworked with Susan Lynch. Other actors also differed, as we can see documented in the cast lists published together with the text of the play. Furthermore, shifts between particular productions of *Mnemonic* are clear in the published textual variants, and the most dynamic element is—as was the case in *A Minute Too Late*—the highly improvised prologue. Finally, *Lionboy* significantly changed between the original 2013 production directed by Annabel Arden and the 2014/15 version by Clive Mendus and James Yeatman. As Judith Dimant stresses, the latter underwent further shifts when it was taken from London to New York (Dimant in conversation).

In all these examples, the echoes of structures worked out in *A Minute Too Late* are striking. That performance established the pattern for the long-lasting creative process, which may be schematically presented as:

research and development

↓

improvised rehearsals

↓

fluctuating performances

↓

further changes resulting from feedback

↓

subsequent productions

Diagram 4.2

Each stage of the creative process allows for experiment, compositional shifts and more general transformations. In other words, the principle of fluctuations and the improvisational skills of performers constitute the type of onstage communication that is analogous to the notion of an 'open work'. The parallel to the concept conceived by Umberto Eco seems interpretatively useful. The analogy involves, among other issues, a shared fascination with:

- indeterminate meanings that coexist within one signifier,
- communication that presupposes ambiguities occurring between interlocutors of artistic communication,
- the paradox of intentional multiplication of interpretative contexts and preservation of internal integrity,
- the aesthetics of implication that leaves much ground to interpretative actions on the part of the addressee,
- the capacity of certain symbols to create universally ambiguous meanings,
- the intellectual co-operation between the encoder and the decoder during the process of communication,
- the poetics of the work in movement (fluctuations),

- the unrestricted interpretation that yet operates within the provided codes and fields of associations,
- the internal capacity of an artistic work to defamiliarise its codes and structures,
- the incompleteness of a finished work.

Pet Shop Boys Meet Eisenstein

Among the events in which Complicite was involved, the open-air presentation of Sergei Eisenstein's silent film *The Battleship Potemkin* is of particular relevance. On the rainy evening of 12 September 2004, a crowd of several thousand people participated in a 'happening' in Trafalgar Square, London. It was opened by Simon McBurney addressing the crowd from the roof of Saint Martin-in-the-Fields with social and political manifestos from the nineteenth and twentieth centuries, including fragments of Karl Marx's *Capital* (Martorell 2004). The action was accompanied by the projection of visuals documenting the broad history of demonstrations held in Trafalgar Square: from the suffragettes at the beginning of the twentieth century, through pacifist objections to the war in Vietnam, farmers' disagreement on a new tax and riots against the policy of Margaret Thatcher, to the more recent anti-Gulf War protests. This happening was followed by the main event, which was the large-scale presentation of *The Battleship Potemkin* accompanied by a concert by the Pet Shop Boys. The event was framed by the final manifesto, namely the on-screen inscription: 'EXISTENCE = RESISTENCE' (Costa 2004; Smyth 2004).

In many ways, McBurney's contribution to *Pet Shop Boys Meet Eisenstein* reflects his fascination with popular music[4] and the medieval tradition of public processions.[5] Both their 'liveness' and 'openness' find a reflection in this one-time event that exploited ambiguities, multiplied interpretative contexts and increased the notion of unrestricted interpretation. It was an open event, not only in the sense that everyone could participate in it for free, but also as one which presupposed considerable dispersion of meanings.

The Noise of Time

The second example of the way in which the aesthetics of an 'open work' is reflected by Complicite is *The Noise of Time*. Stephen Knapper discusses the juxtaposition between McBurney's 'role of dictatorial director' and that of 'collaborative spirit in Complicite's rehearsals' (2004: 69). Knapper, whose article 'Complicite's Comintern. Internationalism and *The Noise of Time*' makes extensive use of interviews with various members of the company, claims that there appears to be a significant degree of ambiguity in the communicative intentions of the performance. In other words, he delineates obstacles in answering the question of where the main agent responsible for the creation of meanings should be placed: in the musical element or in the performative.

Knapper makes it clear that an interpretation of Dmitri Shostakovich's *15th String Quartet* is accompanied by an independent audiovisual performance devised by Complicite.[6] According to the scholar, *The Noise of Time* caused serious generic uncertainty among members of the audience:

> At its first British performance ... the critic from *The Times* remained unconvinced by the conflicting grammars of visual, verbal and musical languages: 'This was indeed a marvellous event, but the test of its success must be the answer to its own question, "What happens when we listen to music?"'. Sometimes, we close our eyes and when all that imagery disappears, it doesn't make the slightest difference. At its premiere the *New York Times* theatre critic loved the theatrical elements but was unsure about the music, its music critic having the opposite reaction. (70–1)

Critics' reaction to *The Noise of Time* illustrates the receptive uncertainty of where to place the dominant mode of the piece, or how to evaluate the intrinsic constructional dichotomy of its being simultaneously a theatrical and a musical event. Characteristically, such duality indicates at least two different types of receptive strategy and thus enlivens the aesthetics of an open work: the meanings cannot be reduced to the elements of various channels of communication but rely on the tensions arising between them.

Mutual relations between dichotomies are crucial for Complicite. This analytical model is equally useful when applied to the paradox of simultaneous individualisation, and the universalisation of communicative processes. When analysing *The Noise of Time*, Knapper observes a disturbing contradiction in the way in which the creative process is described by the company members (he is less attentive to the members of the Emerson Quartet):

> ... the performers could be seen to move like marionettes. For Liam Steel this is an exigency of the form of multimedia ... that the company are employing here: 'You are part of a much bigger picture. As a performer you are another technicality alongside music, video and recorded sound. ...' Such an impression from within might lead one to conclude that the form is

reflecting the content, that the director, is echoing the 20th century dictator in a denial of spontaneous expression by the performer's volition. At first glance this might appear to be backed up by Charlotte Medcalf's description of the devising process: 'Simon comes to rehearsals, perhaps unconsciously, with a strong sense of some of the shapes that he's going to use and some of the key ideas. ... There's always collective feelings about things but in the end it's always going to be Simon's call. ...' However, on closer examination, to cast McBurney in the role of dictatorial director would be a false and somewhat facile conclusion ... Medcalf was at great pains to stress how the challenge for McBurney was to subjugate his own strong sense of rhythm to the demands of Shostakovich's score. (68–9)

In the case of *The Noise of Time*, the 'open' character of aesthetics is based on the generic discrepancy between the rigidly prescribed musical origins of the piece and its superimposed dramatic and performative dimension. Bound onstage in a reciprocal relation, Shostakovich's score and Complicite's performance make use of two divergent systems of communication. As in some other productions by Complicite, the musical component predetermines the visual and the verbal.[7]

Shostakovich is presented as an ingenious composer, who is confronted with the totalitarian world around him. It seems that some of his decisions cannot be separated from the political circumstances by which he is circumscribed. Knapper reports McBurney saying:

> ... In Shostakovich's *15th String Quartet* there are echoes of Soviet funeral marches, parodies of popular music, themes and silence that beset each other leading to a kind of vertigo. ... As with all music, the sounds of the landscape of the composer are always present. **We do not need to know, nor can we, every nuance of the composer's political and physical life to hear his song. We only need to know that it is not irrelevant to the way we listen**. (quoted in Knapper 2004: 73, emphasis added)

The performance develops a specific potential for the polyphonic dispersion of semantics. The simultaneous impact of musical and theatrical traditions cannot be underestimated. For example, Liam Steel associates shaping the movement of actors with that of a marionette, with an increase in the multimedia element. There is, I think, one other way of interpreting the echoes of the marionette and the development of the visual means of communication on the early twenty-first-century stage: it follows the tradition of those innovations introduced by Gordon Craig and cultivated, among others, by Tadeusz Kantor.

FRAMES WITHIN THE CONSTRUCTION

In the case of Complicite, the aesthetics of a fluctuating 'open work' is paired with a contradictory principle of exploring the semiotic capacity of the rigid and explicit framing of divergent structures functioning within a theatre performance. On the one hand, this is the way of establishing constructional foundations that provide a rudimentary basis for ever-changing variants, and on the other hand, the company charge the device of framing with crucial meanings.

Endgame

In its production of *Endgame*, for example, Complicite pursues textual suggestions imposed by Samuel Beckett. There are no major shifts in the characters' depiction, their utterances or the sequence of stage images, except strictly performative ornamentation resulting from the physical qualities of the actors and the carnival predilection of the director.[8] Although the play is performed in a form that will satisfy the regulations of the Beckett Estate, the company manages to indicate their own interpretation of the play by non-verbal means attached to the delimitation of the performance. Unlike in the text of *Endgame*, but more akin to the concept proposed by Beckett in a later play entitled *Not I*, theatre communication is initiated when the audience enters the auditorium and not when the curtain rises. Ambient music prepares for the performance when spectators are gathering and taking their seats, and the initial tableau of Hamm already sitting in his armchair is seen through a transparent crimson curtain. The situation is echoed in the ending. When the main action finishes and the transparent crimson curtain falls, Clov remains for a moment in a beam of light coming from the right window (perspective of the audience). The tableau is followed by the re-emerging ambient music that is heard from now on in the auditorium. The visual (transparent crimson curtain) and sonic (ambient music) framing of Beckett's play add subtly to the overall semantics of the performance.

The frame lays emphasis on the artistic/communicative status of the play and thus juxtaposes the world vision it proposes with the world vision of the audience. The added musical component, which marks the mediating state between 'normal life' and 'onstage *semiosis*', signals the special role of the audience in theatre communication. The hierarchy of structures emerges in which the semantics of a play (internal structures) is the subject of interpretation for the spectator (external perspective). By adding the beam of light coming from the right window to the final tableau, Complicite strengthen the possibility of a somewhat lyrical interpretation of Beckett's highly ambiguous ending. The passing suggestion of moonlight hints at the romantic tradition of lunar poetics.[9] It is noteworthy that this addition is 'hidden' beyond the crimson curtain and thus detached from the main body of the performance.[10]

The Elephant Vanishes

The second example of the functional treatment of a frame comes from the London production of *The Elephant Vanishes*. Prior to the proper performance, a Japanese actress emerges who explains to the audience in her broken English and unofficial manner that, owing to the incongruence of Japanese and British technical systems, the performance will be delayed since 'They don't understand each other'. Interestingly, the pseudo-improvised introduction functions similarly to the Prologue of *A Minute Too Late*, not only by its diminishing the convention of the fourth wall, but also in employing the motif of a delayed performance. As an optional element of the performance, the introduction hints at fluctuating structures and simultaneously defines the twofold quality of the model audience. By intermingling Japanese elements (e.g. the language, source material, styles of acting and storyline) with the non-Japanese features (e.g. the stage language of Complicite and work methods of the director and other members of the creative team), *The Elephant Vanishes* establishes an interesting onstage *semiosis* whose meanings differ depending on the type of audience. The London introduction brings to the fore the obstacles of theatrical communication, and thus underscores the phatic burden of the inter-cultural performance that is delivered by Japanese actors, conceived by a London company and presented to a British audience. As the introduction suggests, the two systems—this time cultural, not technological—are highly incongruous.[11]

The Magic Flute

The third example comes from the production of *The Magic Flute*. In this case the framing involves a gradual darkening of the auditorium accompanied by a musical introduction, followed by a screen projection of an unidentified hand writing in chalk on a blackboard the title of the opera, the name of the author, the date of writing, the title of the first act and a simple, symbolic drawing of mountains. Each time the inscription is wiped out by the hand 'dancing' in accordance with the rhythm dictated by the music. As we soon discover, the figure of the person actually writing is present onstage and delineated by a beam of light. The device is repeated at the climax of the opera, when the hand draws, in an anticlockwise way, the symbol of a moon that soon turns into a sun.[12] We observe an example of the integration of two different theatrical channels of communication in the course of a performance—the onstage action (writing on a blackboard) and the screen projection (live broadcast)—an important feature of the aesthetics of Complicite.

But the integration of divergent channels of the onstage *semiosis* and of its internal segmentation is certainly not the sole function of framing in Complicite's *The Magic Flute*.[13] Unlike in the original Amsterdam version, the 2013 production presented by English National Opera in London sets an interesting frame at the beginning of the second part of the opera (at least in the performance on 14 November 2013). After the interval, there is no clear-cut delineation that would fulfil the rudimentary role of a curtain and distinguish the onstage communication (internal structures) from the sphere of everyday life (external structures). On the contrary, the multitude of performers (including singers, musicians, actors and dancers) enter the stage in a disorganised manner—but dressed formally—so as to sit down in one of the dozens of chairs dispersed around, and they then get involved in group mime representing casual conversations. What becomes clear after a long while, when the stage is fully crowded (i.e. nearly all chairs have been taken), is that the stage situation fulfils the role of a frame in which the audience is mirrored. The motif of impatient waiting, involvement in informal talk, formal dress code and official conduct: these and many other similarities suggest the parallel between the world of the stage (and the fictional reality it depicts) and the world of the spectators.

Interestingly, the meanings created in the opening of part two of the London 2013 production of *The Magic Flute* are precisely opposite to the ones originating in the sonic frame of *Endgame*. Whereas the former implies congruity between the world of the stage and the world of the audience (i.e. stresses that both are part of theatre communication), the latter lays emphasis on the dissimilarity of the fictional world and the theatrical *semiosis* (i.e. provides an interpretation of Beckett's play).

In the case of Complicite, highly functional, and dynamic, treatment of the frame invigorates the semantic potential of rudimentary features of theatre communication. Elements which normally seem to be at the margins (e.g. the temporal frame and spatial demarcation) may be thus charged with pivotal meanings. The focus is on 'associative peripheries' rather than on 'core meanings'. If the principle of fluctuations hints at Eco's 'open work', the exploration of the semiotic capacity of rigid and explicit framing reflects a broader phenomenon studied by Boris Uspienski in his comprehensive book *The Poetics of Composition*. As the Russian semiotician proves, the functional treatment of framing has allowed for the artistic arrangement of the semiotic material on many structural levels ever since Dostoyevsky and Bulgakov (Uspienski 1997).

SPATIO-TEMPORAL IMAGERY AND COMMUNICATION

The Magic Flute abounds in interesting solutions in the domain of spatio-temporal imagery. Not only does it integrate various spheres of communication (e.g. onstage action and its screen projection) but also multiplies divergent points of reference for the onstage communication (e.g. by setting equivalence between the stage and the audience). The course of the main action challenges the most conventional delineation of functions ascribed to the stage, to the orchestra and to the audience, a number of times. Some of the most striking examples include:

- actors who are put in the role of an audience when watching multi-media projections,
- a portable internal stage installed over the main stage (the convention of a stage on a stage),
- Papageno's excursion through rows of spectators and the live screen projection of this 'journey',
- musicians' intrusion onstage so as to assume the role of actors (e.g. the flautist),
- handing a prop to the orchestra and musicians delivering it from one end of the stage to the other.

Needless to say, the orchestra pit is open and visible throughout the entire performance. The enumeration is illustrative and aims to show the degree to which the space of *semiosis* is enlarged from the microcosm of the stage to the macrocosm of the opera house. As in the initial frame of part two, the principle of congruence between the internal (onstage) and external (offstage) structures takes the most prominent role. Actors, just as spectators, are placed within a broader framework of operatic communication.

Measure for Measure

The potential of spatial imagery in theatre is explored in a similar way in *Measure for Measure*. Yet, it is achieved by the means of different tools, and is endowed with different functions. The central juxtaposition confronts the verbal tissue of the play with its theatrical interpretation. Even though the text is delivered in many dialects and styles of acting by an international cast, the verbal tissue is unmistakeably determined by the Shakespearean English. The non-verbal components of the performance stress its contemporary context. It is achieved, for example, by introducing to the stage *semiosis* a variety of structures that hint at theatre, culture and politics at the turn of the twentieth and twenty-first centuries.

By juxtaposing the verbal to the non-verbal (especially the visual), Theatre de Complicite provides a contemporary context for *Measure for Measure*. In one aspect of the performance, the company makes use of the universal semantics of Shakespeare in order to criticise the political situation in the world around them, which in itself is nothing new in terms of the modern approach to the plays of Shakespeare and other classics. The universal and the personal (this time political views) are again bound together. The following enumeration illustrates some of the more striking allusions to contemporary theatre, culture and politics. First, *Measure for Measure*, like much of experimental British theatre in the 1990s ('in-yer-face'), is explicit with physicality. This can be seen in scenes set in a brothel and presenting oral sex.[14] Second, the visual explicitness of violence is magnified in prison scenes and by a multi-scale projection of cutting veins. Third, as in minimalistic theatre, the playing area is mostly restricted to a square delineated onstage, or is submerged in overwhelming darkness. Fourth, the prop of an umbrella is used more than once and by different characters as if to echo the theatre of Tadeusz Kantor. Finally, as in the everyday spectacle of contemporary media, the on-screen image of George W. Bush is presented so as to introduce a political—sharply critical—context for interpretation.[15]

This illustrates the degree to which the performance is subordinated to the ongoing theatre communication. Unlike in *The Magic Flute*, where spatial relations aim primarily at enlarging the sphere of *semiosis*, *Measure for Measure* juxtaposes the verbal with the non-verbal (visual) so as to strongly activate the perspective of the audience. The role of spectators is not so much to recognise themselves as part of an overwhelming communication (*The Magic Flute*) as to interpret the whole variety of incongruous structures and systems. It is obvious that Shakespeare did not intend to criticise the Gulf War (the picture of George W. Bush), but *Measure for Measure*, when filtered through the theatrical language of Complicite, succeeds in preserving its universality (mankind was the same in 1603/4 and at the beginning of the second millennium) while simultaneously explicating a more immediate critique of the contemporary world. All in all, the production exemplifies one of the ways in which theatre communication may thrive on the intersection of diachronic structures/codes (the verbal) with synchronic ones (the visual).[16]

The Master and Margarita

The complexity of spatial imagery is further intensified in *The Master and Margarita*. The performance operates within several neatly intermingled fields of spatial reference. They may be provisionally grouped as:

- the depiction of places originating in the fictional world of Bulgakov's novel (e.g. Moscow, Jerusalem and the underworld),
- historical allusions that hint at the biographical context of the novel (e.g. the image of Josef Stalin, and the final comment directed by Woland to the audience),
- auto-referential devices that underscore the communicative status of theatre (e.g. the live screen projection of the audience),
- devices aimed at universalising generalisation (e.g. 3D projections of the globe and cosmos),
- hints at the immediate context of contemporary London (e.g. the opening comparison of a park in Moscow with Russell Square in London).

In the work of Complicite there is certainly no intention of preserving the classical unity of space in structuring the fictional world. On the contrary, multiplication of places conceived onstage by the whole range of multimedia devices available in the twenty-first century theatre is tremendous.[17] The locations range from the mimetic (the park in Moscow) to the anti-mimetic ones (the night in hell), from metaphoric structures (the palace of Pilate) to those whose character is either symbolic (Moscow as a madhouse) or archetypal (the global perspective), from presenting the stage as the place of a blasphemous ritual (naked Margarita drinks the blood of Berlioz, and the dark mass takes place when Yeshua Ha-Nostri is on the cross), through endowing the stage with features of popular culture entertainment (the Rolling Stones' 'Sympathy for the Devil', the obscene cabaret) to the meta-theatrical release of the lyrical potential of the stage (when Woland explains to the audience the biographical context of the novel). Crucially, the tempo of transforming one scene into another is very rapid, as can be exemplified by the opening interspersing of the scenes designating Woland's arrival in Moscow with those of Pilat's inter-rogation of Yeshua Ha-Nostri, which rapidly and repetitively moves the audience from Moscow to Jerusalem within the temporal framework of two thousand years.

In spite of such an atomisation of spatio-temporal arrangement, one aspect of the construction remains constant in *The Master and Margarita*, and it is the world of the stage. The ongoing *semiosis* may seem overloaded with an amalgam of multifarious and constantly changing meanings, and thus challenges the cognitive capabilities of an audience.[18] Yet, the role rigidly ascribed to the stage in the ongoing process of theatre communica-tion is determined with much rigour. The model of semiotic processes in which the world of the stage is involved may be schematically summarised as follows:

- the **stage** as one in a sequence of places set within → the **fictional reality** and related to both → other *loci* of the action (possibly also depicted onstage) → and the indicated *spatium* of the fictional world,
- the **stage** as a place of *semiosis* that is confronted with → the **audi-ence** in an act of → **theatre** communication,
- the **stage** as a place of **ritual**,
- the **stage** as a congruous part of → the **surrounding world** whose selected aspects are involved in the onstage communication (e.g. the images hinting at Guantanamo prison and the war in Syria).

The Master and Margarita confirms yet again that, in the case of Complicite, spatio-temporal imagery is grounded in the onstage *semio-sis*. The stage is the foundation of all communicative processes. For this reason, the stage accumulates all of the meanings generated by the whole variety of codes and conveyed through divergent channels. Conceptually, it is the world of the stage where diverse and incongruous structures interplay when creating singular meanings in accordance with the company's aesthetics.

THE ONSTAGE WORLD AND THE FICTIONAL WORLD

Notwithstanding the prominence of fragmentation in arranging the fictional world, the world of the stage is intrinsically involved in imposing a sense of internal coherence, be it at least through:

- the stable identity of actors involved in a performance (even when they shift their roles),
- the temporal linearity of the onstage *semiosis,*
- and/or the spatial congruence of the relation between the stage and the audience on the level of theatre communication.

Rather than subordinate these features to the 'realistic' conventions reigning in more traditional kinds of British modern drama, Complicite makes extensive use of the rudimental paradox of theatre communication: there is a firm ontological discrepancy between the onstage world and the fictional reality it depicts. This is to say that Complicite explores the semantic potential of the intrinsic juxtaposition between the three-dimensional unities (actors, time and space), designating the world of the stage with the atomised fragmentation of the fictional world it depicts.[19] This original application of the device that Brecht named 'Verfremdungseffekt' ('the distancing effect') is as much visible in *A Minute Too Late* as it is in later performances.

Shun-kin

The minimalistic imagery of *Shun-kin*, for example, sharply distinguishes between the conventionality of the presented images and the fictional reality they create. When accurately arranged by 'invisible' actors,[20] the same bamboo sticks delineate a door, a room, a shelter, a path, and other spatial notions depending on the requirements of the given episode. In one scene, red ribbons, when thrown accordingly, depict the emotionally moving, masochistic act of Sasuke's self-blinding, through which he expresses his ultimate and unrestricted devotion to his blind mistress.

The eponymous protagonist herself further stresses the discrepancy in question. In the 2010 production, she was represented onstage by both puppets and performers, including the actress Eri Fukatsu as 'Shun-kin' and puppeteers (Eri Fukatsu as 'Shun-kin's Voice, Head, Left Arm', Junko Uchida: 'Right Arm' and Yasuyo Mochizuki: 'Feet').[21] In addition to this, when, in the fictional world Shun-kin, 'a blind *shamisen* player' is supposed to play the music, it is performed onstage by a musician. The fluctuations are succinctly, and accurately, described by Eleanor Margolies in 'The Street of Animation':

> In a circular movement, Complicite and Blind Summit use *bunraku* puppets to dramatise [Tanizaki's] story about … the blind musician Shunkin. Young Shunkin appears first as a two-foot-high puppet with a porcelain-like face and a fall of straight black hair. Two female puppeteers, wearing modern black skirt suits, manipulate her using a rod on the back of her head. At one point she sweeps past in the half-light, nothing but an empty kimono with a human hand emerging from the sleeve.
>
> Later a female actor wearing a smooth white mask plays Shunkin. A short black rod protrudes from the back of her head, and the two puppeteers manipulate her. The movements of this 'puppet-actor' are beautifully precise but highly restricted. She swings through the same arc over and over again as she beats her servant-guide-lover Sasuke; she has become a machine.
>
> Finally, one of the two puppeteers throws this puppet-actor aside to take on the role herself. She initially screams and stamps in an excess of emotion, only for her face to be concealed by another mask, this time of white bandages. The sequence of transformations—from puppet to puppet-actor to actor—recalls Poh Sim Powright's suggestion … that human actors in Asian theatre sometimes modelled themselves on string puppets, emulating their precision and non-naturalistic gestures. (Margolies 2010: 6–7)

The delineation of the central female character involves a puppet, puppeteers, an actress and a musician. To make matters even more complicated, in certain episodes the musicians turn into actors and play as individual characters (Aso as 'Maid, Shun-kin's Mother' and Hidetaro as 'Master Kengyo') or as part of an ensemble. There is neither a one-to-one relation between actors and characters, nor an iconic similarity between the two agents since, in their stage language, Complicite interweave all available means of creating metaphoric meanings. Be they verbal or non-verbal.[22]

In *Shun-kin*, the world of the stage and the fictional world also differ substantially in other aspects. The live presentation of the Japanese traditional music by Kaho Aso (*tsuzumi*) and Honjoh Hidetaro (*shamisen*) lays emphasis on the linearity of the performance and the aesthetic quality of aural communication. Interestingly, Clive Bell mentions both these features (i.e. the linear and the aesthetic) in his essay 'Beyond All Endurance', which is included in the programme to the 2010 Barbican production:

> Everything is **linear** in [Japanese] melody. In **ensembles** we all play variations of the same line, thereby producing momentary clashes and timbral variation. ... In Japan ... the music is not teleological, not concerned with a goal, but an encounter with **the physicality of sound in the present moment**. ... When watching *Shun-kin* don't let the shenanigans on stage blind you to the fact that you are seeing one of Japan's premier league musicians in action—Honjoh Hidetaro and his *shamisen*. (Bell 2010: 12, emphasis added)

Some features of the Japanese music—linearity, ensemble playing, insistence on the physical presence in the given moment—are much in tune with the aesthetics of Complicite (see Chap. 2). By stressing the high quality of Hidetaro's performance, Bell hints at the musician's contribution to the artistic value of the onstage communication as this may pass unnoticed by those who are less familiar with Japanese music.

This observation brings us back to the dichotomy inscribed in Complicite's Japanese plays (i.e. *Shun-kin* and *The Elephant Vanishes*). For obvious reasons, theatre communication proceeds differently for Japanese and Western audiences. In the case of the latter, the aesthetic, but non-semantic, quality of the language uttered onstage predominates and this sets up an interesting equivalence between musical and verbal communication. In Japanese plays the Western audience is put in the role of an outsider confronted with an aesthetic experience, in which codes may be endowed with functions that differ from their original objectives. Because the Japanese language functions as music, it underscores not only the aesthetic potential of the verbal but also 'the physicality of sound in the present moment'. From the perspective of those who do not understand Japanese, both the natural language and the music decide the internal coherence of the world of the stage.

The arrangement of the fictional world in *Shun-kin* is hugely disjointed by:

- the introduction of three levels of narration,
- its episodic and fragmentary construction,
- the fragmentary nature of spatio-temporal imagery.

The fact that the principle of ellipsis is crucial here may be, perhaps, best illustrated by a brief description of the structuring of the narrative. Complicite shapes the frame narration as the contemporary (i.e. twenty-first century) recording of the novella for radio. An actress arrives at a studio and reads *A Portrait of Shun-kin* aloud. During the breaks she talks on her mobile phone and thus reveals details of her personal life, developing her own subplot.

Now, as the novella is read aloud onstage, the twenty-first century narrative level is set and progresses not only verbally but also through the onstage action. In a similar way (by intermingling the visual with the verbal), the world of *Shun-kin* is depicted. In accordance with the narrative structure of Tanizaki's novella, the narrative situation set in the 1930s emerges. It is from this perspective that the proper story of Shun-kin, set in the mid-nineteenth century, is told. During the performance, the Chinese-box structuring of the narrative is not that straightforward and needs to be reconstructed by the spectator from episodes interlacing all levels of narration. An additional communicative obstacle results from the non-chronological delivery of the plot. For these reasons, the narrative structure contributes significantly to the impression of structural disintegration and fragmentation that juxtaposes the principle of linearity imposed onstage with the physicality of the actors, the music and—in the case of non-Japanese audiences—the language.[23]

Foe

The juxtaposition of the world of the stage with the fictional world is structured in a slightly different way in *Foe*, the 1996 adaptation of J.M. Coetzee's novel, directed by Annie Castledine and Marcello Magni.[24] In spite of its rather unusual—for Theatre de Complicite—scenography, the play interweaves the verbal, visual and aural so as to operate within complicated spatial imagery that is already evident in the opening scenes. The stage depicts an open space on a desert island. Its surface is rugged. Upstage left (perspective of the audience) there is a bare tree, a cubed block of rock, suitable for the characters to sit on, and a bonfire. Some earth is spread in the centre, and downstage right there is a pool of fresh water. These rudimentary features of design stress the diagonal line of the stage (tree → rock/bonfire → earth → pool) and underscore the naturalistic simplicity of the presented world. In the course of the action, the wooden scaffolding is additionally revealed to rise vertically, beyond the rocks at the back of the stage.

The opening of Theatre de Complicite's *Foe* employs the convention of equivalence between the stage and the island,[25] making extensive use of the structural parallel between the two. For example, the sharp spatial delimitation of the stage/island, and its opposition with the offstage/sea, is stressed by an anticlockwise procession, when Robinson Crusoe marks out the territory of his white male world, followed by mute Friday (Patrice Naiambana) and Susan Barton (Kathryn Hunter). The female protagonist, a newly arrived castaway, is reluctant to accept the rules imposed by the robust Crusoe. Still, she is the one who, from the perspective of theatre communication, dominates the world of the stage, not only through her wit but also the fact that she is—as the audience is aware—the main narrator. It is striking that Crusoe speaks for the first time several minutes after Susan's narrative begins, when he responds to her inquiry as to why he stays on the island by saying: 'And where should I escape to?' Crusoe's strange axiology, in which the prison of the desert island is evaluated positively, is further confirmed when he refers to the place of the action as 'his castle'. All this establishes the main field of associations structuring one aspect of spatial imagery. It is based on the juxtaposition between the world of Robinson Crusoe (stage/island/castle/white/male/physical) on the one hand and the world to which Susan Barton aspires (offstage/sea/Brazil/female/suggested/idealised) on the other.

But this is certainly not the only way in which spatial imagery operates in the opening of *Foe*. The world of the stage quite explicitly aims at archetypal universalisation. The four elements (earth, water, fire and wind) are hinted at incessantly through visual, verbal and sonic codes. Kathryn Hunter's opening mime resembles the 'dance' of a tree resisting the wind (the mime is echoed later in the performance when Barton—not a tree—struggles with the winds of the island). In the meantime, the general darkness covering the rest of the stage is lit by an invisible actor who lights the bonfire.[26] The initial mime finishes with the sounds of waves stressing that Barton comes from the sea. After a while, when seeing Friday for the first time, Susan utters her first word on the island—'aqua'—but misunderstands Friday's intentions and expresses her fear he is a cannibal. As she cries towards the audience before fainting, 'I have come to the wrong island I thought to myself. I have come to the island of cannibals'. Contrary to her suspicions, Friday soon realises Susan is thirsty and in a most human gesture hands her fresh water.

Not only the action but also the sonic signals stress four elements. In due course we can hear, for instance, the sounds of a thunderstorm (it functions as the opening 'curtain'), rain and waves. The four elements are also made equivalent to colours visually dominating the stage in particular episodes. As it turns out, the opening brownish yellow stands for the earth, the blue light implies the water, the vivid red—the fire, and darkness—the wind.

A degree of abstract universalisation is added to *Foe* by numerous analogies to the imagery of Samuel Beckett's *Waiting for Godot*. Examples supporting the parallel abound: the open space, the bare tree, the stone, Susan/Estragon's preoccupation with bare feet and their need for new shoes, the master and slave relation between Robinson/Pozzo and Friday/Lucky, ordering the slaves to entertain the others ('Sing Friday') and the numbness shared by Friday and Lucky. In addition to this, Robinson's first question, 'Where should I escape to?', unmistakeably echoes Clov's attitude from Beckett's *Endgame*. It would be an interpretative mistake to reduce the semantics of *Foe* to the meanings derived from Beckett. But the parallel certainly delineates the legacy of abstract universality of the Beckett drama in the performance of *Foe*, and thus determines the mode of its interpretation.

One other parallel between *Foe* and *Waiting for Godot* is their insistent meta-theatricality. Yet, in *Foe*, the role ascribed to the auto-referential devices is original and does not owe much to the poetics of Beckett. The type of communication in which spectators actively participate in recognising meanings, underscores the perspective of the audience. As it happens in Complicite, in *Foe* the addressee is bound to be attentive, not only to visual, verbal and sonic signals, but also to the various relations between them. The audience is fully aware of this communicative strategy from the very beginning. At the opening of the performance, Barton's mime (the dance of a tree resisting the wind) is accompanied by the recorded dialogue between her later self and Mr Foe (Rob Pickavance), in which she introduces herself and attempts to convince him that the story she is about to deliver is interesting. The visual (the mime) and the verbal (the recorded dialogue) intersperse the meta-theatrical (actor → audience) with the meta-narrative (Barton → Foe → reader). In other words, theatre communication imposes upon the spectator the role of a reader. Because of the narrative derivation of the performance, whenever Barton speaks directly to the audience, we hear the words which are in fact her textual account delivered to the character of Foe, and, within the narrative structure of Coetzee's novel, to the general reader. The intersection of the meta-textual with the meta-theatrical leads in the case of Theatre de Complicite's adaptation of J.M. Coetzee's *Foe* to an eruption of auto-referential meanings.

Yet, we need to remember that the most immediate 'intertextual' contexts of J.M. Coetzee's *Foe* and Daniel Defoe's *Robinson Crusoe* further enlarge peripheral associations of the performance, most significantly of the fictional world it depicts. As in any adaptation, it is more the fictional world than any other aspect of the stage language that is involved in this type of relationship. After all, the semantics of the performance is hugely autonomous and should not be reduced merely to the context of J.M. Coetzee's novel, just as it should not be reduced to the meanings implied by the subtext of Beckett's poetics. It is the world of the stage that, in the aesthetics of Complicite, is crucial for the originality of the created meanings in which Defoe's and Coetzee's texts play as prominent a role in creating the fictional reality as the principle of archetypal universalisation and the poetics of Samuel Beckett do for the world of the stage.

There was also considerable interest in the mimetic dimension of *Foe*. Professor David Attwell, who was at the time Head of the English Department at the University of Natal, Pietermaritzburg, mentions a visit by the company members (i.e. Kathryn Hunter and Mark Wheatley) to South Africa in search of islands that might have inspired the setting. Attwell remembers meeting

> the actor who played Susan. … [T]hey wanted to know more about the setting that John [Coetzee] had in mind for the island. They reported him as saying that if the text said it was an island off the coast of Bahia, then they should look there. I suggested they visit the Cape Point nature reserve, with its wild beaches, kelp, sand-fleas, and of course, baboons. I believe that is what they did. In the notebook, it turns out, at one point John [Coetzee] mentions the coast of Namibia. (email correspondence)

As so frequently with Theatre de Complicite, *Foe* makes use of the paradoxical intermingling of aspirations towards universal generalisation and strategies aiming at minute verisimilitude.

CONCLUSIONS

Unlike in the modern realistic dramatic theatre that dominates more traditional British theatre, Complicite has pursued the tradition of developing highly autonomous stage communication by means of verbal and non-verbal codes. The metaphoric/symbolic/poetic character of meanings Complicite creates arises from the intersection of multifarious codes that are involved in onstage communication. Strong activation of meta-theatrical devices results in embedding the world of the stage within the outward structures of theatre perspective, where interlocutors are clearly delineated as stage (encoder) and audience (decoder).

In general, the principle of juxtaposition organises relations on various levels of both the world of the stage and the fictional world. Whereas the former is additionally correlated with the imperative sanctioning coherence of the involved actors, the temporal linearity of performance and the spatial imagery within the model of theatre, the latter is subject to the strong influence of the principles of incongruence, ellipsis and indeterminacy. The confrontation of the two opposing levels of creating meanings develops networks of signs that explore 'associative peripheries' rather than pursuing 'core meanings'.

In this book, stage language is understood as an inter-systemic 'supercode' that establishes singular mechanisms responsible for the artistic arrangement of meanings in the given production. Unless it is deprived of artistic aspirations,[27] the language of the stage needs to be recreated anew from the actual onstage *semiosis* each time. It is the distinctive feature of the stage language that, despite clearly visible parallels, it substantially differs from one production to another. On the one hand, the stage language is built upon the materially more concrete semantics of an individual performance, and on the other hand the sum of stage languages created in the entire *oeuvre* develops a more abstract notion of the aesthetics of the company.[28] To illustrate the distinction, we can note that the ingredient of improvisation allows Complicite to utilise the individualisation of each performance. As an invariant constituent in the *oeuvre*, the fluctuation becomes one of the principles characterising the aesthetics of the company. In each production, however, the principle of fluctuations contributes to the stage language in a singular way. All this reveals one of the main objectives of the company, namely the individualisation and personification of the communicative status of each physical (material) encounter between the world of the stage and the audience. The principle of fluctuations increases the singularity of each communicative act (in the sense given to this term by Derek Attridge) as much as the quality of the overall aesthetics guarantees its communicative value (as understood by Lotman in *Culture and Explosion*).

Developed between 1983 and 1989, the stage language of Théâtre de Complicité found its most explicit and comprehensive manifestation in *A Minute Too Late*, where it canonised the following mechanisms as those crucial for the whole aesthetics of Complicite:

- dynamic fluctuation of structures, meanings and the onstage *semiosis*,
- exposure of the onstage communication to the external structures and codes,
- semiotic explosions resulting from multifarious intersections of internal and external signs/structures/systems,
- predilection for the non-systemic, the pre-linguistic, the irrational, the improvised and the non-literal,
- insistent multiplication of codes, channels, levels of communication and setting their mutual relations,
- structuring the plot in accordance with the logic of syntagmatic ellipsis, incongruence and indeterminacy,
- exploration of 'peripheral associations' rather than 'core meanings',
- extensive pursuit of the semiotic potential resulting from the confrontation of the world of the stage and the fictional world.

The stage language of Théâtre de Complicité encompasses more than one production, yet the theatrical enterprise of the company before *The Visit* formulates a distinctive set of principles that suggests its forthcoming evolution. Rather like Simon McBurney's artistic signature and the poetics of *Who You Hear It from*, the stage language of Théâtre de Complicité participates as a formulaic factor in the aesthetics of Complicite. An analysis of it is as fruitful for comprehending the semiotic mechanisms that operate in the company's *oeuvre* as the earlier study of McBurney's artistic signature.

The distinction between the two paradigms fosters further consequences. Their juxtaposition shapes the model of communication valid for the aesthetics of Complicite. Because of its collective derivation, the stage language of Théâtre de Complicité lays emphasis on the dispersed nature of the onstage communication, while the signature of McBurney underscores its individualised and personified features. As we know, the relation between the collective and the individual is both dynamic and fluctuating, but the general tendency is shaped as:

the collective leads the individuals (Théâtre de Complicité)

↓

the collective is led by the individual (Complicite/McBurney)

Diagram 4.3

The direction of this evolution may be perhaps put in the context of a more general observation of George Steiner: 'progress towards textuality necessarily comprised perceptions and paradoxes of authorship. Orality is grounded in the collective and the anonymous. ... Authorship is an altogether different phenomenon. Familiarity has eroded its inherent strangeness' (2002: 287–8).

NOTES

1. Clive Mendus stresses that Kathryn Hunter, who trained at Royal Academy of Dramatic Art (RADA), brought new acting techniques to the ensemble (email correspondence). Her involvement may be treated as another kind of semiotic eruption in the evolution of the company's aesthetics. Miranda Carter describes Hunter's performance in *Help, I'm Alive!*: 'Her tiny body seemed both immensely supple and slightly askew, her use of movement at once acrobatically skilled and utterly un-English. There was something exotic and mysterious about her' (Carter 1994). See also Jacques 2011.

2. The scope and extension of the research and development phase of creative work, which precedes rehearsals, is worth mentioning here, as it contributes a lot to the improvised material and is well documented in the company's archive. See also Jane Edwardes' article 'Directors: The New Generation' (in Shank 1994: 205–22) and McBurney's essay 'On Directing' (2002).

3. It is less obvious in the multi/inter-media and multi-cast performances as they necessitate minute coordination of the performance.

4. McBurney speaks about an intriguing parallel between theatre and popular music when discussing the origins of Complicite: 'We wanted, consciously or unconsciously, to create what I would see whenever I used to go to rock concerts in the 1970s: an event which people lived through! It seemed to me that very often there was more theatre in a rock concert, or more theatre in contemporary dance' (in Knapper 2010: 237). See also McBurney's remark on the concert of the Beach Boys at the Hammersmith Odeon (in Giannachi and Luckgurst 1999: 70).

5. McBurney is reported to have said: 'A great aspect of medieval theatre were the processions, and commentators remarked on the piteous beauty of the poor and dispossessed processing through the streets. This kind of theatre is a form of community theatre and is still very present. It is a collective ritual theatre of celebration and we need it. I link this form of theatre to sporting occasions which play a similar role in our society' (Giannachi and Luckhurst 1999: 72).

6. Originally played by the Emerson Quartet, the musical element of the performance was taken over by the Brodsky String Quartet in 2002 (Knapper 2004: 61). It seems of some relevance that Complicite was commissioned by the former to endow the already existent musical piece with a performative element.

7. Opera productions of *A Dog's Heart* and *The Magic Flute* are certainly other such pieces. The prominence of the audio component in Complicite's work, and its intriguing parallels with the tradition of Polish theatre, is discussed in Paul Allain 2013.

8. The play was directed by Simon McBurney. The cast consisted of Mark Rylance (Hamm), Simon McBurney (Clov), Miriam Margolyes (Nell) and Tom Hickey (Nagg).

9. Both Samuel Beckett and Simon McBurney have revealed their interest in German romanticism. Whereas Caspar David Friedrich's painting *Two Men Looking at the Moon* is the basis for the main image of *Waiting for Godot* (Knowlson 2003: 43–95), Simon McBurney opens the collection of his essays with a quotation from Novalis.

10. In her detailed review of Complicite's *Endgame*, Julie Campbell writes: 'McBurney's direction demonstrated care and respect towards the play … This was a worthwhile and thoughtfully directed production, and McBurney deserves praise both as director and for admirable portrayal of Clov' (2010: 3). John Calder, on the other hand, complained about not taking all the opportunities for Beckett's black humour (conversation, and Calder 2009). See also Murphy 2009.

11. In the Paris production it was Keitoku Takata who addressed the audience in French (Poppy Keeling in conversation).

12. As in the Amsterdam production (watched on 17 December 2012).

13. There were some interesting consequences of this when *The Magic Flute* was introduced in French by Simon McBurney at the International Festival of Lyric Art, Aix-en-Provence.

14. Although he mentions neither the name of the company nor its performances, Alex Sierz stresses the importance of Martin Crimp for setting specific trends in the British theatre of the 1990s (2001: 33). Crimp's translation of Ionesco's *The Chairs* was commissioned and first produced by Theatre de Complicite.

15. Direct reference to the situation in Iraq was a rather conventional gesture in British theatre at that time. Allain and Harvie's *The Routledge Companion to Theatre and Performance* contains a separate entry on the Gulf War (2006: 97–8). Giesekam writes: 'it has become a commonplace in recent productions of classic texts to do with war to insert television footage of contemporary war-zones in the Balkans, or the Middle East, as in Peter Sellar's version of Aeschylus' *Persians*' (2007: 11). See also Sierz 2001: 136, 206.

16. Giesekam refers to Complicite in the introduction of his book: 'Simon McBurney's production of *Measure for Measure* (2004) employed large-scale projection onto cyclorama and floor for setting purposes. CCTV footage created the atmosphere of a surveillance society, and royal arrivals and pronouncements were ... accompanied by camera crews: all this from someone who made his name as an imaginative deviser/director of physical theatre with Théâtre de Complicité, where the focus has always been on the performer's inventiveness' (2007: 2).

17. For a more detailed discussion on the multi/inter-media theatre see Allain and Harvie 2006: 173–4, Limon and Żukowska 2010, Giesekam 2007.

18. This mechanism is usual for contemporary (continental) theatre.

19. In his theoretical analysis, Rozik observes 'existential gaps between text and two worlds' (Rozik 2008: 84–6). Rozik distinguishes between the stage reality (actors), the theatre text (characters) and the fictional world (fictional referents of textual descriptions), and concludes that '[p]erformance analysis should ... focus not on the inscribing function of actors, but on the inscribed text ...' (86). In my view, certain aspects of the aesthetics of Complicite promote ontological discrepancies resulting from contradictory structuring of the world of the stage and the fictional world. I insist that, from the perspective of spectator/interpreter, both of these worlds—and their mutual relations—are equally prominent for the creation of meanings.

20. By 'invisible' actors I mean those whose onstage presence is motivated solely by the requirements of the stage machinery.

21. Names as in the 2010 Barbican production programme.

22. In *The Street of Crocodiles*, the Spanish actor Antonio Gil Martines takes the onstage role of Emil. In the fictional world Emil becomes three different characters: a cousin, a schoolboy and a client. Because the qualities exposed by the actor and his style of acting suggest the cliché of Capitano, Martines/ Emil functions in the play as a direct implication of the convention of *commedia dell'arte*.

23. Non-linear narrative and numerous other features of its structural arrangement reflect shifts that occurred in British prose fiction between 1978 and 1992. For a formal analysis of these shifts see Malcolm 2000.

24. The analysis is based on the recording of the opening part of the performance, as presented in Copenhagen in 1996, and interviews.

25. The convention has been frequently employed in Irish drama, John Millington Synge's *Riders to the Sea* being one of many examples. Obviously, it is decisive for Shakespeare's *The Tempest*.

26. Similarly to the prop of the carpet used in *A Minute Too Late*, 'the real elements of fire, water and earth' echo stage solutions that were used by Peter Brook (see concise entries on Brook and *The Mahabharata* in Allain and Havre 2006: 31–3 and 103–5).

27. The term 'artistic function' is understood in the formal sense as the search for innovative solutions that are capable of defamiliarising pertrified structures and codes and thus bringing forward original meanings and achieving an aesthetic effect.

28. In spite of some straightforward parallels, the stage language does not equal the concept of mise en scène as understood by Patrice Pavis (2013). This is due to my taking into account authorial intentions, the stress put on fragmentary accessibility of stage language, and attention given to the interaction between the stage and the audience.

CHAPTER 5

The Textual Tissue of Theatre de Complicite

Cultural Memory

Marcello Magni associates the main shift in the history of Complicite with the late 1980s and early 1990s, when increasing prominence was given to the textual tissue of a performance. Not only did it strengthen the status of the verbal element but also necessitated the unification of the 'stage language'. Because, at this time, Theatre de Complicite was gaining a reputation—at least in professional circles[1]—as an innovative British theatre company, the role of native speakers of English, as well as British and Anglo-American styles of acting, was more strongly pronounced so as to meet the expectations of a newly emerging type of audience. So, at the turn of the decade, the overtly international—mainly European—endeavour of early Théâtre de Complicité gave way, if only for a moment, to a slightly more British-centred venture. Magni describes this transformation in the following way:

> As a company we came from training at the Lecoq school in Paris. In the first year at the school there were ... actors from all over Europe, Africa, South America, and other places. Complicité wanted to embrace the international spirit of the Lecoq school. We all wanted to express ourselves in slightly different ways. Not through the text where dialogue was based on ideas, but through interaction of events, performers, and personalities.
>
> Our collaborators were mainly from Europe but whenever we had a chance, we invited people from South and North America. ... The initial spirit of Complicité was to gather a variety of cultures, and to present not

© The Author(s) 2016
T. Wiśniewski, *Complicite, Theatre and Aesthetics*,
DOI 10.1007/978-3-319-33443-1_5

119

so much England but Europe onstage. All this took us some time because England has an extraordinary veneration for the text. So, we had to take onstage Shakespeare and other such plays. This caused some problems to foreign performers because they were very aware of delivering a text in the English language, and yet they had to compete with British actors. This is why at this stage Complicité worked mainly with performers from Britain. (Magni 2015: 140)

The shift in aesthetic focus resulted from the mediatory aspirations of Theatre de Complicite. In the 1980s, the company introduced the continental tradition emerging from the pedagogy of Jacques Lecoq into Britain. This, in turn, necessitated the subsequent acceptance of selected features of British theatre (Shakespeare, textuality, accent, style of acting) as part of the company's 'stage language'. The preservation of balance between the two theatre traditions required shifts within the mediating agent, namely Complicite. In consequence, the 'extraordinary veneration for the text' in the British theatre necessitated the permanent and widespread infiltration of the mechanisms of cultural memory. In the above quotation, Magni encapsulates the phase during which the previously ignored textual tissue emerged as one of the constitutive elements of the company's aesthetics.

Since the first production of a modern play (i.e. Friedrich Dürrenmatt's *The Visit* in 1989),[2] the textual tissue of Complicite has been manifested in a variety of ways. Other pieces of dramatic theatre include William Shakespeare's *The Winter's Tale* (1992), Bertolt Brecht's *The Caucasian Chalk Circle* (1997), Eugène Ionesco's *The Chairs* (1997), Shakespeare's *Measure for Measure* (2004) and Samuel Beckett's *Endgame* (2009). The company devised a performance inspired by the 'Russian surrealist and children's writer Daniil Kharms' (complicite.org)—titled *Out of a House Walked a Man* (1994)—and was recently involved in the co-production of two operas: Alexander Raskatov's *A Dog's Heart* (2010) and *The Magic Flute* by Wolfgang Amadeus Mozart (2012).

However, the main body of the text-inspired work of *Complicite* is to be found in numerous adaptations of prose narratives collected from various parts of the world. Two of them are based on collections of short stories—Bruno Schulz's *The Street of Crocodiles* (1992) and Haruki Murakami's *The Elephant Vanishes* (2003)—and three on long-short stories, novellas or essays. These are: John Berger's *The Three Lives of Lucie Cabrol* (1994), Jun'ichiro Tanizaki's *Shun-kin* (2008) and

Mikhail Bulgakov's *A Dog's Heart*. There are also four stage adaptations of full-scale novels: J.M. Coetzee's *Foe* (1996), Torgny Lindgren's *Light* (2002), Mikhail Bulgakov's *The Master and Margarita* (2011) and Petru Popescu's *Amazon Beaming* (2015). In addition to this, *Lionboy* (2013) is an adaptation of a sequence of novels written by Zizou Corder (i.e. novelist Louisa Young and her daughter Isabel Adomakoh Young). One should add a separate category for the two devised pieces—*Mnemonic* and *A Disappearing Number*—because both are inspired by a number of texts (the 1999 printed version of *Mnemonic* includes a bibliography consisting of several texts).

The remaining part of this chapter demonstrates that, when confronted with the stage language of Théâtre de Complicité and the artistic signature of Simon McBurney, the textual tissue develops into a code/system that effectively participates in the creation of meanings. This will be illustrated, first of all, by an analysis of Complicite's persistent employment of the convention of reading onstage.[3]

The second aspect that will be discussed concerns the more abstract and structural consequences of implementing textuality. Because they belong to the mechanisms of cultural memory, textual matters led Complicite into the publication of specific plays derived from devised theatre. In this way, we witness the process of infiltration of strictly theatrical—not necessarily verbal—modes of creating metaphoric meanings into the sphere of the textual and the verbal. The publication of plays enables the juxtaposition of:

- the artistic[4] mechanisms responsible for creating strictly theatrical meanings onstage,
- the fully autonomous artistic artefacts that adapt the devised work of the company to the textual tradition of dramatic literature.

Although they are credited with identical authorship, the performance of *Mnemonic* does not convey exactly the same meaning as the text of *Mnemonic*, or the radio play endowed with this title. All these variants differ as much as the novel of Mikhail Bulgakov differs from Complicite's adaptation of *The Master and Margarita*. Overall, the autonomy of theatre performance is as categorical as the autonomy of dramatic literature, or that of a radio play. For this reason, the multiplication of channels and levels of communication may at times bear most surprising consequences.

ONSTAGE READING

In a Complicite performance, persistent employment of meta-literary devices is linked with highlighting connotations of literature with theatre. Books are frequently used as props that may designate books (Peirce's 'icon') or other notions such as, for example, birds (*The Street of Crocodiles* and *The Magic Flute*), in which case they stress the discrepancy between the stage world and the fictional world. Reading is also a very typical activity that may have many manifestations. In numerous performances, we come across such divergent modes of reading as reading in bed (*Please, Please, Please*), reading aloud (*Shun-kin*), reading in silence (*The Master and Margarita*), silent group reading, reading music (*The Noise of Time*) and group reading aloud in a classroom (*The Street of Crocodiles*). Moreover, the routine of reading may be the subject of hilarious mockery (*The Elephant Vanishes*).

In the opening scenes of *The Street of Crocodiles*, Joseph's prolonged silent reading becomes an ominous one-man show that anticipates tensions introduced later in the play. The activity is echoed later in the performance, when Jewish/Polish schoolchildren read Goethe's poem in German in their classroom. In *The Elephant Vanishes*, the presentation of a similar scene results in outbursts of laughter. The reason for this is that, for the main character, reading a newspaper is part of his morning routine, presented in a mime sequence lasting over three minutes.[5] Dressed in pyjamas, slowly eating breakfast and sipping his mug of coffee, he is reading every single sign in the newspaper before he gets to the article he decides to read aloud. An additional comic effect is achieved by the growing exasperation expressed by the actors who remain in the background and do not represent any characters in the fictional world. As it turns out, this is the inciting moment for the entire onstage action. The protagonist reads aloud the article about an enigmatic disappearance of the elephant from the Tokyo zoo.

As a Japanese performance, *The Elephant Vanishes* multiplies the channels of communication that the non-Japanese members of the audience had to face (the performance toured in Europe and North America).[6] The tasks given to them vary between reading surtitles, listening to the non-semantic (but for the sonic gag based on the word 'ki-tchen') beauty of the Japanese language and watching the visual tour de force presented onstage. Since the performance—at least its 'English' version—takes into consideration the linguistic barrier between the world of the stage and the audience (see Chap. 4), the activity of reading undertaken by the audience underscores its involvement in the process of theatre communication. They are made aware that they are part of an external scheme, in which those who do not know Japanese need to rely on translation. What is at stake here is the sense of ignorance, incomplete knowledge, the mystery of the world around and things one does not know. In a sense, we come back to the motif of epistemological alienation as an aspect of Simon McBurney's signature.

Mise-en-page

W.B. Worthen's *Print and Poetics of Modern Drama* makes a number of distinctions and observations that are crucial for the practical analysis of published plays. Worthen lays emphasis on the semantic value of the *mise-en-page*. By this, he understands the process that, being a textual equivalent of mise en scène, consists of mechanisms responsible for enacting the materiality of printed drama. This encompasses the strictly technical matters of print layout and editorial decisions, as well as the more elaborate issues of authorship, the status of the verbal and oral in print and the ambiguous juxtaposition of the performance and the printed play. This leads Worthen to consider the differences between various editions of plays, and his insistence on the semantic role of textual variants.

Endowing the process with a broad diachronic perspective, Worthen distinguishes several models of setting relations between a performance and a printed play that have had a crucial role in Western drama ever since Shakespeare. Throughout his book, the American scholar distinguishes the models epitomised by:

- William Shakespeare (the emerging role of print in the early modern drama),
- Henrik Ibsen/George Bernard Shaw (individual authorship as standard for a modern play),
- Gertrude Stein (the poetic exploration of the material texture),
- Harold Pinter (devices and conventions adapted to textual purposes from the sphere of theatre, e.g. the pause),
- Anna Deavere Smith (the play shaped as a memory of past experience),
- Complicite (collective/collaborative derivation of a play).[7]

Even if Complicite's plays are not discussed in much detail and constitute a general point of reference indicating a rather surprising turn to the collective 'print authorship' (2009: 97), it is interesting to find Complicite as part of such a noble tradition. When taken all together, the textual output of the company on the one hand supports numerous arguments fostered by Worthen, and challenges some of his most prominent assumptions and conclusions on the other.

Surprisingly, it seems to go unnoticed by Worthen that Complicite's attitude to 'the printed culture' echoes that which dominated in the early modern drama. This is most striking when we consider:

- the question of authorship,
- the explicitly pronounced theatrical provenance of a play,
- the declaratively moderate status of the printed play.

In Worthen's chapter on early modern drama, we come across the passage that is particularly relevant to my current argument:

> In the sixteenth and seventeenth centuries the reciprocal identities of printed and performed drama were weighted differently than they are today, after the dominion of print. With a very few, notable exceptions, print played little role in Shakespeare's theatre, as plays were submitted, copied, distributed into parts, and learned from manuscript. It's perhaps not surprising, then, that the theatrical identity of drama is persistently registered in the printform of early modern plays. If we regard the meaning of the 'author' as one sign of the emerging character of dramatic writing as print literature, then many early modern printed plays seem to represent *performance* as defining the drama's identity, and the printed book as a kind of by-product, a memorial record of that event. (24)

Complicite is, indeed, subversive to the 'dominion of print', persistently stresses 'the theatrical derivation of drama' and hints at the convention of approaching 'the printed book as a kind of by-product'. Nonetheless, I would argue that this strategy does not annihilate the artistic autonomy of the plays published by Complicite. Overtly auto-referential exploration of the *mise-en-page*, in the case of Complicite's printed drama is paired with the original and singular infiltration of performative structures into the poetics of print.

It may seem paradoxical that the enlivening of the conventions rooted in early modern drama is accompanied by the extensive use of the achievements of the canonical form of modern drama. As in the model conceived by Ibsen and Shaw, in Complicite 'the play [is] complete in its reading: reading line to line, margin to margin' (55). This is well illustrated by the monologues opening *The Three Lives of Lucie Cabrol*, *Light*, *Mnemonic* and *A Disappearing Number*. Other echoes of Worthen's model include the following observations:

- in the process of literary reception of printed drama, the reader is bound to assume—among others—the perspective of an audience (the 'we' of stage directions),[8]
- on the structural plane of the plot one observes consistently delineated storylines (as in Ibsen/Shaw), which (unlike in Ibsen/Shaw) do not necessarily obey the principle of chronological presentation onstage (*Mnemonic*, *A Disappearing Number*),
- the world of the stage strongly pronounces the epical and narrative elements, as do the stage directions,
- the style of the printed play avoids the technical jargon of theatre and the printing model of acting editions (41),
- as with Shaw and Stein, the company 'evokes complementary strategies for booking the play' (73) and makes use of narrative and poetic devices,
- it shares the view 'that the *mise-en-page* can have semantic value' for both reading and performing (73).

THE COMPARATIVE SPIRIT

In spite of the considerable accuracy of the proposed distinctions and their practical usefulness, Worthen is reluctant to draw conclusions from his thought-provoking study. The fact that Complicite makes original use of the two contradictory models of shaping relations between print and performance diminishes the concept that certain axiology is ascribed to particular modes of communication. The case of Complicite proves that there is neither 'ideology of print' (8) nor 'politics of performance'. The mechanisms shaping *mise-en-page* and mise en scène are mere conventions and the meanings they convey do not depend on any sort of axiology ascribed to their paradigms. As in the case of natural language, the semantics originates in the concrete syntagmatic employment of the paradigm of the given convention. This is to say that the juxtaposition of print and performance is functional on the semiotic rather than semantic level. It allows for answering the question *how*—rather than *what*—meanings are created. There is a vast difference between the semiotics of a code/paradigm/system and its semantic manifestations. Worthen does not pay due attention to the fact that, when used for artistic objectives, semiotic mechanisms take responsibility for creating fluctuating networks of 'peripheral associations' rather than lead to establishing rigidly schematic 'core meanings'.

Even though his study explores primarily the poetics of printed drama, Worthen is sceptical with regard to the artistic autonomy of dramatic literature.[9] This is perhaps best illustrated by his firm rejection of Lucas Erne's concept of 'the theatre of the mind' in which 'the playwright's authority extends across the page, absorbing the signifier of the stage into the narrative structure of literary drama' (34). Worthen's fascination with the textual tissue does not prevent him from pursuing immediate links between published plays and their theatrical productions.

Contrary to this view, I insist on the firm discrepancy between the type of discourse provoked by the stage performance and that structured in the printed play. Axiomatic premises of the stage language are incongruous with those determining the semiotic potential of a printed play. These are two divergent types of medium. Because the relation between a play and its theatrical production is frequently shaped in accordance with the principle of inter-semiotic translation/transmutation/interpretation/adaptation/parody, the two spheres—despite superficial parallels—make use of divergent mechanisms for the creation of meaning and for this reason conceive completely autonomous pieces of art even when they are credited to the same author and endowed with the same title.

That is not to say that reciprocal relations between, for example, Complicite's *Mnemonic* as a performance, a published play and a radio play are deprived of interesting implications. But the element of rivalry between the page, the stage and the phonosphere is, at least in the case of Complicite, superseded by the comparative spirit. There are both similarities and differences between theatrical, textual and radio variants which are worthy of further scrutiny. One might perhaps say that, in this way, the prescriptive/evaluative approach is replaced by a descriptive one. Questions that matter here are 'how do the relations between variants function?', 'how do the play and its production differ?', 'which meanings are stable and which are added, or transformed?', 'how is the dialogue between the playwright and the director shaped?' rather than 'is the production an accurate realisation of the authorial concept?', 'did the theatre artists appropriately understand, and react to, the authorial intentions?' or 'does the play satisfy the requirements of the stage?'

PLAYS BY THEATRE DE COMPLICITE

Perhaps contrary to the initial intentions of the company, plays published by Theatre de Complicite are at the centre of emerging discussion. Because they are 'by-products' of the company's theatrical productions, the plays explicitly highlight the infiltration of the stage language into *mise-en-page*. An insistent auto-referentiality of each employed medium (something that is typical of Complicite) underscores differences between each variant of a given production.

All this abounds in practical consequences. The virtual perspective of audience/spectator, assumed in printed drama by the reader, does not equal that which is normally taken by the real audience/spectator in an actual performance. As its abstract equivalent, the implied/virtual audience occupies the sphere of literary imagination in which the theatre communication is delineated (not experienced) on the basis of verbal signs (not sensory signals). Similarly, making extensive use of the world of the stage and the stage language, the play operates within the model of theatre, but it does so—again—by means of the verbal language. In 'the theatre of the mind', the very word 'curtain' enlivens the visual signal commonly used in the stage language to delineate the temporal borders of the world of the stage. Overall, the stage language, the world of the stage and the model of theatre function in published drama as verbally delineated structures that actively participate in the eruption of strictly literary meanings. By definition, the textual meanings are autonomous but they function in the comparative context of theatrical productions.

As the case of Complicite suggests, printed plays are not necessarily the origin of theatre performances, so it is risky to postulate that, by writing for a 'reading audience', one (Shaw and Ibsen, but why not Complicite?) 'incarnated the dominance of the book form of the play over its theatrical representation, confirming a sense of the performed play as an after-effect to its literary book-bound being' (54). Because of the discrepancy of theatrical and literary modes of communication, 'the reading audience' does not determine the pre-theatrical 'book-bound' semantics of a theatre production but establishes its primary comparative context. In a parallel way, theatre productions of devised plays such as *Mnemonic* or *A Disappearing Number* do not diminish the artistic autonomy of printed plays that derive from them.

The conclusion is that, even though Complicite seems not to be preoccupied with the status of their printed texts, the company participates in juxtaposing conventions emerging from contrasting models. What initially appears to be subordinated to the mechanisms of cultural oblivion (i.e. non-literary/non-verbal derivation of drama) brings back from beyond the sphere of cultural consciousness the long-forgotten codes and structures that dominated early modern theatre. It is the particular artistic achievement of Complicite that the company managed to:

- defamiliarise these conventions within the language of contemporary theatre,
- implement these structures in the poetics of modern printed drama,
- infiltrate these codes into their own innovative aesthetics.

This certainly results in an artistically valued eruption in which the clash of a number of divergent traditions is projected into a singular and idiosyncratic utterance.

PUBLICATION DETAILS

Since 1995 the company has published nine volumes containing their plays. Notwithstanding whether they were credited to Theatre de Complicite (three books) or to Complicite (six books), their group authorship has remained unchanged, the only exception being Eugène Ionesco's *The Chairs* in the new translation of Martin Crimp. Five books were published by Methuen, two by Oberon Books, one by Faber and Faber (*The Chairs*) and one by Nick Hern Books (*Lionboy*). Most volumes contain a single play but there is also one—*Plays 1*—that comprises three plays republished in a new edition. In the latter case, *The Three Lives of Lucie Cabrol* and *The Street of Crocodiles* involve only minor editorial changes, but *Mnemonic*, which is the coda of the volume, must be treated as a new published version of the play. There are substantial editorial, structural and semantic differences between published variants of *Mnemonic* (Table 5.1).

In all the books—including *The Chairs*—the main text of the play is accompanied by an extensive peritext that provides:

- specification of publication,
- supplementary essays,
- details documenting their theatre provenance (including stills and promotional material).

Table 5.1 Summarises the publication details of all volumes

No	Title	Authorship	Adapted from	Adaptation/ translation by	Publisher	Year
1.	The Three Lives of Lucie Cabrol	Theatre de Complicite	John Berger	Simon McBurney and Mark Wheatley	Methuen Drama	1995
2.	The Chairs	Theatre de Complicite (first production)	Eugène Ionesco	Martin Crimp	Faber and Faber	1997
3.	The Street of Crocodiles	Theatre de Complicite	Bruno Schulz	Simon McBurney and Mark Wheatley	Methuen	1999
4.	Mnemonic	Theatre de Complicite			Methuen	1999
5.	Light	Complicite	Torgny Lindgren	Simon McBurney and Matthew Broughton	Oberon Books	2000
6.	Mnemonic	Complicite			Methuen	2001
7.	Plays 1: The Street of Crocodiles, The Three Lives of Lucie Cabrol, Mnemonic	Complicite	Accordingly	Accordingly	Methuen	2003
8.	A Disappearing Number	Complicite		'Conceived and directed by Simon McBurney'	Oberon Books	2008
9.	Lionboy	Complicite	Zizou Corder	Marcello Dos Santos	Nick Hern Books	2014

The data, which conventionally appeared in the programme, provided an immediate context for these publications. The elements of the peritext of individual volumes are enumerated in Table 5.2. As can be seen, some elements stress the textual tissue of these books (editorial, supplementary texts) and others allude to its theatrical derivation (production details, biographies and photographs). There are also promotional materials hinting at the mercantile aspect of theatrical enterprise and publishing. Overall, the mechanisms of cultural memory find fertile ground in the variety of

Table 5.2 Summarises the details of the textual arrangement of all volumes

	Title	Editorial details and the text proper	Supplementary texts	Details documenting their theatre provenance				Other materials
				Production details	Biographic details	Company promotional materials	Photographic documentation	
1	*The Three Lives of Lucie Cabrol* (1995)	Ed. (1 page) Play (51 pages)	'John Berger on Theatre de Complicite' by John Berger (1 page), 'Collusion Between Celebrants' by Michael Ratcliffe (4 pages)	1 page	1 page	None	2 photos in the body of supplementary texts	Promotional materials of the Royal Court Theatre (7 pages), 'Ionesco's Notes' (2 pages)
2	*The Chairs* (1997)	Ed. (1 page) Play (60 pages)	None	3 pages	2 pages	4 pages	None	
3	*The Street of Crocodiles* (1999)	Ed. (1 page) Play (63 pages)	'Bruno Schulz: a chronology' (2 pages), 'Note on the script' by Simon McBurney and Mark Wheatley (2 pages)	Introductory announcement (1 page), 'Music' (1 page) and 2 pages after the main title page	6 pages	2 pages	6 black and white performance stills between pp. 30–1.	Promotional materials of the Royal National Theatre (1 page) Promotional materials of Methuen (5 pages)
4	*Mnemonic* (1999)	Ed. (1 page) Play (72 pages)	'Collisions' by Simon McBurney	1 page	4 pages	2 pages	8 black and white performance stills between pp. 38–9	'Appendix' (2 pages) 'Bibliography' (1 page) Promotional materials of Methuen (5 pages)
5	*Light* (2000)	Ed. (1 page) Play (70 pages)	'Rehearsing *Light*' by Steven Canny (pp. 85–103)	1 page	6 pages	1 page	8 black and white rehearsal photos between pp. 64–5	

6	*Mnemonic* (2001)	Ed. (1 page) Play (75 pages)		1 page	5 pages	1 page	8 black and white performance stills between pp. 38–9	Methuen promotional materials (5 pages)
7	*Plays 1: The Street of Crocodiles, The Three Lives of Lucie Cabrol, Mnemonic* (2003)	Ed. (1 page) Plays *TSoC* (62 pages) *3LLC* (48 pages) *Mn* (80 pages)	'Contents' (1 page), 'Prologue' by Simon McBurney (4 pages), 'Bruno Schulz: a chronology' (2 pages), 'Note on the script' by Simon McBurney and Mark Wheatley (2 pages)	3 pages (*TSoC*) 3 pages (*3LLC*) 2 pages (*Mn*)		'A Chronology' (2 pages)	16 black and white performance stills between pp. 116–17	
8	*A Disappearing Number* (2008)	Ed. (1 page) Play (70 pages)	'Contents' (1 page), 'Introduction' by Simon McBurney (5 pages), 'A most romantic collaboration' by Marcus du Sautoy (3 pages), 'A note on the text' by Ben Power (1 page)	2 pages	2 pages		4 colour stills on the covers, 8 black and white rehearsal photos between pp. 32–3	'Appendix. The Functional equation of the Riemann zeta function' (1 page)
9	*Lionboy* (2014)	Ed. (1 page) Play (45 pages)	'Introduction' by Annabel Arden (3 pages), 'Adapter's Note' by Marcello Dos Santos (1 page)	2 pages	2 pages	1 page	1 colour still on the cover	List of adaptations published by Nick Hern Books

editorial and publishing strategies that prove the prominence of the material (physical) aspect of the textual tissue (*mise-en-page*) for the company.

ARTISTIC AUTONOMY OF PLAYS

For a study on the aesthetics of Complicite, the shift from the orthodox reliance on performativity to the attraction of the textual tissue marks a pivotal turning point in the evolution of the company. Rather than simply guaranteeing the authorised documentation of particular performances (which was, perhaps, the company's initial objective), the volumes provide fully autonomous artistic artefacts that may be read and interpreted without previous awareness of the performance. What is more, some of these plays inspire productions and workshops by other companies; thus, the texts acquire the codex function,[10] serving both as dramatic literature and theatre script.

In general, the company's approach to the texture of a book evolves. This can be seen, for instance, when we compare the somewhat ascetically issued *The Three Lives of Lucie Cabrol* (1995) with the splendid edition of *A Disappearing Number* (2008). The nine volumes published by (Theatre de) Complicite extend the scope of the creative process by adding a third phase to it. The experience of inter-semiotic translation (transmutation) also turns out to be useful when transcribing a devised performance into print. In this context the process of creation is structured in accordance with the following scheme:

narrative(s) → improvised rehearsals → devised performance → printed play

Diagram 5.1

In addition to this, a study of the evolution of publications reveals an increasing mastery of introducing artistic solutions originating in improvised performativity into strictly textual structures. This is, however, not to say that, in the case of Complicite, the company should treat a published play as the ultimate objective of artistic enterprise. On the contrary, the play proposes one of many variants of the production. It is the communicative status of a textual work that distinguishes the play from the whole set of fluctuating performances. The conflict between the mechanism of cultural memory and that of cultural oblivion bears serious semantic consequences.

The following part of this chapter will demonstrate that the published plays function primarily as autonomous pieces and are subject to the structures of literary communication. This will be illustrated by an analysis of three plays: *The Street of Crocodiles, The Three Lives of Lucie Cabrol* and

Light. The chronological character of the sequence results from the fact that the textual character of *The Street of Crocodiles* is much more explicit—hence more illustrative—than that of *The Three Lives of Lucie Cabrol* and *Light*. The three plays in question are textual variants of performances based on adaptations of narrative prose.

COMMUNICATION IN *THE STREET OF CROCODILES*

Mutual relations between mechanisms of confrontation and unification of the internal and the external spheres are functional in the aesthetics of Complicite. *Who You Hear It from*, for example, fosters a possibility of unification on personal, social, artistic and archetypal planes (see Chap. 2). *The Street of Crocodiles* illustrates a different artistic solution because dispersing self-identity, internal disintegration and the menacing intrusion of the external element play such a prominent role in this play.

The Street of Crocodiles echoes the tradition of initiation to evil forces. Still, at the most general level, the piece balances the demonic and destructive forces by celebrating the artistic, at times religious, ordering of the universe. Thus, there emerges an internally disjointed model of the world grounded on oxymoronic combinations of signs/structures/systems and paradoxical juxtapositions of contradictory principles. This is one of the most significant features of the aesthetics of Complicite: the principles organising the model of the presented world are echoed in the construction of their plays.

Fragmented and dejected as it is, the semantics of *The Street of Crocodiles* expresses a profound sense of disagreement with the absurdity of killing a writer. By 'enlivening' Schulz's imagery in a new language (English) and media (theatre→drama), Theatre de Complicite creates an original and autonomous work which not only appreciates the mastery of the provincial artist, but also gives his death a universal status. A strong disapproval of circumscription and demarcation of the human lot arises.

The communicative situation that structures the predominant part of the onstage action of *The Street of Crocodiles* is quite original for late-twentieth-century British drama (if not for drama and theatre in general). Ternary in nature, the stage communication confronts Joseph's internal soliloquy (i.e. the dramatic convention of displaying the protagonist's psyche onstage) with polyphonic discourse delivered in the form of dialogue by numerous speakers inhabiting the onstage world. In this way, the play puts at its extreme Jan Mukařovský's statement concerning mutual interdependence of monological and dialogical tendencies. As the Prague scholar claimed, reciprocal tensions between aspirations to univocal authorisation of drama on the one hand, and an expression of divergent—though equivalent—visions of the world on the other, are decisive for communicative structures in drama. Just as dialogic overtones are very likely to be found in a piece of monologue (e.g. a doubt, a second thought, a citation), argues Mukařovský, it is also vital to be attentive to monological aspects in all dialogic structures (e.g. wherever interlocutors share the vision of the world) (see also Bakhtin 1984b).

In *The Street of Crocodiles*, Complicite broadens the scale by putting the internal soliloquy at one extreme and incongruous polyphony at the other. Moreover, both individualistic idiosyncrasy (Joseph's internal world) and the communal polyphony of all inhabitants of the world of the stage are overtly subordinated to the predominant level of artistic communication. Monological in nature, this kind of theatre communication transfers meanings from the encoder (Complicite) to the decoder (reader). In *The Street of Crocodiles*, the usual complexity of dramatic communication undergoes further atomisation, and yet immense complexity is paired, as elsewhere in Complicite, with a clear-cut coherence of the overall ternary communicative structure:

- the polyphony of the introduced speakers
- is embedded in Joseph's internal soliloquy
- and both function within the monologically structured act of stage communication.

The Prologue and Epilogue fulfil the function of a constructional framework and, thus, constitute the basis for the semantic coherence of the entire play. The role of the onstage setting is analogous here to that of a narrative situation whereas the main onstage action, which is presented from Part One to Part Four, is an introduced story just as all characters except for Joseph and Nazi soldiers belong to the internal world of Joseph.[11] The stage reality of *The Street of Crocodiles* confronts the external perspective of Drohobycz in 1942 (the frame/narrative situation) with the internal perspective of Joseph's psyche (the main onstage action/narrated events).[12] Whereas the logic of the Prologue and the Epilogue derives from the plodding universalisation of biographical verisimilitude, the proper action (Part One → Part Four) allows for the oneiric unpredictability of events.

THE ONSTAGE ACTION

The rudimentary action developing in the world surrounding Joseph may be illustrated by the following sequence:

1) the delivery of books to be sorted out,

↓

2) Joseph's reluctant obedience to sort out the books,

↓

3) his involuntary, if hazardous, fascination with books and their content,

↓

leading to 4) his abandonment of the oppressive world of war for the world of his imagination

(transgression into the internal perspective),

↓

5) his internal experience, presented as the on-stage action, gradually turns out into a

nightmare

↓

that finds its culmination in 6) the final change to the war reality of the Drohobycz warehouse

↓

where 7) Joseph is killed in what develops into an on-stage, elaborate rite of passage to the

world of the dead.

Diagram 5.2

In this scheme, all of the external events are shown in the Prologue and the Epilogue, the only exception being stage 5, which delineates the internal onstage action presented from Part One to Part Four (i.e. the main onstage action).

The visual depiction of the narrative situation is static and underlines the complete alienation of the protagonist and anticipates its fatal consequences. Joseph's estrangement is reflected in spatial terms through a conventional contrast between the onstage *locus* and the offstage *spatium*. The initial safety of the warehouse (onstage) is increasingly endangered by the inevitable reality of war, which is metonymically implied by the orders delivered from offstage in German (voices of Nazi oppressors), and the ominous sound of marching feet. In *The Street of Crocodiles*, the duality of spatial relations is the basis for a compound field of associations:

(on-stage: Jew/victim/reader-artist/recluse)

vs.

(off-stage: Nazis/oppressors/soldiers/group).

Diagram 5.3

Whereas the world of the stage is shaped as a shelter, the offstage epitomises the growing menace. The confrontation of the two worlds (onstage and offstage) leads to the initiation to the evil element of the world. Even this brief account illustrates the way in which the spatial imagery is endowed with the developing 'metaphoric' potential. The final intrusion of the martial values associated throughout the play with the offstage world is decisive for the total annihilation of the vulnerable world of an artist.

FUNCTIONS OF LETTERS

The narrative situation is decisive for the overall meanings of *The Street of Crocodiles* in yet one more way. By clearly referring to the circumstances of the death of Bruno Schulz, the framework motivates a curious equivalence between the protagonist of the play and the writer. The biographical dimension is further vindicated by strictly textual quotations which appear as mottos justifying the shape of particular scenes. Even though, in the majority of cases, the quotes are taken from Schulz's narratives, the Prologue and the Epilogue open with a biographical account of Schulz's death (fragments of Tadeusz Lubowiecki's letter to Jerzy Ficowski). In two other scenes, biographical quotations accompany the narrative ones: a letter by Jacob Schulz—Bruno's nephew (Part One, scene 2)—and Bruno Schulz's own letters (Part Two, scene 1). Interestingly, the beginning of another letter by the latter is read aloud by Adela in Part Two, scene 9:

'Dear Sir, I need a friend. I need the closeness of a kindred spirit. I long for some outside affirmation of the inner world whose existence I cherish. I need a partner for voyages of discovery. One person becomes reality when reflected in two pairs of eyes. ... My world has been waiting for this two-some, as it were. What was once a closed tight place with no further prospects now begins to ripen into colours in the distance, burst open and reveal its depths. ...' (1999: 44–5)

In this way the biographical potential of the play (Joseph's equivalence with Bruno) is paired with its meta-literary aspect (epistolary expression of the authorial search for the reader). In the perspective of the addressee, Joseph (the protagonist of Complicite's play) is confronted as much by Bruno Schulz as by Joseph (the narrator of Schulz's narratives). Simultaneously, the letter read by Adela inscribes the relation between the author and the reader into the structure in which interlocutors are bound together ('I need a partner for voyages of discovery').

DUALITY WITHIN THE INTERNAL PERSPECTIVE

The Street of Crocodiles is constructed in accordance with the principle of dichotomy. The model of the world which is presented in the play confronts, among others, the following notions:

- the brutality of the surrounding world vs the vulnerable world of imagination,
- the narrative situation vs the narrated events,
- the biographic vs the oneiric,
- the constructional framework vs the main onstage action.

Within the world of Joseph's imagination, the principle of dichotomy is concisely indicated by the appearance of the motif of twins (Theodore and Leon) and the prop of a half-plate. The latter is owned by Maria, who is incessantly searching for the other half (of the plate, and the beloved one). Intense and enormously diversified application of the principle of dichotomy leads us to the exploration of the relation between the theme of Joseph's alienation and selected aspects of spatio-temporal imagery (the classroom, the sanatorium and the Father's shop).

Joseph is constantly put in the role of a vulnerable outsider, someone whose nature does not fit well with the requirements of the brutal reality around him.[13] It is explicitly visible in the classroom situation. As a teacher, he is horrified by the need to make basic decisions—such as the subject matter for a class—and is incapable of imposing rudimentary discipline upon his pupils. This goes so far that at one point Joseph falls asleep, and the pupils take complete control of the events. As the stage directions have it, at the beginning of Part Two, scene 1—entitled 'The class'—Joseph is *'not sure what he is supposed to teach today'* (1999: 13), and in its concluding part

... remains asleep. The class hatch a plan. **Charles** *makes a wooden spoon with* **Leon** *and* **Theodore**. *He leads the sleeping* **Joseph** *round the classroom in a dance of death, the class providing the rhythmical accompaniment.* **Joseph** *ends by standing on a chair in the middle of the room.* **Agatha** *'shoots' him.* (17)

The teacher is put in the position of a victim and the situation antici-pates his final death. What initially seems a rather mimetic—overtly bio-graphic—depiction of the everyday horror of a classroom, turns into an elaborate visual anticipation of the climactic assassination.[14]

The classroom is not the only place where Joseph appears in the role of an outsider. In Part Three, scene 2—entitled 'Sanatorium'—his alienation is endowed with a supernatural character. Accompanied by his Mother, Joseph arrives at the otherworldly 'sanatorium under the hourglass' to meet his dead Father. The principles governing this space are clearly anti-mimetic so that the visit acquires qualities of a nightmare. The motifs of an everlasting night, permanent sleep of all patients, and cumbersome bureaucracy, together with the allegorical figure of Death (**'Leon** *is still dressed in black as the figure of Death'* [49]) make it clear that Joseph and his Mother are in the position of the living-among-dead. As the follow-ing quotation illustrates, Joseph feels awkward in such a situation and is uncertain of what is happening around him:

> **Leon** We received your telegram. Are you well?
> **Joseph** Is my father still alive?
> **Leon** [who is Death] Of course. Within certain limits. In your country, your father is dead, but here he is very much alive. Here we turn back the clock. Go straight through. It's the first door. The first door!
> **Joseph** *advances DSR.* **Leon** *exits USL.*
> **Father** (*appears on the back wall*) The six days of Creation were divine and bright. But on the seventh day, God broke down.
> **Joseph** Father!
> **Father** How good of you to come... (49)

The actual meeting with Father proves that the world model of the play allows for an encounter between those who are alive and those who are dead.

For obvious reasons the role of an outsider is closely related to spatial imagery. The semantics of the classroom stresses the alienation of Joseph/Schulz/teacher in confrontation with his pupils. Besides, the sanatorium scene highlights the meeting with the world of the dead. Even though the semantics of the Father's shop operates within the same type of imagery, it introduces relations that are more dynamic.

The play presents three different, though interlinked, types of relations between Joseph and the shop. Characteristically, in all of them the protagonist takes the role of an outsider who is faced with others in an increasingly threatening way. In 'Part Two: The Age of Genius', scenes 2 and 3 are entitled, respectively, 'The shop of childhood memory' and 'Father's beautiful shop'. Joseph appears here as the one who enlivens in his memory the events of the past, endowing them with a mythical dimension. The opening tableau presents him as the one who revisits the scene from his childhood: '*in a playful mood*' he watches the sleeping shop inhabitants. He blows, then, '*on his father's head*' and, thus, brings forth '*the sound of birds flapping*' (18), which wakes Father up. This is followed by the equally surreal image of finding an egg in Mother's hair, the action which also awakens her.

There emerges an intriguing parallel between this scene and the recollection of McBurney's Cambridge home, which was narrated in the opening essay of *Who You Hear It from*. In 'To kill a caribou (and feast on its guts)', Mother and Father's awakening under the frosty quilt epitomised their initial awakening from the sphere of memory. In both cases, a living son is given the power to enliven the memory of his dead parents and return to the mythical world of his childhood. In *The Street of Crocodiles* the awakening is followed by enlivening the memory of the Father's shop: Leon and Theodor (the twins) are accompanied by Adela as shop assistants, Emil becomes an eccentric client who contemplates the extraordinariness of an electric bell, Joseph (as a boy) shows the first signs of his erotic fascination with Adela, and Maria breaks her plate in two halves.

A different arrangement of the discussed network of associations is presented in 'The empty shop', which is the third scene of 'Part Three: The Republic of Dreams'. The scene begins with the following stage directions:

> **Joseph**'s *growing sense of desperation in this scene is not only about an attempt to reverse time and refind his childhood but also a sense of foreboding about the future. In the repetition of the gestures, he not only expresses his anger and hurt at the disappearance of his father and by extension his past, but also is attempting in some way to hold up time.* (53)

These 'directions' do not reveal any meta-theatrical connotations such as what the actors are supposed to do. On the contrary, the description of Joseph's emotional state provides some interpretative clues concerning the development of the onstage action. The quotation presents a narrative way of explaining the protagonist's behaviour, which is to be conveyed onstage by means of non-linguistic codes. The written text offers a straightforward and one-dimensional interpretation of what theatrically is likely to cause a considerable degree of ambiguity.

Joseph is aware that, after Father's disappearance, the action took a fatal course. His desperate attempts to reverse automatisation are confronted with the growing dehumanisation of the remaining characters (e.g. actors are becoming dummy-like) and increasing disintegration of the presented reality. Notwithstanding Joseph's actions, Father's shop has transformed from the place of nostalgic recollection of childhood safety to that of contemporary nightmare.

The following quotations illustrate the futility of Joseph's struggle to avert disintegration. Contrary to his desires, 'the empty shop' is the place where there are still customers, but there is nothing to sell:

> **Emil** [as a customer] I'd like a Royal tartan, please.
> **Assistants**, *extremely rapidly, look in the desks. There is nothing there.*
> **Mother** I'm sorry, we have nothing left.
> **The Assistants** Niet material!
> …
> **Joseph** No…! (54)

This 'directorial' objection suspends the course of the action, makes changes possible, and results in a repetition of the episode. As it soon turns out, the repetition allows for no improvement. On the contrary, duplication underlines increasing disintegration:

> **Joseph** Mother the shop! It is wrong! Do it again.
> *He throws the shoppers out, cruelly throws his* **Mother** *out and makes them do the whole routine again. This time it is a little shorter. <u>All the figures are a little more dilapidated</u>. No-one understands why they are being forced to do this.*
> …
> **Emil** [as a customer] I'd like a Persian cedar please.
> **Assistants**, *extremely rapidly, look in the desks. There is nothing there.*
> **Mother** I'm so sorry, we have nothing left.
> **Assistants** Niet material!
> …
> **Joseph** No!
> …
> **Joseph** Do it again! Again! Do it again! (54–5, underlining added)

The second, even more desperate, 'directorial' objection is followed by the third, and again unsuccessful, repetition of the episode:

Emil I'd like a Royal tartan, a Persian cedar, an electric bell—
Charles The calaphony—
Emil The calaphony from Malabar.
Assistants, *extremely rapidly, look in the desks. There is nothing there.*
Mother I'm so sorry, but we have absolutely nothing left!
Assistants Niet material!
Joseph No!

...

Everybody is turning as at the end of a nightmare. ... (55–6)

The threefold repetition of the increasingly frustrating uselessness of 'the empty shop' marks the shift in Joseph's attitude to the place from the nostalgic myth of an idealised childhood to the ill-omened nightmare of 'manekination' (Schulz's neologism), dehumanisation and automatisation. As it occurs, the repetition—similarly to the earlier classroom application of the convention of the dance of death—suggests the ritual dimension of *The Street of Crocodiles*. The action is shaped as regression and disintegration.

For this reason, the worse is yet to come. Scene 1 of 'Part Four: The Act of Destruction', which is entitled 'The worshippers of Baal', presents the ultimate confrontation of Joseph with all other characters. This time they are neither protective family members nor acquaintances but intruders representing the menace of the offstage world. The previous balance separating the onstage shelter of memory from the external danger (the sound of marching feet) is irrevocably destroyed. The shop is set as the venue of the final—though not permanent—triumph of the evil element of the universe.

Notwithstanding his insistent attempts to preserve the *status quo* ('The shop is closed!', 'Come back tomorrow!', 'I'm sorry but we are in the middle of stocktaking'), the shoppers interfere with Joseph's mental world and the course of their movement establishes '*an ominous square space around the shop*' (61). In other words, the spatial imagery undergoes a complete redefinition: the shop—initially the secure place of idealised childhood—has been transformed into the setting of the forthcoming ritual of initiation to evil.

We can see the variety of ways in which the ritual dimension of the scene is underlined. The others (shoppers/intruders) turn into a group character, and as a chorus either intensify the mode of disintegration ('*The group breaks once more into the cacophony of demands*') or increase, by univocal singing, the ceremonial aspect of the event. As the stage directions have it: '*Their chorus of demands to* **Joseph** *to open the shop grow and grow until they break into song "Worthy is the Lamb" from Handel's* Messiah ...' On the one hand, the substitution of the initial line of the psalm ('Worthy is the Lamb that was slain') with the one of immediate deictic relevance ('Joseph,

Joseph, open the shop' [62]) firmly and unambiguously sanctions the parallel between Joseph's death and the sacrifice of the Lamb, while on the other hand testifying to the process of implementing Christian imagery for artistic purposes. The ritual interpretation of the murder of Joseph/Schulz is conceived less as a sacrifice in the religious sense of the word, and more as a sense-endowing archetypal analogy. In this way, the theatrical vision of the absurd death of Joseph/Schulz becomes Complicite's tribute to the writer and the books that survived him. In this context, the legend of the novel, entitled, as with Handel's oratorio, *Messiah*—apparently completed by Schulz but lost to the world (Jarzębski 1998: xix)—forms a significant point of biographic reference.

There is one more religious allusion in 'The worshippers of Baal', since Joseph's final monologue consists of an adapted quotation from the Book of Exodus (1999: 64). By setting the analogy between the story of Joseph/Schulz and that of Moses, Complicite provide an additional interpretative context: this is a story of the artist/prophet whose death does not annihilate the artistry of his vision. Permanent as it is, the imaginative creation of Bruno Schulz—just as the task fulfilled by Moses—is directed to the generations to come, which is auto-referentially exemplified by Complicite's *The Street of Crocodiles*. The play, just as the performance, thrives on the abrasive powers of Schulz's imagination.[15]

The discussion of the Father's shop prompts some important conclusions. The three occurrences of the same space setting formulate three different—though interlinked—structures. Their semantic potential is intrinsically related to the storyline of Joseph and the dense tension between the internal world of his imagination and the menace caused by the unavoidable intrusion of the external war reality. Moreover, the direction of transforming the semantics of the shop (idealised myth of childhood → the nightmare of the empty shop → the initiation into the evil) points to the prominence of the principle of regression. The automatisation of actions, the dehumanisation of characters and the general disintegration of the world model testify to a theatrical/dramatic application of Schulz's concept of 'manekisation'. This exemplifies Complicite's fascination with the autotelic: the construction of the play is arranged in accordance with the features of the presented world vision.

The broad meanings ascribed to the Father's shop invariably put Joseph in the position of an outsider. The confrontation with the memory of childhood, the empty shop and the ritual murder enable the addressee to define the meanings ascribed to the protagonist. It is the question 'who was he?'—and not 'who am I?'—which is crucial for the semantics. Even though the play thrives on a tragic contemporary myth based on both Bruno Schulz's art and his biography, the signature of Simon McBurney imposes its rather positive interpretation. The allusions to the Lamb and Moses provide a broad human perspective: the absurd lot of Bruno Schulz (and by extension the atrocities of the contemporary world) acquires an archetypal dimension in which the story of Joseph epitomises the condition of human beings/artists.

CONFRONTATIONS

In *The Street of Crocodiles* the theme of alienation is embedded in the structure of spatial relations. The main onstage action develops fields of associations, which either result in numerous, frequently unpredictable, paradigmatic equivalences of auto-referential, oneiric, surreal, irrational, archetypal character or combine in accordance with the biographical accuracy and realistic verisimilitude. All these contradictory means of the combination of signs find application in the play.

It is, however, also true that the main onstage action of *The Street of Crocodiles* multiplies dichotomies and cultivates the dualism of the presented world. The following enumeration extends the list of oppositions by introducing new aspects. On the one hand, the arrangement of characters establishes clear-cut, if multidimensional, juxtapositions, such as:

- son vs father/mother/family,
- Joseph vs Adela/Maria/women,
- Mother vs Maria/Adela,
- Maria vs the beloved one/the other half of the plate,
- Jew vs Nazis,
- Emil as a cousin vs Emil as a pupil vs Emil as a shopper,
- Leon as an assistant vs Leon as the figure of Death.

On the other hand, major fields of association are based on the same principle. Again, examples abound:

- life vs dream/memory/semblance/imagination,
- dream vs nightmare,
- biography vs fiction,
- victim vs oppressor,
- the living vs the dead,
- teacher vs pupil,
- artist vs reader/audience.

The initiation to the evil element of the world is not the only type of initiation operative in the play. Whereas in some episodes there emerges a visualisation of the rite of passage into death, the theme of erotic initiation to maturity is suggested by Joseph's fascination with Agatha and Adela. It is also hinted at by the robust subplot of cousin Emil and autoerotism of Part Two, scene 6. The broad auto-referential potential of initiation into the world of imagination, memory and art should also be mentioned as it pervades the entire play.

THE THREE LIVES OF LUCIE CABROL: THE COMPOSITION

There are numerous parallels between *The Street of Crocodiles* and *The Three Lives of Lucie Cabrol*. This results not only from interpretative possibilities provided by their printed versions, but also from the fact that both plays examine similar structural solutions, such as dichotomous construction, spatio-temporal contrasts, juxtaposition of communicative levels and frame composition. Nevertheless, the meanings created on analogous foundations are not the same. This is explicit when we take into consideration that, as a stage adaptation of narrative fiction, *The Three Lives of Lucie Cabrol* makes no hints at the biographical context of the plot.

In *The Street of Crocodiles* the distance between the performance and the fiction written by Schulz is rooted in Theatre de Complicite's interweaving of fragments chosen from numerous short stories and the mixing them with biographical detail. There is no doubt the audience deals with a piece that has been inspired by Schulz's fiction rather than with an attempt at its 'faithful' theatre adaptation. Also the printed play lays emphasis on its artistic autonomy. There are numerous overtly editorial remarks, such as the titles of compositional units and added quotations from letters.

The Three Lives of Lucie Cabrol makes use of a different constructional strategy. Based on the long-short story by John Berger, the play integrates narrative structuring with numerous conventions that are rooted in dramatic literature and/or derive from the medium of theatre. Its debt to the plot adapted from the narrative is balanced by auto-referential devices. As the title suggests, Berger's story consists of three main parts that present three different lives of Lucie Cabrol. The play, by contrast, condenses the second and third lives into one part and in this way juxtaposes the title (three lives) with the construction (two parts). The printed play is textually divided into 12 titled scenes, whose distribution is asymmetrical because the seven scenes in Part One (the first life) are followed by five in Part Two (the second and third lives). The scenes are numbered continuously from 1 to 12, which underscores the chronological logic of the plot. The sequential nature of the performance is further stressed by the compositional framework. Part One begins with the Prologue and Part Two finishes with the Epilogue.

In other words, it is the printed play that sanctions the logic of the onstage action and its relation to the plot. The episodes which were selected from Berger's narrative are visible already when we have a look at their textual arrangement:

Part One

Prologue

1. Birth

2. The Naming of the Cocadrille

3. The First War and the birth of Edmond

4. The mountain pastures

5. Marius's funeral and Marie

6. The maquisards

7. The casting out

Part Two

8. Jean's return (forty years later)

9. Lucie's hut

10. Lucie's funeral

11. Blueberry picking

12. Building the Chalet

Epilogue

Diagram 5.4

Unlike in *The Street of Crocodiles*, the compositional framework is integral to the major division into the two parts of the text. Yet, in both plays the Prologue and the Epilogue function similarly since they delineate the narrative situation embedding the main onstage action and in this way establish the main dichotomy within the construction (i.e. the narrative situation vs the main story).

THE FRAMEWORK AND THE NARRATIVE SITUATION

In *The Three Lives of Lucie Cabrol*, the Epilogue mirrors the Prologue in a very clear way. The play begins and ends with the stage direction '*Music*' (1995: 3, 54). In the ending, it is followed only by the word '*Fade*' (54). Verbally, the framework is dominated by Jean/narrator's recollection of the dead, the world of the past, and by the memories of his earliest childhood. Exact repetitions of certain phrases appear (e.g. 'Before I was six, perhaps I was only two or three…' [4, 53]), and close variants of longer passages ('Now when I light the stove in the morning, I say to myself: I and the fire are the only living things in the house; my father, mother, brothers, sisters, the horse[s], cows, rabbits, chickens, all have gone. And Lucie Cabrol [, who was known as the Cocadrille,] is dead' [4, 53]).

Similarities between the Prologue and the Epilogue abound also in the visual imagery: when delivering his monologue, Jean is moving towards—and later is sitting at—the stove. He is constantly confronted with the characters who inhabit the internal stage of his memory/imagination. In the initial tableau (before Jean's appearance) all other characters are sitting upstage with boots placed irregularly in front of them. After his entrance, Jean washes himself and drinks 'fresh water' so as to purify himself before enlivening the dead. Then, he '*comes down centre*' and begins his introductory monologue:

> **Jean** (*indicating a pair of boots*) Émile Cabrol, who died of his war wounds nearly twenty years after the Great War. Émile. Eldest son of (*Indicating another pair of boots.*) Marius Cabrol and his wife La Mélanie. (*Another pair.*) Henri Cabrol, second son of Marius and La Mélanie, who was to say of his sister, 'This woman has never brought anything but shame on my family.' (*Another pair.*) My schoolteacher, André Masson, killed at Verdun. (*He gestures towards other pairs.*) Joset. St Just, the maquisard. Georges, who electrocuted himself because he knew he would become a pauper. The dead surround the living, and the living form the core of the dead. (3)

In this passage, Jean defines himself as the narrator whose story is to be conveyed from a stage to an audience. An element of alienation appears, as all the characters are French, whereas the language used is mainly English. By indicating boots—not actors—when introducing particular characters, Jean employs the figure of visual metonymy[16] and in this way puts strong emphasis on the conventional nature of theatre communication. The juxtaposition of the fictional world and the world of the stage not only enlivens the meta-theatrical potential of the performance but also establishes major fields of association.

Jean's introductory monologue gives the primary role to family relations and in addition to this establishes the pattern in which Lucie—the eponymous protagonist of the story—is shaped as an existential outsider, the one who is despised even by her younger brother, Henri ('This woman has never brought anything but shame on my family'). Furthermore, the dead are confronted with the living, and the dynamic nature of this reciprocal relation is defined in the final sentence ('The dead surround the living, and the living form the core of the dead'). As it turns out in scenes 11 and 12, a physical encounter between the two is feasible not only on the plane of storytelling (as the narrator, Jean enlivens the memory of the dead), but also within the fictional reality (as the character, Jean is taken by the now-dead Lucie to the wood where the dead live).

Unsurprisingly, the fields of association that are established here are based mainly on contrasts and revolve around such juxtapositions as:

- Jean vs other characters/spectators,
- rural France vs contemporary English-speaking actors and spectators,
- the living vs the dead,
- past vs present,
- verbal vs visual,
- stage vs audience.

Interestingly, the Epilogue introduces one new element to the semantics of the play. The field of associations built upon the metaphor of the forest, a roof built from trees, Lucie's equivalence with the blue sky, and Jean's nostalgic dream of reversing time, hints at the ending of Berger's narrative. Unlike in the Prologue, the Epilogue stresses the compositional debt of the play to the original text. Even if its verbal component echoes the Prologue, Jean's final monologue is positioned in the same place as in Berger's narrative.

LUCIE AS AN OUTSIDER

But the main contrast in the play is based on the confrontation of the idiosyncratic world vision of Lucie Cabrol with the views of all the other characters. The protagonist is shaped as an existential outsider who is incessantly facing the hindrances imposed by the hostile world around her.

In scene 1 (Birth), we learn that Lucie was born in 1900 as a dwarf with an ominous 'red mark of a carving', and her parents were slightly disappointed with her sex as they expected a second son. Her physical strangeness quickly becomes the object of derision for other villagers, including children. It is Henri who, in scene 2, names Lucie the 'Cocadrille' and insists that she killed rabbits simply by looking at them. By ascribing supernatural powers to Lucie, her younger brother cultivates her increasing social alienation. His other similar acts include spitting at her in public, teasing her at school and disapproving of sharing their parents' heritage. In fact, after their parents' death, Henri, Marie (his wife) and Edmond (the youngest brother) alienate Lucie completely and multiply the public accusations of her misbehaviour, which results in her being expelled from the village. This is how Part One of the play—and the first life of Lucie Cabrol—ends:

> **Marie** It was the mayor's wife who came up with the solution which he finally proposed to Henri and Edmond. They accepted it enthusiastically.
> **Edmond** *comes round the table, sweeps the debris from it and sits in* **Lucie's** *place.*
> **Marie** And with this proposal the first life of the Cocadrille came to an end.
> **Lucie** *walks. She is loaded up with possessions—a sack, a spade, a chair, a blanket, her scythe—until she is bent under their weight. She circles the space and goes off up right. Fade.* (30)

Disinheritance and banishment are not the only misfortunes to strike Lucie in her first life. She is also thoroughly disillusioned by Jean's decision to leave their village for the wide world, after their intense, if short-term, romance in the summer of 1924. What for Lucie seemed the only predicable prospect of a marriage was treated by Jean as a rather shameful act of unrestrained passion ('What was it that made me go back the following night? Why did I deliberately go up alone, avoiding my companions?' [20]). Whatever the consequences of this decision, Jean leaves the village for Paris, and then Buenos Aires, moving after another 20 years to Montreal.

When, towards the end of his life, he decides to come back to the village, Jean learns of the enormous detachment of Lucie and her increasing shrewdness. In scene 8 ('Jean's return [forty years later]'), the narrator recollects his first encounter with Lucie after all those years. The reminiscence takes the form of a duologue:

> **Lucie** ... So you've come back.
> **Jean** Yes, I've come back.
> **Lucie** (*staring at him*) You were away too long.
> **Jean** I remembered the way up here.
> **Lucie** You came up here to spy on me.

...

Lucie Whilst you were away, everything changed.

Jean I suppose a lot must have changed when you left the farm.

Lucie I didn't leave it. They threw me out. Did you marry out there?

Jean Yes, I did.

Lucie Why did you come back alone then?

Jean Because my wife died.

Lucie *crosses herself.*

Lucie Oh. You're a widower.

Jean I am a widower.

Lucie Do you have children?

Jean Two boys. They are both working in the United States.

Lucie America. America. Money can change everything. Money can eat and dance. Money can make the dirty clean. Money can make the dwarf big. I have two million!

Jean I hope you keep it in a bank!

Lucie Fuck off! Fuck off and get away! (32–3)

Detached from other people, Lucie earns a fortune, which changes hardly anything in her harsh lifestyle, or in her coarse nature. Suspicious, malicious, shrewd and mean, she is uncompromisingly rude and unsentimental even to the only one whom she seems to have once loved. There is no way in which she may be persuaded to come to terms with the surrounding world. The other should remain her enemy for ever. In scene 9, she is murdered for her money and thus finishes her second life.

THE ADDRESSEE

Even though *The Three Lives of Lucie Cabrol* by Theatre de Complicite echoes the title, the storyline and much of Berger's narrative, its semantics does not exactly mirror the long-short story but provides an innovative response to it. The textual tissue of the printed play illustrates how the narrative material was selected and combined for the purposes of the theatre company. In this view, the performance and the printed play turn into an account of an artistic response to the singularity of Berger's narrative. In George Steiner's terms, one would say that the play completes the hermeneutic process with its fourth stage, that of compensation and reiteration (Steiner 2008). Pronouncement of the constructional autonomy of the play is, thus, made functional. On the one hand, it stresses the independence of meanings created by the play, and on the other emphasises its involvement in a more general plane of communication where Berger's narrative was followed by Complicite's performance, which was followed by Complicite's printed play.

There are some practical consequences of this. On a more general communicative level between the stage and the audience, Jean's introductory monologue takes on a double role for the implied addressee (i.e. audience/spectator/reader). The monologue anticipates the events that are to happen and, simultaneously, suggests dichotomies that dominate the presented world vision. It builds up suspense and hints at concrete questions concerning the development of action: 'what's the shame mentioned by Henri?', 'why are the Great War and Verdun mentioned?', 'what happened between the war and the death of Émile?', 'what is the story of Georges?' But when considered from the perspective of someone who is familiar with Berger's narrative, the very same monologue indicates the characters and events that refer back to the long-short story. When assuming such a perspective, another major compositional shift introduced by Theatre de Complicite is revealed. The words uttered by Jean in the opening monologue are those that appear only at the ending of Berger's narrative. Unlike in Complicite, in Berger there is no compositional framework. A more detailed comparative interpretation of these works would reveal plenty of equally intriguing correspondences.

The Prologue and the Epilogue underscore the juxtaposition of two kinds of reception, the one focused primarily on the development of onstage action (with no awareness of the original story), and the other taking into consideration the subtext of Berger's narrative. Whereas the former type may be labelled as the 'naïve spectator' that follows primarily the stage signals, the latter requires more active participation in the communicative process and should be perhaps labelled as the 'model reader'.[17] None of these perspectives should be treated as the privileged one; on the contrary, their relation is of a complementary nature. From the perspective of the 'naïve spectator', the image of Jean's initial washing and drinking constitutes an important frame for the performance, and for the 'model reader' the same image is primarily the signal of intertextual prominence as it signals that the play distances itself from Berger's narrative.

The double role of the addressee is not, of course, anything new in theatre or dramatic literature. But in *The Three Lives of Lucie Cabrol* the juxtaposition contributes in a particular way to the singularity of artistic experience. The complementary roles of the 'naïve spectator' and 'model reader' underscore how watching a performance differs from reading a play. They also reveal necessary shifts between perceiving a piece of art as autonomous and as rooted in the cultural context. When exploring the multiple roles of the addressee in other shows, Complicite creates numerous other meanings. These are just some of the most striking examples:

- street shows involve casual passers-by and those who intentionally follow the performance,
- multi/inter-media performances such as *Measure for Measure, The Disappearing Number* and *The Master and Margarita* necessitate rapid shifts of receptive roles within the whole spectrum of channels of communication (e.g. spectator, reader, listener),
- the Japanese plays differentiate between the Japanese and non-Japanese speaking members of the audience,
- *Lionboy* presents slightly different stories for teenagers and adults.[18]

LIGHT: THE COMPOSITION

In *Light*, an adaptation of Torgny Lindgren's novel, the roles ascribed to the addressee are similar to those I discussed in *The Three Lives of Lucie Cabrol*. Yet, they create different meanings. Whereas the 'spectator' is, this time, made more aware of the dialectics of the 'liveness' and conventionality of the performance, the position of the 'reader' is less omnipotent. One of the reasons for this is the fact that the textual composition is less explicitly marked. When compared to *The Street of Crocodiles* and *The Three Lives of Lucie Cabrol, Light* redefines the role of the textual tissue in the aesthetics of Complicite.

The printed version of *Light* is divided into two untitled acts, with no further subdivision into scenes, not to mention explanatory or biographical quotations. In consequence, reading is made more laborious, as it necessitates interpretative decisions when, for example, recognising the composition. In this sense, the role of the 'reader' is closer to that of the 'spectator': neither of them is privileged by overt textual guidance.

On closer inspection, however, the composition of *Light* does not differ that much from the previously analysed plays. The onstage narrator establishes a firmly depicted compositional framework that embeds a chronologically arranged storyline of the main episodic onstage action. Unnamed as they are, both the Prologue and the Epilogue begin with the narrator's comments on the unsolvable 'riddle of the rabbit'. The final monologue is far more concise and spectral than that from the beginning. Moreover, it is no longer the narrator, but his recorded voice, that repeats the two crucial paragraphs of the introduction:

Man can never comprehend the rabbit. No, not even if we live to be a thousand can we solve the riddle of the rabbit. Their fur is soft and warm; it's like the hair in a woman's armpit. Stroking a rabbit is like dripping your hand in warm milk straight from a cow. And the flesh is as soft and white as butter. You're full for a whole week when you've eaten rabbit, even the cooked meat seems to have offspring and multiply itself.

Man may be made in the image of God, but there is also a God who created the rabbit in his own image, a God of liveliness and quivering and fear and fecundity. Yes. The rabbit is a creator. (2000: 13, 82–3)

Needless to say, even though the wording is exactly the same, the meanings created at the beginning differ substantially from those at the end. The anticipatory dimension of the Prologue introduces the theme of human curiosity, the mystery of the animal element, the sensory fascination with rabbits and puzzling values ascribed to them.

In the Epilogue, the naturalistic/symbolic vision of the world of the introduction is retrospectively endowed with a more metaphorical dimension. At this point, the entire story of the Great Sickness brought by the plague-ridden rabbit to the northern village of Kadis has been told. Therefore, the theme of 'a God of liveliness and quivering and fear and fecundity' that 'created the rabbit in his own image' (83) is more immediately linked with the question of morality and the fear of unrestrained annihilation of 'the natural order of things' (32). As we learn throughout the play, it is the bringing of the rabbit by Jasper that incites the obliteration of the natural and moral conduct of the 'old world'.

While the exact repetition of the verbal utterance sets the compositional framework for the play, the visual images that accompany the words stress contrasts between the semantics of the opening and the ending. As the performance begins, the Narrator '*enters a bare stage with a live rabbit in his arms*' and forecasts reactions of the audience by saying 'I know what you're thinking, is she real or is she a fake? Is it true or is it a fiction?' In a moment, the world of the stage is additionally occupied by the crowd of puppets representing the villagers: '*During the NARRATOR's speech a number of puppets come into view and gather for a church service*' (13). This sets the opening frame for the main onstage action, which takes us back 650 years.

Even though the textual tissue of *Light* is not as explicitly segmented as *The Street of Crocodiles* and *The Three Lives of Lucie Cabrol*, all these plays are grounded on similar foundations. We can see the following structuring of the onstage action of *Light*:

ACT ONE

Prologue

1. The Great Sickness in Kadis.

2. The musk gland of the beaver.

3. The heir of Avar.

4. Seven survivors.

5. Avar's bath death.

6. The birth of Blasius.

7. Redistribution of inheritance.

8. The Room and the devil.

9. The law from Umeå.

10. The slaughter of rabbits.

11. The births of Maria and Kare.

12. Könik's fight with Önde and his attempt at Kare's life.

ACT TWO

1. Könik's release from the lock-up.

2. The disappearance of Kare.

3. The passing of seasons.

4. The arrival of Nikolavus, King's messenger.

5. Blasius eats Maria.

6. Grief.

7. The trial.

8. Nicolavus expelled.

9. The arrival of a Priest, Maria, Kare and a rabbit.

Epilogue

Diagram 5.5

What we observe is, however, a slightly different textual strategy that aims at stressing the theatrical—rather than narrative—provenance of the printed play. The role of the reader is, above all, to consider the perspective of a spectator of a Complicite performance and not so much to get involved in comparative analysis of the printed play with the novel by Lindgren. Hence, the play abounds in more consistent allusions to theatrical conventions, such as the ritual, the procession and the chorus of villagers. The cause-and-effect logic of the characters' actions is bound to the immoral themes of incest, sodomy, greed, kidnapping, hanging and other vicious deeds that lead to an annihilation of the natural order of the world.

LIVENESS AND CONVENTIONALITY

The model of theatre and, hence, theatre conventions, are much integrated with the textual tissue of *Light*. This is revealed, for instance, when the stage directions establish equivalence between the perspective of the reader and that of the audience by using the pronoun 'we' (as in '*We are back in ÖNDE's room*' [23]). This is just one of many examples when the printed play disregards discrepancies between the experience of reading and the experience of watching the performance. For this reason, the spectator—'the reader as a spectator'—is particularly exposed to the interplay of liveness and the conventional.

The opening of *Light* multiplies the complexity of semiotic relations within the world of the stage. The meanings are created by actors, their utterances, gestures, actions and their proxemic relations with other elements of space-time setting. Notwithstanding other typically theatrical conventions that are employed, there appear numerous puppets and the live rabbit. The spectrum of stage conventions thus revealed may be schematically presented as the one that encompasses the following extremes:

- the live animal (liveness),
- the live actors playing fictional characters (theatricality),
- the puppets representing fictional characters/animals (conventionality).

The ending shapes these relations in a slightly different way. The verbal element is subordinated this time to the visual. Actors move backwards in a line, a process which deprives them of their individual qualities. In addition to this, there is no actor/narrator but his recorded voice. The monologue focuses, yet again, on the nature of rabbits and, thus, enlivens the images of rabbits accumulated in the course of the performance: plague-ridden rabbits, puppet rabbits, newly born rabbits, slaughtered rabbits, and the ones hammered on the cross.

The world of the stage is shaped by the interplay of actors, puppets and the live rabbit. Spatio-temporal imagery is dichotomous as it intermingles the meta-theatrical level of the frame narrative with the past story of those who survived the plague in Kadis. Moreover, the narrator assumes certain roles within the narrative. In Act Two, for example, he turns into Nicolavus, who is an outsider, a king's messenger, a judge, and the one who gives an account of the story of Kadis to the wide world. It is he who aims to reinstate secular axiology in which wealth and material goods prove to be merits that overshadow 'trifles' such as the moral code distinguishing what is good from what is bad. Overall, *Light* presents a moral parable, in which straightforward presentation of the storyline is subordinated to the theatrical devices of creating meanings.

MODEL OF COMPOSITION

Even if the meanings conveyed by the printed versions of *The Street of Crocodiles*, *The Three Lives of Lucie Cabrol* and *Light* vary from those created by the theatre productions, the published plays play a vital role in preserving some of the features that are decisive for shaping the aesthetics of Complicite. One of these features is the composition. Divergent as the presented stories are, their artistic arrangement consistently follows the pattern established by *A Minute Too Late*:

the Prologue (narrative situation/now)

↓

the main on-stage action (narrated story/the past)

↓

the Epilogue (narrative situation/now).

Diagram 5.6

Each play makes use of this general scheme in its independent way. In other words, by reinventing the earlier solutions, Complicite manages to enliven artistic qualities in its subsequent productions. The compositional variants may seem subtle but they are of the greatest prominence.

So, whereas in the case of *The Street of Crocodiles* the above pattern is applied as:

The Prologue

↓

[Part One (2 scenes) → Part Two (9 scenes) → Part Three (6 scenes) → Part Four (2 scenes)]

↓

The Epilogue

Diagram 5.7

in *The Three Lives of Lucie Cabrol* it takes the following structure:

Part One (The Prologue → [scenes 1-7])

↓

Part Two ([scenes 8-12] → The Epilogue).

Diagram 5.8

Compared with this, the textual composition of *Light*:

Act One

↓

Act Two

Diagram 5.9

seems to be the least developed, but—as we have seen—this is a wrong impression.

NOTES

1. A separate entry on Théâtre de Complicité appears in J.A. Cuddon's *The Penguin Dictionary of Literary Terms and Literary Theory* as early as the 1991 edition. There are just a few other theatre groups mentioned in the volume as the dictionary concentrates on literature and not theatre. Still, the entry seems to confirm the high reputation of the company in professional circles at that time (1991: 964).
2. *Help, I'm Alive!* was a contemporary adaptation of a script by Ruzzante (www.complicite.org).

3. For a comprehensive study of functions of complex relations between onstage reading of books, see Frances Babbage's article 'How Books Matter: Theatre, Adaptation and the Life of Book', where *The Street of Crocodiles* and *The Master and Margarita* are discussed. For a slightly different interpretation of *The Master and Margarita*, in which the performance is put in the context of the novel and the tradition of its stage adaptations, see Naz Yeni's 'Multiplicity in Complicite's *The Master and Margarita*'.

4. I argue that, unlike audiovisual materials, which are documentary recordings done for archival purposes, the printed play belongs to the commonly sanctioned tradition of dramatic literature and as such it acquires the full autonomy of an artistic piece. A similar process occurs in radio plays.

5. This can be seen in the video recording of the performance (12:50–15:40).

6. *The Elephant Vanishes* toured: Tokyo, Osaka, London (2003) and Tokyo, New York, London, Paris and Ann Arbor (2004).

7. For a concise summary of print conventions see Worthen 2009: 100.

8. Perhaps Worthen's statement that '[…] Shaw's stage directions describe the play from the perspective of the reader-as-spectator' (2009: 55) needs some modification. As is clearly visible also in Shaw, 'the reader-as-spectator' is one of the roles imposed on the addressee, as he/she is also faced with the narrative organisation of the stage directions, and other strictly literary devices play a significant role both in the primary and secondary text.

9. In the tradition of Polish studies, artistic autonomy of dramatic literature and its divergent relations with theatre studies has been broadly discussed by Irena Sławińska (1990 and 2014), Stefania Skwarczyńska (1970), Janusz Degler (2003), Jerzy Limon (2002 and 2010), Dobrochna Ratajczakowa (2006 and 2015), Sławomir Świontek (1999), Krystyna Ruta-Rutkowska (1999), Małgorzata Sugiera (2005) and Andrzej Zgorzelski (1999).

10. Andrzej Zgorzelski convincingly claims that a dramatic text by definition reveals the tensions between the supercode and the codex functions. This observation has some far-reaching consequences as it reveals the inherent dichotomy of drama—each sign functions as part of both literary communication and prospective theatrical performance.

11. The stage directions lay emphasis on the discrepancy between the semiotic status of Joseph and other characters a number of times, as is the case here: '*The cast gradually appear onstage as if called up by* **Joseph**'s *imagination*' (1999: 7).

12. Boris Uspienski distinguishes between internal and external perspectives and stresses the semantic role of those situations when they are changed (1997: 90–123).

13. McBurney observes that 'There's a sense of being "outside" in the work of Bruno Schulz. Outside of everything: not an outsider in terms of being a Jew, but in terms of his own imagination' (Sebba 2008: 36).

14. Complicite carried out broad research on Schulz. The production files include quotes from many prominent researchers. For more detailed analysis of this see Wiśniewski 2012a.

15. 'We have attempted to create a peculiar theatre language, a fabric that might hold some of the scents falling from the jacket of Schulz's prose. But I must emphasise that the books, the stories, live as themselves. And if any strain of our imagination touches yours then pick up a volume and that which we were digging for will have been found' (McBurney in Sparshatt: 3).

16. I use the term 'visual metonymy' and not 'iconic sign' on purpose. It is interesting that even Rozik speaks of 'rather obscure definitions' of the terms 'icon', 'index' and 'symbol' as provided by Peirce (2008: 21). In theatrical practice, various aspects of one and the same sign frequently—if not habitually—interweave the three functions. For this reason, Pavis's view that Peirce's typology introduces unnecessary confusion to the complicated discipline of theatre studies is convincing.

17. When Rozik discusses the term 'implied spectator' (2008: 161–73), he does not make much use of theoretical differentiation between the 'model/ ideal spectator' (most competent), 'the implied spectator' (constructed by the play/performance), 'the virtual spectator' and so on. Neither does he delineate their possible roles. In principle, as a semiotic construct 'the implied/model/virtual spectator' is ontologically discrepant with 'the real reader' and for this reason the latter cannot achieve the perspective of the former (such aspiration is suggested by Rozik 2008: 163). For further discussion on the matter of textual reception see, for example, Wolfgang Iser 1978 and 2000, Umberto Eco 1984, Michał Głowiński 1973, Andrzej Zgorzelski 1999 and Grzegorz Maziarczyk 2005.

18. In his review for the *New York Times*, Charles Isherwood writes: 'The vibrant cast and the exotic storytelling combine to propel *Lionboy* forward at a heady pace, although the adaptation is always clear enough for children to follow. In truth, adults accustomed to more linear narratives may have a harder time absorbing its twists' (Isherwood 2015).

CHAPTER 6

The Aesthetics of Complicite

Yuri Lotman's Semiosphere

The argument which has been presented in this book is based on the assumption that Lotman's semiosphere is suitable for approaching the aesthetics of Complicite.[1] Indeed, the practical usefulness of the concept proves the far-reaching consequences of the radical shift in semiotic studies stimulated by Lotman in the early 1980s. His proposal diminished the analytical primacy of 'the atomic element' of 'an isolated sign', which characterises approaches originating in the premises of Peirce-Morris on the one hand and those of Saussure and the Prague school on the other (Lotman 2005: 205–6). Rather than initiating exclusive semiotic scrutiny in the study of a sign, Lotman proposes redefining the primary perspective in view of 'a specific semiotic continuum, which is filled with multivariant semiotic models situated at a range of hierarchical levels' (206). This implies that a given semiosphere may on the one hand be embedded in a more universal semiosphere, and on the other hand may comprise a number of more specialised ones.[2] There emerges something like a network of non-schematically structured semiospheres.

Lotman argues that, being analogous to the 'biosphere' and the 'noosphere' (understood in V.I. Vernadsky's sense), the semiosphere should be defined as a specific abstract space that is integral, enclosed and dynamic. It consists of multigeneous signs, hierarchical structures and autonomous systems, whose unpredictable, reciprocal relations are endowed with the potential to create meanings. In addition to this, Lotman accentuates the

© The Author(s) 2016
T. Wiśniewski, *Complicite, Theatre and Aesthetics*,
DOI 10.1007/978-3-319-33443-1_6

diachronic dimension of the semiosphere and, hence, its dynamic character. In short, the semiosphere is a fluctuating entity that incessantly undergoes significant transformations.

Perceived as a delimited space, the semiosphere is by definition idiosyncratic (at one point Lotman speaks of its '"semiotic personality"' [209]) and is surrounded by non- or extra- semiotic[3] space. It is, then, vital to recognise those elements which, at a given moment of time, are situated within its boundaries and those which are beyond. As Lotman convincingly argues, the semiosphere is necessary not only for the formulation of either an individual language (*langue*) or a particular utterance/text (*parole*) but also for initiating all 'communicative processes' and 'the creation of new information' (206). In other words, in his view, the semantics of an individual network of signs in the micro-scale of communication correlates to the macro-scale arrangement of the semiosphere, and all the levels of semiotic organisation that emerge between these extremes.

Among 'a range of attributes' (207) of a semiosphere, the following are the most relevant when describing the aesthetics of Complicite:

- the delimitation of communicative space,
- the juxtaposition of the centre and the periphery,
- the prominence of the notion of a boundary,
- the autonomy of constitutive elements (i.e. signs/structures/ systems),
- the potential of equivalent or isomorphic arrangement of these elements.

THE DELIMITATION OF COMMUNICATIVE SPACE

The specificity of each semiosphere makes us aware of its precise distinction from the non- or extra-semiotic space in which it is immersed. When approached from the internal perspective (i.e. from within), the semiosphere appears as an internally 'unified mechanism' (206), and the outer sphere emerges as a 'chaotically' disorganised one. Even though the enclosed space of the semiosphere is by definition continuous, it consists of multigeneous signs/structures/systems. The meanings created by such constructional units are directed in two contradictory ways: internally and externally. Each of them aims to delineate its communicative independence, which means that each sign—just as each structure and each system—strives to create autonomous senses. Simultaneously, they are all involved in external relations with the remaining elements of the semiosphere.[4] This is the main paradox covered by Lotman's concept: even when they emerge on diverse levels of the construction, signs/structures/systems are subject to the principle of equivalence. For this reason, even when they are not immediately associated with each other, their comparison and/or confrontation may turn out to be fruitful for analysis and interpretation.[5]

Compositional units increase their capacity to create meanings by underscoring both similarities and differences. It should be stressed that the principle of equivalence is indifferent to the status of compositional units and is equally attentive to the relations between various systems, to those between a particular sign and a system, a structure and a sign, a structure and a system, and so on. Moreover, the principle operates in a similar way when setting 'horizontal' or 'hierarchical' relations between semiospheres. When discussing the questions of equivalence and isomorphism, it is possible to draw conclusions from analysing relations between an individual sign and the entire paradigm.

The aesthetics of Complicite proves the practical validity of the above observations. Not only does it define itself in stark opposition to the external world (everything that Complicite is not), but also establishes a complex, idiosyncratic and enclosed paradigm of communicative elements and artistic mechanisms.

FOUR LEVELS OF THEATRE COMMUNICATION

The aesthetics of Complicite is founded on the hierarchy of four major levels of theatre communication. The levels may be provisionally described in the following way as ranging from the most concrete to the most abstract:

- the individual performance,
- the production,
- the complete piece,
- the expanding *oeuvre* of the company.

Each of these levels requires a slightly different analytical treatment. The proposed typology is shaped so as to illustrate the increasing generalisation of the interpretative perspectives and to reflect the hermeneutics of Complicite rather than to sketch a theoretical model encompassing all possible examples that might emerge in the theatre practice of various theatre companies.

An individual performance is an elementary act of theatre communication. By assuming immediate sensory contact between the interlocutors (actors/stage → spectators/audience) in a given theatre at a given time, it highlights the transience of the physically, verbally, aurally or visually constructed communication. Precise spatio-temporal delimitation of each performance allows us to perceive it as a straightforward semiosphere (paradigm/system). It is a distinctive feature of theatre communication that, notwithstanding invariant elements of the entire production, each performance differs from others and in this way multiplies more or less distinctive variants.[6] Associates of Complicite repeatedly stress that the immediate contact between the ensemble of actors and the audience is of primary importance for this company. Examples confirming this attitude abound[7] but its most concise expression is that provided by Simon McBurney: 'Audience and the acknowledgement of audience are fundamental to me: there has to be that thread of companionship' (In: Giannachi and Luckhurst 1999: 73, compare McBurney's essay 'I'm Going to Die').

The production, which consists of an increasing, or finished, set of individual performances (variants) presented in one, or more, venues on a certain number of occasions, establishes a more general mode of communication. Fleeting as it is, the production constitutes an enclosed, singular and internally coherent entity that may be described as a semiosphere consisting of a set of performances (i.e. smaller-scale semiospheres). If this perspective is irrelevant for those who expose themselves solely to the sensory mode of theatre experience, it is central for all those who wish to take the role of a spectator/interpreter that assumes a more general (i.e. even less concrete) perspective. This is not to say that either of these perspectives should be treated as better or worse. The distinction is necessary for differentiating between watching a performance and the procedure of its analysis.

It is intriguing that, in the model of artistic communication that predominates in Complicite, the increased sensory complicity between interlocutors within individual performances is paired with the sense of amplified fragmentariness of reception on the level of a production. By experiencing the singularity of a one-time performance, the audience is made aware that they participate in one of many variants of the theatre work. In the case of Complicite, the collocation of singularity and incompleteness is functional and derives from the asymmetrical epistemological status of the ensemble of artists (encoder) and the audience (addressee). This mechanism is even more intense on the more general communicative levels.

The complete piece consists of a set of its different theatre productions and other forms of artistic expression. In the case of Complicite, these are, for instance, radio plays, audiovisual recordings, scripts and/or printed plays. For various reasons, the semantics of one production is bound to differ from the meanings created by other productions so that their comparative analysis sketches the evolution of a piece. Also, this level of communication shapes a kind of semiosphere. This time it comprises variants (individual performances) within variants (particular productions). In comparison to the level of a given production, the cognitive asymmetry between the theatre-makers and the addressee increases substantially. To put it in an illustrative way, it is hard to imagine a non-company member who is fully aware of all the performances of all the productions. Some of the essays presented in *Who You Hear It from* suggest that this broad perspective is also taken into consideration by Complicite/McBurney. In 'You must remember this', for example, the European tour of *Mnemonic* is compared with the earlier (1999/2001) productions of the play, and in '*The Elephant Vanishes*' McBurney seeks to make directorial alterations to the new production of *The Elephant Vanishes*, so as to improve on the earlier version.

The complete piece is embedded within a yet broader framework of the still-expanding *oeuvre*. The notion is understood here as the kind of paradigm that comprises a complete set of variants of all pieces produced by Complicite and other activities of the company (e.g. educational, informative and publishing). It is important that the *oeuvre* is treated as an open system consisting of the previously distinguished levels of communication rather than one resulting from a set of conclusions emerging from their analysis and interpretation. This is an abstract notion and its analysis depends on analytical and interpretative decisions by a spectator/interpreter/scholar. For obvious reasons, at this level, invariant features, rather than fluctuations of variants, dominate analysis and for this reason we are speaking here of a rather singular, and abstract, mode of communication.

The perspective of an *oeuvre* assumes that all creative enterprises of Complicite are likely to establish meaningful (paradigmatic) relations with all other activities. Such an attitude seems justified by numerous examples: variants of the published play of *Mnemonic* not only reflect particular theatre productions but are also involved in the evolution of printed drama; the multi/inter-media solutions of *The Master and Margarita* echo those of *A Disappearing Number* and are placed in stark contrast to the visual solutions used in, say, *The Caucasian Chalk Circle*; the episodic composition of *A Minute Too Late* anticipates that of *The Elephant Vanishes*; and the victim-like physicality of Cesar Sarachu links the *The Street of Crocodiles* with *The Master and Margarita*, whereas Simon McBurney's nakedness in *Mnemonic* is somehow echoed in the naked flight of Margarita. All this illustrates a particular, and very general, perspective for interpretation, in which relations between the complete pieces underscore significant shifts in the company's aesthetics and bring forth Complicite's artistic and aesthetic decisions.

THE MULTIPLICATION OF VARIANTS

The dynamism within the four levels of theatre communication leads to the growing cognitive asymmetry between the encoder and the decoder. When the *semiosis* within an individual performance originates in a set of stage signals that are materially accessible to the audience, the communication on the level of the company's *oeuvre* intrinsically privileges the perspective of the ensemble of artists over that of spectator/interpreter. In the case of an individual performance we may speak of some kind of cognitive symmetry, whereas in the case of an *oeuvre* the perspective of the addressee is increasingly fragmentary.

As with many companies today, Complicite makes extensive use of such asymmetry. The multiplication of variants, which is functional on all four levels of communication, develops into a universal principle: an awareness of the fragmentariness of reception increases. In the case of *A Minute Too Late*, for instance, individual performances are bound to differ from one another owing to extensive use of improvisation and techniques derived from *commedia dell'arte*. Shifts in the selection and combination of the already performed material become the intrinsic manner of the company's creative work.

This is furthered by Complicite's predilection for national and international tours. On the one hand they necessitate constant adaptation to the conditions of concrete theatre buildings, and on the other they transform the dynamics of theatre communication by confronting actors with incessantly changing types of audience. Whereas variants encouraged by changing theatre spaces are well illustrated by the adaptation of *The Master and Margarita* to the open stage constructed within the walls of Avignon castle,[8] the meaningful shifts in the types of audience are most striking in the Japanese plays, depending on whether they were performed in Tokyo or in the West. Variants also multiply whenever the creative team rotates and this is frequent in Complicite where actors are loosely and temporarily associated with the company.

The multiplication of variants is achieved not only by the shifts in material conditions of a performance (e.g. space, involved artists, addressee) but also by using a variety of mediums for one and the same piece. The most developed case is that of *Mnemonic* where three theatre productions are accompanied by its three published versions and a radio play. A similar number of variants characterises *A Disappearing Number* where theatre productions are supplemented by a published play, a radio play and the DVD recording of the live broadcast done for 'National Theatre Live'. The change of medium always results in auto-referential implications and substantially re-evaluates created meanings.

The aesthetics of Complicite encompasses all four levels of communication and is immersed in the entire spectrum of external non- or extra-semiotic phenomena. Its delimitation is immediately related to the analytical decision as to whether or not the given element is involved in at least one of the above described levels of communication. Owing to the cognitive perspective of the spectator/interpreter, the repertoire of signs/structures/systems and the catalogue of principles that are functional for the emerging aesthetics testify to the singularity of communication. This means that, in theatre studies, the confrontation of the worlds of the ensemble of artists and spectator/interpreter/scholar results in a prolonged semiotic eruption.

THE CENTRE AND THE PERIPHERIES

Internal relations within the aesthetics/semiosphere are based on a gradual scale merging its centre with peripheries. Whereas 'nuclear structures' that are placed in the centre are vital for its general character, 'inherent internal irregularity of peripheries' generates fluctuating ways of meaning creation. Due to the 'bilingual' character of peripheries, they participate in assimilation of external elements. According to Lotman, the semiotics of periphery is characterised by elliptic fragmentation and incongruence. It is frequent that random signs, partial structures or incomplete systems function in their own ways and do not reflect roles they would fulfil in their original environment. Yet, the mechanisms of reconstruction, which are strongly operational here, allow for re-enacting past structures and systems into new ones whenever it is encouraged by changing attitudes.[9]

Complicite attempts to elude petrification of central structures and insistently explores the potential of fluctuating peripheries. Their *oeuvre* involves a number of radical alternations that stimulate constant defamiliarisation of artistic achievements. The hugely improvised spirit of *Anything for a Quite Life* was followed by the stage production of Friedrich Dürrenmatt's play *The Visit*. After the multi/inter-media extravagance of *A*

Disappearing Number, the company decided on the technical minimalism of *Shun-kin*. Their ascetic adaptation of Samuel Beckett's *Endgame* preceded international cooperation on the premiere production of Alexander Raskatov's opera *A Dog's Heart*. The multicast *The Master and Margarita* was followed by a one-man show entitled *The Encounter*.

Complicite's predilection for radical alternations of artistic solutions may be best summarised by the company's self-description:

> … Complicite is a **constantly evolving** ensemble of performers and collaborators … Complicite's work has **ranged from** entirely devised work to theatrical adaptations and revivals of classic texts. The Company has also worked **in other media**; a radio production of *Mnemonic* for BBC Radio 3, collaborations with John Berger on a radio adaptation of his novel *To the Wedding* for BBC Radio and *The Vertical Line*, a multi-disciplinary installation performed in a disused tube station, commissioned by Artangel. **Always changing and moving forward to incorporate new stimuli**, the principles of the work have **remained close to the original impulses**: seeking what is most alive, integrating text, music, image and action to create surprising, disruptive theatre. (Complicite 2003: 1, emphasis added)

The sole core of the aesthetics of Complicite revolves around the preservation of vigour in the course of theatre communication between the stage and the audience. The concept clearly derives from the rudimental sense of 'complicité' that was adapted from Jacques Lecoq. Notably, even the work 'in other media' participates in the search for 'surprising, disruptive theatre' by broadening the scope of artistic solutions and enforcing the unpredictability of the company's objectives. Everything else is subordinate, optional and its positioning on the scale, spread between the centre and peripheries, evolves in time. This is true of entire systems (e.g. the natural language), particular structures (e.g. the composition) and individual motifs (e.g. the chair).

THE QUESTION OF THE NATURAL LANGUAGE

Even the role of the system of natural verbal language undergoes significant transformations. From the very beginning the multinational cast challenged the conventional supremacy of the 'well-delivered' standard English on the British stage. Still, dialects, strange foreign accents and the occasional intrusion of other languages did not cause as much controversy in *A Minute Too Late* or *The Street of Crocodiles* as they did in adaptations from Shakespeare (*The Winter's Tale* and *Measure for Measure*). It is one thing to allow for subverting the supremacy of English in improvised performances (peripheries of British theatre) and another to risk a confrontation of the genius of the language with external usurpers. Marcello Magni describes the problems he encountered when acting in *The Winter's Tale*:

> In the initial version of [*The Winter's Tale*], I was Autolycus. He is a thief, a cheater. So when I appeared on stage for the first time I said 'Mi chiamo Autolycus.' I continued the lines in Italian first and, then, I spoke Shakespeare, which I introduced as an 'original translation.' The audience did not understand what I was doing so I specified that this was 'the Shakespearean translation.' And then I continued with 'a bit fantastic translation.' Little by little I twisted the spirit of Shakespeare but I thought it was well justified because Autolycus was a thief. When you play at the National Theatre in London that kind of liberty is considered going a bit too far. The higher you go the less freedom there is. (Magni 2015: 141)

The question of the natural language functions differently in the productions of *The Elephant Vanishes* and *Shun-kin*. Here, the non-Japanese part of the audience was exposed to the non-semantic aesthetic quality of the language (see Chap. 4). The analogy is furthered in performances such as *The Noise of Time* and *A Dog's Heart* where music determines the increased sonic quality of the language. The strong pronouncement of the trochaic pace in the libretto of *A Dog's Heart* serves as a very good example, as does the final dominance of music over language in *The Noise of Time*.

When employing verbal language for theatrical purposes, Complicite revitalises the language in a number of ways: by shifting its semantic potential, by stressing its musicality and by confronting the musicality of various languages. There are, however, performances where the verbal language functions in a more conventional way. This is the case, for example, in *The Caucasian Chalk Circle* and *The Three Lives of Lucie Cabrol* where—notwithstanding the fact that, unlike the actors, the characters do not speak English!—the fundamental role of the verbal communication in conveying the storyline and depicting the fictional reality remains unquestionable. In Complicite, the roles ascribed to the natural language oscillate between the most conventional (i.e. as in dramatic theatre) and the peripheral (e.g. when musicality overshadows semantics). Although the central role of the communicative functions of the language is never fully subverted, the prominence given to peripheral ways of its functioning certainly defamiliarises prototypical employment of the language in British modern theatre (see Rebellato 1999: 71–99).

STRUCTURING THE COMPOSITION

Initial insistence on structuring the onstage action in accordance with the principles of episodic sequencing and compositional framing has been reinforced by the textually derived logic of dramatic theatre (since *The Visit*). It has been additionally strengthened by the integration of narrative structures into the requirements of the stage. This epical dimension is achieved differently in adaptations of narrative texts where the storyline is preconceived (e.g. *The Street of Crocodiles, The Three Lives of Lucie Cabrol, The Master and Margarita*), and differently in originally devised performances where the epical dimension does not follow schemes left by earlier artistic structuring (e.g. *Mnemonic* and *A Disappearing Number*).

Yet, there are some other ways of structuring the composition that are used by Complicite. In *Shun-kin*, for example, the company adds the narrative framework of a radio recording to the elements emerging from Tanizaki's text. At one point in Act Two of *The Master and Margarita* (DVD recording Act Two 1:00:20–1:01:10), the novel's epigraph is announced and the biographical context of the book is discussed, and this substantially re-evaluates the narrative structuring of the theatre communication. Then, the text of *The Street of Crocodiles* reveals the rules that shaped the composition of the play (epigraphs, mottos, fragments of narratives and letters).

Significantly, Complicite's decisions concerning structuring the composition have always explored the tensions between the centre and peripheries: solutions that at one point dominate the aesthetics tend later to be marginalised. If it is true to say that episodic composition of *A Minute Too Late* emerges primarily from strictly theatrical conventions such as improvisation and *commedia dell'arte*, Complicite's productions of Beckett's *Endgame* or Ionesco's *The Chairs* are determined mostly by structuring derived from dramatic theatre. Although the two mechanisms are not identical, their roles within the aesthetics of Complicite are equally prominent. For this reason the aesthetics of the company eludes straightforwardly comprehensive categorisations.

THE MOTIF OF A CHAIR

The kind of dynamism that characterises the aesthetics of Complicite may also be illustrated by the fluctuating semantics ascribed to the rudimentary theatre motif/prop: that of a chair.[10] In general, the chair is not only endowed with the function of delineating spatial relations but is also firmly associated with certain actions undertaken by actors/characters (e.g. sitting, reading and thinking).[11] In scenes 7 and 9 of *A Minute Too Late*, Martin Webster recalls his dead wife when sitting by the table in his living room. In the Prologue to *The Street of Crocodiles*, Joseph is engrossed in reading when sitting on a chair in the Drohobycz warehouse. The action of his sitting/reading is pivotal for the entire play as it dominates the frame of the presented plot: in *The Street of Crocodiles* the main story originates in the imagination of the sitting protagonist. Similarly, the role of sitting is seen in *The Elephant Vanishes*, where the inciting moment is related to eating breakfast. While sitting in pyjamas by the fridge, the male protagonist is reading a newspaper and at one moment comes across the information that the elephant has vanished from Tokyo zoo. In these situations, the chair interweaves various aspects of the onstage communication: the development of action, the character delineation and the construction of spatial relations. In this way it becomes a prominent and consistent element of the stage language, though of course it is just one of many similar elements.

As an element of visual communication, the chair frequently participates in depicting different means of transport. In *A Disappearing Number*, for instance, a particular arrangement of chairs delineates a plane, a taxi or a train. Notably, the train tableau, in which Ruth is sliding down the chair/seat, is repeated several times, as it presents the pivotal image of her death when travelling through India. In *The Master and Margarita* two chairs depict, among other things, the bench in the park where Ivan Nikolayich Bezdomny and Mikhail Alexandrovich Berloitz are approached by Woland (Act One 0:08:19) and the tram where, surrounded by the throng of commuters, the master encounters Margarita (e.g. Act One 1:13:05–1:13:06). Later in the performance, the visual echo of the tram tableau is endowed with new functions. When the master's empty chair is tenderly approached by Margarita (Act Two 0:03:53–0:05:29), it hints at her love and longing, stresses the absurdity of the couple's separation, and becomes a firm non-verbal announcement of the Master's absence. All in all, the meanings ascribed to the chair in the later tram tableau make the prop function as a minus sign that highlights what/who is not present onstage.

These examples illustrate the capacity of a prop like a chair to create metaphoric/symbolic meanings. The chair cannot be reduced to a mere 'iconic' sign that suggests material connotations between the signifier and the signified. It is true that, when located on a stage, a chair may denote a 'chair' as a piece of furniture in the fictional world, but it is simultaneously likely to contribute to the network of literal and/or metaphoric/symbolic/poetic associations. It may, for example:

- participate in motivating the development of the action (*The Street of Crocodiles* and *The Elephant Vanishes*),
- take the role of a visual metonymy/synecdoche that constructs spatial relations (a room, a kitchen, a warehouse and a park),
- suggest the state of being in motion (various means of transport),
- participate in structuring the composition (Ruth's death in *A Disappearing Number*),
- stress the internal states of characters (Margarita's feelings towards the Master in *The Master and Margarita*).

Complicite endows the prop/motif with considerable dynamics and in particular plays uses it in more or less conventional ways. The company's attempts at refreshing the meanings ascribed even to such an elementary prop result in the involvement of the chair in integrating the overall aesthetics. Some of the most significant alterations of the motif may be observed when comparing the central role of chairs in the production of Ionesco's *The Chairs* with the fluctuating semantics of a chair in *Mnemonic*.

THE MASS OF CHAIRS

Complicite's production of *The Chairs* involved an original creative team and the main collaborators were gathered just for this occasion. It was Niall Buggy and Geraldine McEwan who invited Simon McBurney to direct the play. In the course of rehearsals Richard Briers took over the role of the Old Man but, as Catherine Alexander stresses in 'The Chairs. The Story of a Play', Buggy's role 'was instrumental' and he 'participated in the initial workshop' (1997b: 2). When undertaking the production, Complicite was fully aware of those problems caused by the fact that Ionesco's play was originally written in French. Dissatisfied with earlier English translations, the company decided to increase the theatrical attractiveness of the production by commissioning Martin Crimp to provide a new translation of the play.[12] The design for the production was provided by the Quay Brothers, demonstrating that insistence on the fresh quality of the verbal dimension was paired with special attention given to the visual. Cath Binks, the company stage manager at the time, notes that

> For this production, the set design evolves with the rehearsal process. We are now approaching the end of week three (out of six) of rehearsals and the Quay Brothers, our designers, together with Simon McBurney have been

gradually moving away from their original design idea—the ultimate aim being to produce a very pure set design which will complement and enhance the action on stage. (quoted in Alexander 1997b: 24)

The play begins with two chairs placed downstage, side by side. It soon turns out that they are ascribed to Old Woman and Old Man, who inhabit a bare room that is located on a remote island. In the course of the action, guests arrive one by one so that in the climactic episode of the mute Oracle, when the double-suicide of the hosts occurs, the fictional room is crowded. Still, the onstage world is inhabited merely by three actors, namely: Old Man, Old Woman and the Oracle. The sense of a crowd is conveyed not by actors but by a mass of chairs. Such a metonymic representation (chair → character) enables the audience to experience the paradoxical juxtaposition of absence and presence and increases the complexity of spatio-temporal imagery. Theatre de Complicite's resource pack for the production quotes the following words of Ionesco: 'What is needed is plenty of gesture, almost pantomime, light, sound, moving objects, doors that open and close and open again, in order to create this emptiness, so that it grows and devours everything: absence can only be created in opposition to things present' (quoted in Alexander 1997b: 9). In this sense, the play stresses the discrepancy between the fictional reality and the world of the stage.

In the final episode the mass of empty chairs is arranged with their backs to the audience. The attention of the invisible characters is thus directed in the same way as that of the audience: towards the rostrum occupied by the Orator. The earlier action has escalated expectations concerning the prominence of the final tableau. In other words, the onstage *semiosis* leads to the final focus on the far end of the room, which is situated upstage.

The proxemics of theatre communication sets up a disturbing equivalence between the guests of the house (onstage) and the spectators (audience). In spite of their diverse communicative statuses, both assume the same perspective of perception during the dumb speech of the Oracle. In this way the following field of association is sanctioned:

(**audience:** theatre/spectators/presence/people/external world)

vs.

(**chairs:** stage/guests/absence/props/on-stage *semiosis*).

Diagram 6.1

Notwithstanding substantial dissimilarities between the model of the world emerging from the onstage communication and that shaped by the external experience of the audience, an intriguing congruence between the two is suggested. In the finale of *The Chairs*, the guests of the house mirror the audience. Simon McBurney observes the strange parallel between the worlds when describing reasons for undertaking the production:

> ... I seized the opportunity to continue this dialogue which had struck me so forcibly in the seventies; to find out what it was I felt close to, why it thrilled me to play [*Jeux de Massacre* by Ionesco], and, most importantly, why—far from appearing absurd—Ionesco's world had always felt utterly reasonable to me. (quoted in Alexander 1997b: 2)

A similar tableau of the mass of chairs opened the after-interval part of the London production of *The Magic Flute* (see Chap. 4). This time, however, the chairs faced the audience and were increasingly occupied by the crowd involved in the production.[13] Unlike in *The Chairs*, the image offered in *The Magic Flute* functioned as a kind of anti-curtain as it blurred the rigid delineation of the stage communication. For several minutes there was suspense as to whether the interval was still continuing or the performance had already begun anew. Simultaneously, by introducing two contradictory spatial perspectives, the tableau juxtaposed the proxemics of the world of the stage to that of the audience. The actions of the performers seemed to be mirrored by the spectators and the other way round. The suggestion of the interchangeability of their semiotic statuses was constantly suggested throughout the opera. On the one hand, the performers did not hesitate to intrude into the space of the audience, and the huge live broadcast of spectators was projected onto the back of the stage. On the other hand, props and images that suggested the intrusion of the contemporary world into the world of fiction may be exemplified by Papageno's mountaineer's anorak from the opening,[14] and the auto-referential explicitness of the audiovisual technology that participated in creating the world of the stage.

In each case the tableau of the mass of chairs participates in establishing slightly different meanings. Whereas *The Chairs* implies that even most anti-mimetic fiction is capable of communicating otherwise inexplicable aspects of an audience's experience (e.g. the dialectics of absence and presence), *The Magic Flute* suggests that the fiction mirrors life as much as life mirrors fiction.

THE PERSONIFICATION OF A CHAIR IN *MNEMONIC*

In *The Chairs* and *The Magic Flute*, chairs as props are treated en masse. By contrast, *Mnemonic* enhances the individual and profoundly human potential of the chair by involving it in overtly personal fields of association. During Simon/Director's opening monologue the stage is empty *'except for a chair and a stone'* (2001: 3). One might expect that during the course of the performance some prominence will be given to these sole visual elements accompanying the speaker in the introduction. The chair remains only an 'iconic' representation of a chair until its emotional burden is revealed when Simon/Director claims it belonged to his father and was used in earlier performances:

> So ... I thought about my father because this chair was his. I *know* it. He sat on it. And so did my grandfather. In fact, it's a chair I know very well because I have used it in several of my shows. It was in a show called *The Chairs* ... (5)

The episode ascribes to the visual sign of a chair clearly autobiographic connotations and it does so by strictly verbal means. In this way, the motif turns into a 'bilingual' sign that integrates not only the visual with the verbal but also the onstage communication with meanings emerging from without the semiosphere of the piece.

On the one hand the meanings ascribed to the chair multiply in the course of the performance, and on the other hand the emotional attitude is not diminished once the performance is finished. In addition to this, the episode highlights the epistemological discrepancy between the encoder (Simon/Director) and the decoder (audience) since the former reveals his emotional attachment to what, from the perspective of the latter, was initially the mere 'iconic' stage sign of a chair.

In the course of performance, the situation turns out to be increasingly complicated. The introductory monologue finishes in a darkness that completely reverses the stage situation. At this point the audience experience two levels of the world presented onstage and is made aware of its increased fictionality. When the lights come up again, Simon/Director is sitting on the chair as Virgil, who is a character inhabiting the fictional world. In addition to this, Virgil turns out to be a member of an imaginary onstage audience and follows instructions given by the now recorded voice of Simon/Director. Moreover, he *'has a mask and is holding a leaf*

(8). At this point, spectators gathered in the theatre are aware that Virgil mirrors activities undertaken by them.

The episode is an interesting application of the theatre-within-a-theatre convention in which the 'macro-play' is metonymically created by the recorded voice of Simon/Director and the 'micro-play' conceived by the visual synecdoche of Virgil sitting on the chair. Both these roles are fulfilled by one actor—Simon McBurney (respectively his voice and his appearance). In the context of Limon's article 'The Play-Within-The-Play: A Theoretical Perspective' it is of much relevance that the entire episode leads to the explicit presentation of Virgil's unappreciative reaction to the inner-spectacle. For Limon: 'What counts is not only what is being performed within, but the reaction (or lack of reaction) of the figure-spectators to it and equally relevant are all sorts of possible relationships that the play within creates with the macro-play' (Limon 2005:18).

The semantic nature of the chair has substantially changed. Functioning on several levels, it is now dominated by meta-theatrical connotations. Virgil's words and actions turn the chair into a visual synecdoche of an audience that, in turn, metonymically implies the space of the imaginary theatre. From the perspective of the 'real' audience, this is the only visual element of the fictional theatre in which Virgil watches the performance. As in *The Chairs*, we are confronted with the paradox of activating imag-ination by stressing absence. In *Mnemonic* the chair enhances the rec-ollection of Simon's father and grandfather and later depicts materially non-existent audience and the fictional theatre it belongs to.

But the meanings ascribed to the chair undergo further alternations. At one point in Scene 2, when Virgil is completely engrossed in the phone conversation with Alistair, the chair unexpectedly collapses, which not only introduces slapstick humour but also suggests the emotional loss of the piece of furniture. There are also more conventional uses of the motif. In Scene 22, chairs delineate a Greek migrant's taxi, and in Scene 33, a row of chairs situated downstage in front of the plastic curtain is occupied by researchers in what develops into a parody of an academic congress. In these cases, chairs participate in delineating spatial relations and fulfil a subordinate role.

The situation changes again in Scene 34 where the chair turns out to be portable and takes the role of a puppet that is involved in the final des-perate march of the Iceman. As we read in the stage directions that open the scene:

Over the following text, the chair slowly becomes the puppet of the Iceman. The rest of the company come around the table and take the puppet. It has a stick and its face is suggested by a towel. The puppet of the Iceman follows the final moments of the Iceman in his gully, 5,000 years ago. (2001: 72)

Yet again, the chair triggers the imagination so as to enliven what is absent and inaccessible. Yet again, the prop is completely deautomatised and endowed with an unexpected function. It once again underscores the discrepancy between the material character of stage signs and the meanings they construct. Onstage, the chair may simply signal a chair (the introductory monologue), conceive complex spatial relations (audience, theatre, Virgil's room), motivate emotional recollections (father), inspire metatheatrical statements (Virgil as a spectator) and be the centre of the most lyrical mime sequence (Iceman's death).

THE PROCESS OF COMMUNICATION

In *Mnemonic* the semantics of one prop/signal/motif may rapidly alternate between more and less conventional applications. All this highlights the epistemological asymmetry between the encoder and the decoder that is operative in the course of an individual performance. The ensemble of actors expose the very nature of the communicative process in which they are involved. Fluctuating meanings ascribed to the prop/signal/motif of a chair prove that in this model the audience is to follow (decode) meanings preconceived by the theatre-makers. This is not the cognitive model in which the audience would actively participate in the construction of free associations. Yet, as may be expected, this rule is not treated in a dogmatic way. For example, when spectators are told to imagine the line of their ancestors, the meanings depend on recollections of each individual member of the audience.

When discussing the functioning of natural language, the mechanisms of structuring composition and the dynamics of the motif of a chair, we have concentrated on how these rudimentary features of theatre fluctuate in the aesthetics of Complicite. Since they are frequently deprived of their conventionally determined roles, the features tend to activate their peripheral rather than central (prototypical) functions. The system of the natural verbal language highlights the aesthetic quality of its sonic arrangement when it is exposed to those who are incapable of pursuing the semantics. The mechanisms of dramatic and epical structuring of the composition re-evaluate the performative quality of the stage language of Theatre de Complicite. Besides, the portable chair reveals its highly lyrical potential when it takes on the role of the dying protagonist in his final march through the Alps. It all leads us to the conclusion that, throughout its *oeuvre*, Complicite continues to explore the core of all artistic mechanisms: the company never allows for the petrification of its aesthetic centre. The complicity between the stage and the audience that constitutes this centre is repetitively challenged by the ever-evolving methods of creating meanings that emerge from—and at times from beyond—the peripheries of its aesthetics.

The Prominence of the Boundary

Complicite tends to engage with ever-fluctuating margins for artistic purposes. Because of numerous tensions between the centre and peripheries, the notion of a boundary appears particularly prominent. The company explores the fact that the boundary is prone to artistic explosions. These result from a whole range of intrusions of the external material. Such intrusions are particularly frequent in the history of Complicite. In the majority of cases, the newly absorbed signs/structures/systems are endowed with original functions. Such is the case with the mobile phone in *Mnemonic*: the discharging of the battery is crucial for structuring the composition of the onstage action. In *The Caucasian Chalk Circle*, the theatre-in-the-round arrangement is decisive for creating intimacy between the world of the stage and the audience, which is relevant for a play using the word 'circle' in its title. In *Lionboy*, the onstage monitors threaten Charlie's pursuit with menacing signals emerging from the offstage reality of corporate business. Focus on the delimitation of the aesthetics makes it possible to observe many similar examples in which external signs/structures/systems become an integral part of the company's stage language.

We may distinguish two phases of the creative process that expose the aesthetics to the infiltration of external material. These are research and development, and rehearsals. The process of probing the boundaries is endowed with an exceptionally collective character. It depends not only on the physicality, training, skills and creative powers of the involved theatre-makers but also on their predilection for working collectively and cooperating with the entire team. For obvious reasons, the ethos of collective work is shaped differently in different conventions used by the company. The success of improvised street shows depends a great deal on the immediacy of skilful reactions by the ensemble of performers. In the dramatic the-atre, the playwright's artistic vision predetermines the shape of the fictional world and motivates exploration of the peculiarities of stage language. In the multi/inter-media theatre, technical innovations contribute to an inten-sification of the audiovisual dimension of the onstage *semiosis*. In the opera and other musical spectacles, the sonic tissue dominates all other aspects of the production, and the creative process involves the cooperation of per-formers with musicians. Finally, in the devised theatre, the research, devel-opment and rehearsals lead to the creation of a new play by the ensemble of theatre-makers.

Contrary to what is at times suggested, for Complicite none of these methods acquires the central position. On the contrary, each of them (and some others) fluctuates between the centre and peripheries, and all con-tribute to the overall aesthetics, even if at a given phase in history it is marginalised, seems non-operative, or even excluded from the aesthetics. The company is eager to explore the challenges and possibilities emerging from each new production. For this reason, the notion of a boundary is particularly dynamic and worthy of attention.

The Visual Tissue

The visual tissue of Complicite is subject to equally eclectic intrusions and undergoes transformations as radical as the textual dimension. The initial minimalism of the design focused attention on the physicality of acting, especially on the languages of body and movement. In *A Minute Too Late*, for instance, sparse props (a few stones, a bucket of earth, a carpet, chairs, a table) were subordinated to the craftsmanship of performers who were responsible for creating characters, furniture and other elements of stage design. Such economy in early productions led to establishing major visual features that later developed into the following principles: non-realistic and non-literal design, intense interplay of a sequence of images, frequent employment of visual metonymy and synecdoche, and exploration of the metaphorical and symbolic potential of stage images.

Later in the history of the company, all these features resulted in the increased prominence of theatre machinery. The intense stage design of the opening of *Foe* underscores the isolation of a desert island by stressing the boundaries of the stage with its archetypal universalisation through the suggestion of the four elements. In *The Chairs*, the mastery of the design by the Quay Brothers strengthens the metaphoric/symbolic potential of the play, and in *Endgame* physical tensions between Mark Rylance and Simon McBurney not only highlight the miserable relations between Hamm and Clov but also explore the carnival mockery of Beckett's play. Other performances incorporate conventions such as mannequins (*The Street of Crocodiles, Shun-kin* and *Light*), puppet theatre (*A Dog's Heart, The Master and Margarita* and *The Magic Flute*), theatre of shadows (*The Magic Flute*), acrobatics (*The Elephant Vanishes, Lionboy*), circus (*Lionboy*), Noh theatre (*Shun-kin*) and the Bharatanatyam (*A Disappearing Number*).

The next major intrusion into the visual tissue is related to the incorporation of state-of-the-art technology. Ever since structuring the onstage action upon the device of a mobile phone in *Mnemonic*, the whole spectrum of multi/inter-media devices has become an integral part of the stage language.[15] They include the synecdoche of the eye of an elephant introduced by the portable screen in *The Elephant Vanishes*, the live broadcast of the onstage detail in *A Disappearing Number* and *The Master and Margarita*, the large-scale projections of books that function as a metonymy of a library in *A Disappearing Number* and *A Dog's Heart*. *The Master and Margarita* particularly abounds in multimedia devices. In the latter, the images include the three-dimensional hologram of a horse, the Google map that covers the entire stage so as to place the action in various parts of the globe, the large-scale live broadcast of the audience, the background film projection of a war reportage, and the onstage crossing of Yeshua Ha-Nostri.

By intermingling the more or less traditional means of enlivening the visual imagery, Complicite substantially strengthens the autonomy of its stage language. Devices such as shifts in perspective (e.g. *The Master and Margarita*), paradigmatic equivalence of tableaux (e.g. the class in *The Street of Crocodiles*) and juxtaposing the vertical with the horizontal (e.g. *Foe, The Chairs* and *Endgame*) facilitate the creation of powerful visual meanings. This is probably most explicit in *Measure for Measure* where the visual dimension hints at the contemporary relevance of Shakespeare's play and in this way confirms the universal character of the verbal element.

The meta-theatrical prominence of the visual tissue underscores an additional arrangement of all stage signals: the visual tissue contains an unpredictable and limitless repertoire of signals and devices that conceive networks of signs, and more developed structures. As elsewhere in the aesthetics of Complicite, in the domain of visual relations, the inclusion of external elements is frequently followed by their prompt exclusion, with the possibility of their later re-emergence in a new form and/ or function (e.g. the shadow of an elephant in *The Magic Flute* echoes the performance of *The Elephant Vanishes*). Even though the recent output of

Complicite seems to be dominated by multi/inter-media theatre, there are productions that overtly and insistently elude such categorisation. The visual minimalism of *Shun-kin* on the one hand and the unexpected purity of the dramatic theatre in the production of Beckett's *Endgame* on the other prove that the borderline of the visual tissue is subject to the mechanism of marginalisation of previously assimilated external elements. Complicite's aesthetics embrace the field of rapid relocations between the external world, its fluctuating peripheries and the semantic centre.

THE SONIC TISSUE

In his article 'Ways of Hearing', Paul Allain reveals interesting features of the sonic tissue of Complicite. According to Allain, the aural potential of McBurney's theatre, if frequently underestimated, is crucial for the company's aesthetics, and he said so in 2013, a long time before the idea of *The Encounter* was presented:

> This sonic aspect of [Complicite's] work, its music and its musicality, is frequently overlooked and perhaps forgotten. Just as Complicite's work has an extraordinarily rich visual weave, so does it have a complex and equally rich aural texture. Text sits within this nexus as much as it sits in relation to the total *mise-en-scène*; but I fear that we too frequently need to be reminded of its musical and aural potential. ... It appears at first glance that most scholarly analyses and reviews of Complicite's performances focus on their visual aspects ... And yet McBurney has always (and increasingly more so) embraced music, from the 2001 *Noise of Time* to the 2012 *A Dog's Heart* at the English National Opera. Collaborations with the likes of Nitin Sawney, the Pet Shop Boys, and the Los Angeles Philharmonic all attest to the constant importance of sound within their *mise-en-scène*. (Allain 2013: 149–50)

True, the sonic tissue of Complicite is as dynamic as the visual and the textual. Its functions vary from an examination of the unamplified human voice in theatre and non-theatre spaces (early works), through the employment of technological devices such as microphones, loudspeakers, headphones and sound recordings, to the extensive exploration of live music played during the performance (e.g. *The Noise of Time, Shun-kin*, and the operas). Generically, the music varies from classical traditions gathered from all over the world to rock and popular songs. On the one hand, the sonic tissue may be completely subordinated to the onstage *semiosis* as a background commentary on the onstage action (e.g. Handel's *Messiah* in *The Street of Crocodiles*) or an indicator of spatio-temporal relations (e.g. the offstage sounds of cars in *A Minute Too Late*). On the other hand, music may reveal a more autonomous dimension when arranged in a film-like style (e.g. *A Disappearing Number*). In *The Noise of Time*, it develops into an independent counterpart to the visual plot, whereas in the operas music dominates the remaining aspects of theatre communication. We should not forget that a constant exploration of the musicality of natural language (e.g. the Japanese plays) sets a gradual scale between the human voice and other types of sound, music in particular.

Intrusions: Some Conclusions

In Complicite's theatrical practice the three tissues (textual, visual, sonic) are minutely and inseparably interwoven. Their interrelations vary and establish a repertoire of theatrical devices that participate in the creation of meanings through juxtaposition of these elements. When compared with other British theatre companies, Complicite explores the tensions in a particularly vibrant way. To make such exploration possible, the entire rehearsal process involves the stable collaboration of artists and technicians responsible for particular fields of creativity.[16]

Complicite's ethos of collaboration leads to the careful and meaning-endowed selection of artists, technicians and institutions for particular projects. Such a strategy aims at giving credence to the company's eclectic method of work. The following are just illustrative examples:

- *The Chairs*, which was co-produced with the Royal Court Theatre, to commemorate the original adaptation of Ionesco for the London stage back in the 1950s, involved a collaboration with the Quay Brothers whose earlier commitment to Bruno Schulz guaranteed a similar artistic sensibility.
- When working on an opera, Simon McBurney collaborated with English National Opera in London and De Nederlandse Opera in Amsterdam.
- The company has worked with musicians such as Gerald McBurney, the Emerson String Quartet, the Los Angeles Philharmonic Orchestra, Honjoh Hidetaro, Martyn Brabbins and the pop band the Pet Shop Boys.
- The element of puppetry involves a long-lasting collaboration with the Blind Summit Theatre, just as lighting design does with Paul Anderson, sound design with Gareth Fry and costume with Christina Cunningham.
- The multi/inter-media projections and visual design involve cooperation with Finn Ross, Es Devlin and Luke Halls.

The intense interweaving of textual, visual and sonic tissues within the aesthetics has illustrated the prominence of the notion of a border and the mechanism of semiotic intrusion. Incessant infiltration of external elements into Complicite's aesthetics fosters artistic eruptions whenever the external signs/structures/systems clash with those which oscillate between the fluctuating peripheries and the centre of *semiosis*. In the case of Complicite, the peripheries stock the entire spectrum of artistic solutions conceived by the company at any point of their evolution, whereas the invariant centre incorporates the concrete act of communication occurring between the stage and the audience during a performance. This is by definition a one-time, unrepeatable and transient act whose liveness is crucial. Yet, from the perspective of spectator/interpreter, each performance fosters 'an avalanche of meanings' by getting involved in meaningful relations that occur within the aesthetics of the company.

NOTES

1. In spite of its immediate relevance to the domain of artistic endeavours, the concept of semiosphere has not had much resonance in theatre studies. It is striking that in a broad and extensive historical overview of semiotic/structural studies on theatre done by Rozik neither the name of Lotman nor any mention of his concepts appear (see the sub-section titled 'Main Schools and Trends' in 2008: 2–7).

2. To give the most straightforward example, the semiosphere of the English language is embedded by the semiosphere of all natural languages and comprises the semioshperes of American, British, Irish, Australian and other dialects.

3. 'Non-semiotic space' is that which does not depend on semiotic arrangement (e.g. 'the natural world'). 'Extra-semiotic space' is that which belongs to (an) external semiotic system(s).

4. Lotman discusses internal and external relations in poetry in *Analysis of the Poetic Text* (1976).

5. Lotman speaks in this context of 'symmetrical-asymmetrical pairings'.

6. The case of a one-time 'unplugged' performance of *Measure for Measure* 'that played a 150 seated venue in Mumbai', India is a striking example of this (Rintoul 2013: 121).

7. Victoria Gould puts it this way: 'It is such a cliché to say that in the theatre we share the same air, but I think Simon [McBurney] is looking constantly for that communality of experience, which transcends language or class or culture' ('Nothing is off limits apart from not turning up' in *A Disappearing Number*—programme: 14).

8. Judith Dimant stresses the Avignon open-air space setting was very appropriate for the grand visual scale of the spectacle (in conversation).

9. In terms of Zgorzelski, one may say that the periphery is the domain of equivalents.

10. In his interview with Morris, McBurney refers to the chair as to 'the human body without the body' (27: 30). It is perhaps not accidental that a picture of a chair is emblematic of the company in, for example, social media. For a very instructive—if slightly different—interpretation of the ways in which the chair is used in *The Master and Margarita* and earlier works, see Campos 2014.

11. Enoch Brater analyses the dynamic capacity of the trope of 'the seated figure on stage' in modern theatre. Even though his analysis focuses on Beckett, Brater puts the trope in the broader context of Henrik Ibsen, August Strindberg, Anton Chekhov, Tennessee Williams, Eugene O'Neill, Harold Pinter, Caryl Churchill, Arthur Miller, Edward Albee, Sam Shepard, and then Jean Baptiste Racine and William Shakespeare (2011: 69–85). Brater concludes that 'Beckett draws a rich vocabulary of theatrical convention, analyses his inheritance, then takes it several steps forward' (85). The same, I think, may be said about how Complicite uses the prop of a chair.

12. 'One of the most exciting things about this production is the commissioning of the first new translation of *The Chairs* since the early 1950s' (Alexander 1997b: 13). Similarly, in the case of Bertolt Brecht's *The Caucasian Chalk Circle*, a new translation—this time by Frank McGuinness—was commissioned. It remained, however, unpublished until a later production by the National Theatre.

13. A similar image of the mass of chairs facing the audience was presented in *The Noise of Time*.

14. This is a direct echo of *Mnemonic*.

15. According to McBurney, Complicite always adapts technology to theatrical objectives. In *Mnemonic*, he says, '[t]he central love story in the show takes place between two people who have been talking on a mobile for an hour and a half, having not spoken for a year and attempting to understand what has kept them apart. At the end, it's inevitable that someone's battery runs out and they get cut off. We are not making a heady comment on technology, but the technology itself serves as a metaphor for the breakdown in human communication' ([Mc]Burney 2000: 12).

16. See Michael Levine film interview recorded for Theatre Museum Canada (2011).

CHAPTER 7

Kaleidoscopic Fragmentariness

Dispersed Meanings

The artistic objectives of Complicite involve the pursuit of kaleidoscopic meanings that are created by both autonomous elements of construction and independent compositional units. Of course, dispersed meanings challenge coherence and cohesion. But—as we already know—it is an intrinsic feature of the company's aesthetics to elude the complete unification of semantics and to promote fluctuating peripheries and kaleidoscopic fragmentariness. In practical terms, considerable autonomy of individual signs/structures/systems increases the auto-referentiality of particular elements and stresses their singular features. The process characterises all aspects of communication and leads to another 'avalanche of meanings'. The example of *A Disappearing Number* illustrates the ways in which Complicite makes radical use of the general semiotic principle that determines artistic communication: 'internal diversity' is decisive for the overall 'integrity'.

There were three theatre productions of *A Disappearing Number* (2007, 2008 and 2010) performed in several venues around the globe.[1] In addition to this, the piece was transposed to other mediums. As a printed play, a radio play and a recording of an audiovisual broadcast in the National Theatre Live project,[2] *A Disappearing Number* constitutes three independent, though interrelated, versions of one piece. Each of them makes use of the intrinsic qualities of the given medium. The technology of audiovisual broadcast not only allows for cinematographic shifts in focus (e.g. close-up) and perspectives (seven cameras were used [Dimant

© The Author(s) 2016
T. Wiśniewski, *Complicite, Theatre and Aesthetics*,
DOI 10.1007/978-3-319-33443-1_7

in conversation]), but also expanded the proxemics of communication. Broadcast to hundreds of cinemas, this special performance included references to audiences in Plymouth, London, New York, Melbourne and other cities around the globe (DVD recording 25:04–10).

For obvious reasons, the radio play enhances its sonic tissue by converting selected visual signals into phonic ones. Ruth, Al, Aninda and the other characters are conceived primarily through the recorded voices of actors and not, as is the case in theatre performance, by the physical onstage presence of actors. In terms of composition, the refrain-like repetitions of counting become crucial for delineating particular units of segmentation and stressing the linear development of *semiosis*. Besides, the entire meta-theatrical dimension of the performance is substituted by structures that refer to the primacy of the sonic tissue in a radio play.

Although the broadcast and the radio play reduce the physical indications of the presence of actors, it is certainly the published play that is most radical in this respect. There are neither cinematographic projections of images nor the phonemic materiality of their recorded voices. In this case, the act of communication is grounded in the conventions of the printed word. Yet, the long-lasting tradition of dramatic writing endows *A Disappearing Number* with strictly textual means of creating meanings. They are explored in a profoundly auto-referential way and, by clashing with performative conventions, lead to an interesting eruption of artistic meanings.

Numeric Sequences

Printed drama imposes the textual means for clear-cut segmentation. When compared with a theatre performance, this textual convention increases the autonomy of the precisely determined compositional units such as acts and scenes. In *A Disappearing Number*, the beginning of each of the 15 scenes is marked in the same way by placing numbers in the incipit (centred, higher font, at the top of a new page). Particular scenes substantially differ not only in terms of their structural arrangement but also in the complexity of interweaving numerous spatio-temporal points of reference. As a result of the considerable autonomy of these scenes, each of them demands different analytical treatment.

There appears, however, one additional textual device that firmly divides the play into two parts. Scene '3', which is the only one finished by the stage direction 'darkness', is followed by a sequence of eight black-and-white photographs taken during rehearsals. The photographs suspend the reading process and necessitate 'a break' filled with a concise visual essay.[3] Frequent as they are in books published by Complicite (see Table 5.2), in this particular case the rehearsal photographs mark the division of the text into the opening three scenes and the remaining 12.

Such compositional patterning vindicates the prominence of the darkness finishing scene '3'. Its importance is further maintained on the semantic plane, because the two scenes that follow the rehearsal photographs ('4' and '5') are placed in stark contrast to the communicative overdose served by the introductory section of the play (scenes 1–3). Whereas the spatio-temporal arrangement of scene '3' accentuates the kaleidoscopic fragmentation and may appear as a semantic jumble, the stage situation in scenes '4' and '5' is built in accordance with the principles of verisimilitude, mimetic accuracy and communicative lucidity. The compositional prominence of scene '3' and its meticulous internal patterning suggest that it assumes the function of the semantic core and thus is decisive for the meanings created in the entire play.

Exceptional communicative density is already revealed in the scene's opening. By using strictly textual means, the passage necessitates the consideration of a number of communicative channels that are functional from the perspective of the implied audience within the onstage *semiosis*. It is assumed that the words are to be heard, the numbers written on page watched and heard, whereas the stage images that are verbally described by the stage directions establish one set of correlated visual stage signals. The fragment reads as follows:

3

AL looks at the numbers on the screen.

AL: **1, 2, 3...** (*He turns and stops speaking, but his voice continues to count up. He listens, then begins to count backwards.*) **-1, -2, -3...** (*Again, he stops speaking but his voice continues. Now there are counting voices in both directions. AL listens.*) **And between 1 and 2 there is an infinity of other numbers such as 1.1 and 1.2... and 1.11 and 1.12... and 1.111 and 1.112... and 1.1111 and...**

He stops and, again, his voice continues the pattern. (2008: 30, emphasis added)

The overall dominance of numbers is striking. A particular role is given to the number three. The very number initiates the textual arrangement of scene '3' as the textual incipit. Next, Al is looking at unspecified numbers presented on the screen and begins to count aloud 'one, two, three...'.

Even though, in terms of onstage action, hardly anything happens, the fragment has already enlivened three different channels of dramatic communication:

- the textual (it exposes the fact it is written),
- the visual (it describes a concrete stage image),
- the sonic (Al's counting is to be heard).

In each of these three channels, our attention is focused on numbers; but in each of them the semiotic status of numbers is different. First, the printed '3' at the top of the page stresses the materiality of the written text, but such materiality is completely non-existent onstage. Second, the numbers Al looks at are presented in their written form but this time their material status is achieved onstage: they remain unspecified for the reader (*'numbers on the screen'*). Third, Al's counting '1, 2, 3...' confronts the printed text with the situation presented onstage. This time the voice delivers continuous counting, whereas the written version only describes this activity and, by employing an ellipsis, gives prominence to the number three. (The situation is mirrored in the ending of the play when Ruth is doing exactly the same thing: she is counting.)

Even such provisional analysis of a textual detail reveals the degree of meticulous internal patterning of scene '3'. The situation gets even more complicated when Al balances the monotony of his onward counting by doing it backwards, and then increases the sense of numeric confusion by introducing analogous counting of more and more detailed decimal fractions. In this passage—as elsewhere in *A Disappearing Number*—the numbers convey much more than sheer mathematics. In such a minute episode as this one, they are written (on the page and on screen), watched (by the reader, by Al and by the audience) and heard (by Al and by the audience). They impose patterns and bring confusion (for a more detailed discussion of mathematics in *A Disappearing Number*, see Wiśniewski 2013c).

Numbers take an equally—though differently—prominent role in the opening of the entire play. The onstage action commences with Ruth beginning her lecture on mathematics. Yet, it is well integrated with the theatrical context as Ruth's words establish a proxemic equivalence between her fictional auditorium in the university lecture hall and that of the audience gathered in the theatre. The fragment reads as follows:

1

A university lecture hall, with a large whiteboard in the centre. ...
AL stands next to the desk with his back to the audience. R UTH enters. She
writes '1, 2, 3, 4, 5' on the whiteboard.

RUTH (*Nervous.*) Good evening ladies and gentlemen. I'd like to go
through one or two very basic mathematical ideas that are integral to this
evening so that the recurrent mathematical themes become clear to you all.

Right, OK. (*Beat.*) Let's consider these sets of numbers. (*She writes them
up as she speaks.*) 2, 4, 6, 8, 10... 2, 3, 5, 7, 11... 1, 2, 4, 8, 16... These are
known as sequences, and they have two characteristics. The terms can go on
forever and they have a pattern, which helps you to continue the sequence.
Some patterns are more obvious than others. (2008: 21)

The beginning of scene '3' and the beginning of the entire play are in
many ways similar. They both multiply various modes of counting (textual, written on board, spoken and heard). In both cases, mathematical
sequences are directed to infinity and yet they are evoked by only mentioning their beginnings.

But slight, if meaningful, differences appear between the two scenes.
In scene '1' it is Ruth who is counting and Al who is listening. When seen
in the context of scene '3' (where Al is counting), the activity indicates
the possibility of a complete act of communication, as if to prove that
Al has internalised what Ruth teaches him about mathematics and mathematicians. Moreover, on the compositional plane, Ruth's opening lecture
anticipates her recorded final counting at the end of the performance,
which sets the compositional framework for the entire play.

INTERNAL INTEGRITY

In spite of such intense exploration of the kaleidoscopic aesthetics of fragmentation and dispersion, *A Disappearing Number* constitutes an integral
piece of artistic work. The fundamental integrity of autonomous elements
is determined, among other devices, by the aesthetic, semantic and semiotic potential of the very title. On the one hand the title phrase establishes
the central verbal metaphor for the entire piece (paradigmatic plane), and
on the other, in the course of reception, the semantics of the title is subject
to radical shifts and unpredictable transformations (syntagmatic plane).
In other words, the integrity of general associations is challenged by the
autonomy of numerous employments of the title metaphor in theatre,
print and radio productions. This paradoxical arrangement of the title

echoes the way in which meanings are created within the semiosphere of the whole piece.

The title phrase has an immediate metaphoric implication: the language does not normally qualify 'numbers' as 'disappearing', which suggests a degree of ambiguity and universality. Once the primacy of literal meanings is challenged, the striking poetic quality of the title phrase strengthens. Dense sound orchestration of the phrase 'a disappearing number' reveals a considerable phonosemantic potential. The three uneven words (the syllabic pattern of: 1 [a] + 4 [di-sa-pear-ing] + 2 [num-ber]) establish a regular rhythmic arrangement of the three stressed and four unstressed syllables (_*_*_*_). Next, the length of the central stressed syllable [pɪər] is highlighted since it contains the only diphthong in the phrase. The phonemic strength of the middle syllable is, moreover, counterbalanced by the placement of the short unaccented schwa [ə] at the beginning and end of the phrase (a weak frame is confronted with a strong centre). Furthermore, the assonantal repetition of [ɪ] appears in the extreme syllables of 'disappearing'. Finally, the nasal consonants accumulated in the third word and followed by a voiced bilabial plosive [n/m—b] accentuate the prominence of the noun. In short, the accumulation of all these phonosemantic devices not only proves the intense internal integrity of the title phrase but also suggests the importance of its poetic/aesthetic potential.[4]

Such metaphoric understanding of numbers and mathematics affects the compositional plane of the printed play. Although terms such as acts or scenes are not used here, there are 15 precisely delimited compositional units sequentially labelled as numbers arranged from '1' to '15'. (I refer to them as 'scenes' because the units fulfil exactly this role.) The device proclaims mathematical ordering to be a compositional principle, and makes counting one of the central fields of association. Still, there is no doubt that the composition of the textual version of *A Disappearing Number* varies from that which regulates an ever-evolving, continuous, non-discrete and ephemeral live performance presented onstage or the sonic linearity of the radio play.

ARTISTIC MEANS OF PATTERNING

The complicated and multi-layered arrangement of the play's composition reveals the most rudimentary feature of a communicative system: there is always an ontological discrepancy between a semiosphere and the natural world. Quite appropriately for a play infiltrated to such a degree by scientific jargon, *A Disappearing Number* introduces this rudimental discrepancy as one of the themes discussed by the characters. It is Ruth who, in the compositional framework of scene '14', approaches the theme twice when she says:

> RUTH: (*Voice-over.*) It should be obvious by now that I am only interested in mathematics as a creative art. In that sense it has nothing to do with physical reality. By physical reality, I mean the material world, the world of day and night, earthquakes and eclipses. For me and I suppose for most mathematicians there is another reality, which I shall call mathematical reality. (2008: 81)
>
> RUTH: (*Voice-over.*) For me, and I suppose for most mathematicians, there is another reality, which I shall call mathematical reality. (*Pause.*) Take a chair for example. A chair may be simply a collection of whirling electrons, or an idea in the mind of God; the more we think of it, the fuzzier its outlines become in a haze of sensation which surrounds it. (*Pause.*) But the number 2 or 317 has nothing to do with sensation. 317 is a prime number, not because we think so, or because our minds are shaped in one way rather than another, but because it is so, because mathematical reality is built that way... (82)

By perceiving mathematics as a kind of creative art, Ruth implies the juxtaposition of the natural world and the mathematic/artistic/theatrical modelling systems. In this sense, Ruth's statement has practical consequences for the aesthetics of Complicite: it refers to mathematics as much as it does to the art of theatre.

But there are at least two more consequences of this discussion. *A Disappearing Number* consistently builds up an analogy between mathematics and art, most notably poetry, and theatre. If mathematics is perceived from the position of art, the theatre (drama) is presented as responsible for the meticulous formation of beautiful and manifold patterns. Concise as it will be, the following analysis of the selected textual, compositional, semantic and semiotic arrangements should suffice to illustrate the analogy between mathematical and artistic means of patterning:

> RUTH: ... Clearly this result looks **anomalous**! As G H Hardy said, '**A mathematician, like a painter, or a poet, is a maker of patterns... And beauty is the first test...**' (*She points at the equation.*) Look at this in a new way and **a hidden pattern** emerges which connects the two sides of the equation in **the most extraordinarily beautiful way.** (27)

RUTH: (*Voice-over.*) It may be very hard to define **mathematical beauty** but that is true of **beauty of any kind**. We may not know quite what we mean by **a beautiful poem**, but that does not prevent us from recognising one when we read it. (42, emphasis added)

According to Ruth, the notion of beauty is as relevant in mathematics as it is in poetry, and she adapted this view from Professor Hardy. This, in turn, indicates the ways in which knowledge is absorbed: through complete acts of one-to-one communication.

On a more general plane, *A Disappearing Number* explores a theme at the core of the aesthetics of Complicite: the recognition of beauty in the unknown and incomprehensible. The play ascribes to Al the position of an epistemological outsider. Like many spectators, he is not a professional mathematician, and this makes him feel intimidated by mathematical patterns. As he confesses at one point: 'I haven't understood a word you've said, but I've found it fascinating. You clearly like what you do' (28). The words are directed at Ruth, who finds herself, at times, in a similar position. Ruth's fascination with overwhelming beauty is explicit in her account of the journey to India:

RUTH: ... This is so exciting Al. I'm holding Ramanujan's notebooks in my hands. I'm feeling in the middle of things again. I turn page after page. I'm looking at the numbers. Whole sequences of them. They are scattered across the page like seeds 1... 9... 19... 24. Everywhere the number 24. This is an example of what mathematicians call a magic number. Numbers that continually appear where we least expect them for reasons that no one can understand. And **I don't understand, but they're beautiful...**

AL: (*To himself.*) **How can something you don't understand be beautiful?**

RUTH: (*Turning to AL.*) **Don't we call something 'beautiful' simply because it outpaces us?** (42, emphasis added)

For Ruth, the journey to India epitomises the thrill of the profound experience of the unknown, which somehow resembles one of the roles Simon McBurney assumed in *Who You Hear It from*. The parallel is made even stronger since, in *A Disappearing Number*, the nomadic experience acquires certain auto-referential implications. This, for instance, is the case in scene '1', when Aninda and Al travel through Chennai in a taxi. In spite of its strong mimetic motivation (they speak about Al's first impressions of India), Aninda's question encompasses some meta-theatricality. From the perspective of an audience, Aninda is asking as much about India as he is about the performance:

ANINDA: Are you enjoying **it**?
AL: It's a little overwhelming. (25, emphasis added)

India, and mathematics, are as overwhelming as the performance. The meanings of one monosyllabic pronoun are multiplied. After all, it is typical of Complicite's aesthetics to explore auto-referential potential and to stress the inexplicable constituent of beauty.

EQUIVALENCE AND ISOMORPHISM

Complicite explores singularities emerging from the autonomous elements of construction and composition. These are combined with a contrasting fascination with the sense originating in coherence and homogeneity. An interesting perspective emerges in which elements that derive from the whole range of communicative levels may be potentially interrelated in meaningful ways. For the addressee/interpreter, the microscopic procedures focused on analysing specificity of individual units such as a scene, a phrase or a tableau is correlated with the equally protruding procedures of scrutinising the macro-scale analogies between these elements (i.e. their isomorphism).

The intensity with which this juxtaposition is harnessed for artistic purposes is one of the pivotal features of Complicite. Notwithstanding standards commonly assumed in more traditional theatre, the company insistently sets up equivalence between elements that are at times adjacent but more frequently quite remote. There is no fixed principle predetermining once and for all the rules of setting equivalent and isomorphic arrangements. In *A Disappearing Number* a comparative analysis of the openings of scenes '1' and '3' is as fruitful for the overall analysis of the play as the exploration of the title metaphor in the context of particular versions, individual scenes, episodes, motifs, actions, or the scrutiny of the spatio-temporal arrangement of the fictional reality and the proxemics of the onstage *semiosis*.[5]

Obviously, this does not mean every single compositional element should be compared with every other element. Although such an approach may perhaps lead to some interesting conclusions, both particular elements and the general principles governing aspects of the overall aesthetics define most adequate connections. Such is the case with *Mnemonic*, a devised performance that triggered 'an avalanche of variants' in a variety of mediums.

Mnemonic

Mnemonic is a special play in the history of Complicite because each of its three theatre productions (1999, 2001 and 2002–3) was accompanied by a different printed version. The publication of more than one textual variant does not occur in any other instance. In addition to this, the radio play (2002) establishes an important point of reference as the fourth—materially preserved and artistically complete—variant. As was the case in *A Disappearing Number*, the variants cultivate their status of fully developed and autonomous artistic wholes whose meanings derive from—but do not depend on—theatre productions. On this basis, the textual and radio variants of *Mnemonic* may be compared with the documentary video/DVD recordings,[6] and other archival materials (e.g. preliminary notes, preparatory scripts and brainstormed schemes). *Mnemonic* provides more research material for analysing the evolution of a piece than any other play by Complicite.

The juxtaposition of the mechanisms of oblivion with those of memory functions not only as the prevailing theme of *Mnemonic* but also as the device which is decisive for the communicative processes. Whereas the former is already marked by the title, the latter is explicit when we confront the material status of signals in the theatre performances (transient/one time/visual/aural/verbal) with those dominating in the printed plays (recorded/lasting/textual/verbal) and the radio play (recorded/lasting/aural/verbal). In the medium of theatre, the balance between cultural memory and cultural oblivion is shaped differently than it is in published and radio plays.

In general, theatre communication is subject to the varied experience of all those who participate in this collective act. An aspect of theatre studies may aspire to reconstruct the actual course of performance from memories, recordings, reviews and other available sources. Paradoxically, then, even though the material status of stage signals is pivotal to the immediacy of sensory contact between the stage and audience, it is the sign of a signal (e.g. a recollection and/or recording) that constitutes the primary subject of scrutiny. In this case the analysis depends on the research on signs of material signals rather than on signal material itself. In a similar way to historical—and archaeological—studies, the semiotic analysis of a performance is determined as much by the information that is preserved (mechanisms of memory) as by that which is extricated from the study (mechanisms of oblivion).

In *Mnemonic* the multiplication of theatre variants resulted from three productions that were staged in ten countries in 18 different theatres, and twice at the London Riverside Studios (*Mnemonic* 2003: 128). The structure of the performance was, moreover, fluctuating. The opening monologue provided vast ground for improvisation, and this enabled Simon/Director to underscore the unrepeatable nature of every single performance (its 'liveness'). The audience was thus made aware that they were participating in a one-time *semiosis*. Even though the vast majority of such invariant features are lost forever, Complicite commemorates selected idiosyncrasies and thus introduces them to the sphere of memory. In his essay 'All in the Mind', for instance, McBurney recalls the Balkan war memories bursting from the audience in Zenica, and Kostas Philippoglou's hesitancy as to whether he should speak his lines in Greek when performing in Thessaloniki. A number of similar events would certainly broaden the meanings of *Mnemonic*, but it is significant that these—and not other—recollections testify to the prominence of the juxtaposed processes of oblivion and memory. The process of selection turns out to be prominent also when preserving the memory of theatre communication.

TEXTUAL VARIANTS

For similar reasons, it may be informative to analyse those aspects of *Mnemonic* reflected in the three printed versions of the play. Interestingly, its evolution within the textual tissue is particularly dynamic:

- In Scene One (the prologue), not only the immediate contextual information changes (i.e. added reference to the turn of the millennium [2001: 6, 2003: 135]) but also the name of the speaker shifts from Simon (1999, 2001) to Director (2003).
- The increasingly detailed peritext encompasses theatrical documentation of subsequent productions (e.g. cast, venues and awards), the dedication ('to the memory of Katrin Cartlidge' [2003: 127]) and an added footnote (2003: 136).
- The bibliographical note of sources included only in the 1999 version is omitted.

- There is a shift in the actual transcription of foreign lines, the Greek in particular (compare 2001: 23–4 and 2003: 154–5).
- The role of the (Slovak/Slovenian) Cook from Scene Nine (2001: 21) or Scene Ten (2003: 152) decreases.
- There is a general change in the number of scenes from 35 to 36.

Detailed as these changes may seem, they illustrate a more general evolution in the narrative, spatio-temporal and compositional dimensions of the play. Indeed, these are prominent issues that require more detailed scrutiny (see Wiśniewski 2012b, 2013a, b).

VISUAL COMPOSITION

The archival materials include the recording of the performance played on 3 February 2001. Recording of this particular performance increases its semiotic value as it serves particular purposes not only in shaping the semantics of the piece but also in delineating the aesthetics of Complicite. As a material sign of theatrical *semiosis*, the recording creates grounds for a comparative analysis of *Mnemonic* as produced in different media. In the case of the recording, the audiovisual dimension of the performance turns into a very prominent resource for more detailed study.

Both aural and visual signals activate numerous communicative conventions and stimulate a complex segmentation of the performance. The episodic arrangement of the construction is stressed by the strong diversity of tableaux, rapid shifts in proxemic solutions and fluctuations in spatio-temporal imagery. The recording begins when spectators enter the auditorium. There is no curtain and the chair is the only element to be seen on the bare stage. After nearly ten minutes of presenting this static tableau, Simon/Director appears onstage so as to begin his introductory one-man show based, to some extent, on improvisation. His exaggerated gestures hint at the highly conventional nature of the body language as do numerous occasional jokes ('*lazzi*') that provoke outbursts of laughter. On the one hand, then, when speaking to the audience in a casual manner via the microphone, Simon/Director makes use of the convention of stand-up comedy. On the other hand, by revealing some autobiographical details and stressing the tangibility of the theatrical space, Simon/Director anticipatorily highlights an auto-referential context for the spectacle. *Mnemonic* follows the pattern established by the Prologue to *A Minute Too Late*: the borderline of theatre communication is blurred so as to create an impression that the ontological rules of the onstage *semiosis* do not differ from those that govern in the external world. This is a well-known theatre convention.

At one point in this introductory one-man show, the visual channel is switched off. Spectators are asked to put eye masks on their heads so as to blind themselves, and the theatre space is in complete darkness. Yet, Simon/Director's monologue continues. The character of theatre communication shifts at this point from the collective (audience) to the individual (a group of spectators), which is strengthened by the voice's request to recall concrete personal memories.

Another shift that occurs now is achieved by changing the source from which the monologue is delivered. It is soon revealed to the audience that it is no longer the actor but his recorded voice that is delivering the words. The shift in source fosters a surprising device: when the stage is lit anew and Virgil appears sitting on a chair as a member of a fictional audience. When his telephone rings unexpectedly, he creates a hilarious mime of getting away through a crowd of fellow spectators (though there are no other actors onstage yet) into the fictional onstage foyer where he may continue his phone conversation with Alistair.

By this stage of the performance numerous semiotic points of reference have been established. First, there appears the whole spectrum of deictic frameworks such as those between:

bare stage

↓

one-man show

↓

autobiographic context

↓

the perspective of the theatre audience

↓

fictional audience

↓

fictional foyer.

Diagram 7.1

Second, the semiotic discrepancy between the world of the stage and that of the audience is strongly stressed by numerous auto-referential devices (e.g. the onstage 'audience'). Third, the covertly theatrical nature of the ongoing *semiosis* delineates the shifting communicative roles of the encoder (Simon/Director/actor/character) and decoder (individual spectators vs collective audience) (visual vs aural vs verbal channels of communication).

SONIC AND VISUAL TYPES OF SEGMENTATION

The introductory passage of the performance establishes complex and multifarious principles that distinguish audio and visual ways of segmenting the performance. On the sonic plane, the silent pre-performance image of the chair is followed by the long piece of monologue in which Simon/Director sets frameworks of contact between the stage and the audience. This leads to the sequence of Virgil's phone conversations. He thrice talks to his friend Alistair and twice to his beloved Alice. In fact, phone conversations with Alice are lengthy and constitute the main framework for the remaining onstage action. Notably, even in the introductory fragment, the sonic potential is stressed by the whole spectrum of devices, such as the microphone, the amplified voice, the recorded voice, phone conversations and listening to the voice coming to the audience from the stage in the dark.

On the visual plane, the role of the opening tableau (0:00–9:25) increases as it sets the anticipatory expectations of the audience. 'Why is the chair the only element placed on the bare stage?', 'Who is going to sit on it?', 'What is the purpose of such a minimalistic setting?' The image is followed by the passage in which Simon/Director speaks through the microphone with exaggerated movements, causing much humour (9:25–18:19). Next, the stage is covered by darkness (18:19–26:15), which is followed by a rather conventional depiction of a fictional onstage audience achieved by gestures and body movement.

The next shift occurs when the stage turns into Virgil's room, with clearly delineated walls and props, such as a TV set, a sink, a mirror, a bed, a table and some additional chairs. Throughout the remaining part of the performance (33:30–2:12:22), Virgil's room undergoes numerous transformations but it remains invariably the primary setting for the onstage action. It shifts only at the very end of the performance when Virgil is on his way to the airport. The central image created in *Mnemonic* is that of Virgil talking on the phone with Alice when moving around the room.

This is not to say that the world of the stage is stable. The conventionally realistic character of this image is challenged not only by internal shifts in the arrangement of props (e. g. mirror shifts of furniture, which are well documented in the archive) but also by imposing upon the image of Virgil's room a number of other points of reference. We may conclude that the spatio-temporal imagery appears to be structured in accordance with the device of the palimpsest.

Even though the stage is structured primarily as Virgil's room, *Mnemonic* abounds in audiovisual shifts that result in rapid transformations within the world of the stage. For example, when the ensemble of actors enters the stage (39: 40), the closed space of the room is turned into the open landscape of the Alps by the mere pace of the characters' movement. While climbing among the chairs, bed and table, the mountaineers (this is marked visually by anoraks) discover the naked body of the Iceman (naked Simon/Director/Virgil). The highly unrealistic visual design of the scene (furniture as mountains) is enhanced by the sonic verisimilitude of the sound of veering wind.

A completely different type of audiovisual imagery is used in the episode presenting the piano class conducted by Carlo Capsoni.[7] Set just before the outbreak of the Second World War in Northern Italy, the scene employs visual naturalism, the illusion of the fourth wall and specific ('dated') lighting design. Both the spatio-temporal setting and the technical means contribute to the overall detachment of the scene from the rest of the performance. This is well motivated by its complete autonomy in terms of the storyline. The figures of Capsoni and his student appear onstage only once in this narratively unconnected—if well-crafted and demarcated—episode. Still, their marginal presence participates in the universalisation of the story of the Iceman and in establishing metaphoric parallels between the artistic experience and climbing ('Capsoni: … When we play a piece of music for another person we often feel frightened, sick with fear, like a mountaineer with vertigo' [2001: 19]). The episode contributes also to the metaphoric potential of the theme of reaching the summit.

As we have seen, audiovisual signals promote multifarious types of segmentation. By this they strengthen the episodic construction of the performance. Meanings are frequently created by divergent semiotic means so that their reception/analysis requires constant shifts in strategies of decoding. This type of theatrical *semiosis* is made more complex by multiplying narrative points of reference. As the recording well illustrates, the world of the stage allows for the simultaneous realisation of several of them.

LEVELS OF NARRATION

The complex relations between the segmentation imposed by audiovisual means and the features of spatio-temporal organisation are made even more complicated by the incongruous nature of the narrative structure that typifies *Mnemonic*. The world of the stage incorporates several communicative situations that are mutually, yet inconsistently, interwoven. In this way, the semantics of the performance echoes the principles structuring the overall aesthetics of Complicite. Both of them encompass autonomous elements of varied derivation whose fluctuating arrangement results in reciprocal interactions.

Mnemonic turns into a fragmented performance consisting of varied episodes that on the one hand strive for semantic independence and on the other are grounded in the stable foundation of the stage situation that is decisive for the internal coherence of their arrangement. Virgil's room develops into the pivotal narrative plane of *Mnemonic*. The audience witness various communicative situations happening in this room. Insomniac Virgil is engrossed in his desperate thoughts, drinks beer, smokes cigarettes and erases answer-phone messages, struggling with memories of his ex-girlfriend, Alice, who left him nine months earlier without saying farewell. The TV set is on. Although it does not attract Virgil's attention much, it provides odd information from the wider world such as the weather forecast or the piece of news on the arrival of the body of the Iceman to the Italian town named Bolzano. This enhances the loneliness of the depressed protagonist, his detachment from other people and total engrossment in the attempt at redefining for himself a new life situation (i.e. after Alice left him). The convention of metonymic representation of the internal world of the protagonist through both spatial imagery and visual means is established. The shifts in the messy and fluctuating room epitomise the psychical instability of Virgil.

The room is also the place of five phone conversations. In terms of spatial arrangement, the world of the stage (audiovisual depiction of Virgil's room) is juxtaposed with the offstage world depicted verbally by the voices of Alistair (his flat) and Alice (the hotel room in Bolzano). This type of phone duologue is quite conventional in modern drama and yet the functions ascribed to it in *Mnemonic* are rather original. This is particularly visible in the case of conversations with Alice. So as to reflect the technical facilities of mobile phones at the turn of the millennium and thus highlight phatic obstacles, the lengthy conversations finish abruptly both times as if the coverage was lost or a battery discharged. Though, in the fictional world, they are separated by trans-European distance (London—Bolzano), the couple appears onstage together in several episodes (e.g. when Alice mentions the night spent in Vilnius, Lithuania). Interaction between the actors not only reveals the metaphoric/symbolic character of the stage world but also exploits the juxtapositions of various channels (visual vs verbal) or conventions (realistic vs non-literal) that are used by Complicite.

Configuring the onstage action around the structure of a phone conversation fosters the possibility of introducing two simultaneous and interweaving narratives. The internal story delivered by Virgil (the story of the Iceman) and that told by Alice interweave and complement each other. This culminates towards the end of performance, when the audience learn that Alice is in Bolzano. This means she may visit the museum where the body of the Iceman is exhibited. At this point, the focus of the narrative changes. The dominant perspective of Virgil is challenged when events are presented from Alice's internal perspective. At least in two episodes the audience witness what remains unknown to Virgil. When Alice talks about her meeting with the BBC correspondent, she avoids mentioning that she was in bed with him. Simultaneously, the audience witness the visual tableau where the two strangers who met on the train are actually in bed. The other episode occurs at the end of the performance when Alice is describing the body of the Iceman exposed in the museum in Bolzano. Although the words are directed to Virgil, they are not involved in a conversation, so it seems she is talking to him in her mind. By juxtaposing Virgil's and Alice's internal monologues, Complicite enlivens the dialogic (polyphonic) fragmentation occurring within the world of the stage. Patrice Pavis concludes that the paradox of *Mnemonic* results from the fact that 'the blending of all ... elements does not form a homogeneous discourse, no subject centralises or homogenises the materials, and nevertheless the cleverness of the dramatic structure allows a network to locate the centre of the work' (2013: 48).

The phone conversations of Virgil and Alice assume the role of frame narratives for a number of more or less integrated stories that are set around Europe over a period of roughly five thousand years. The communicative status of the introduced narratives oscillates between verbal description (e.g. the narrative delivered by Konrad Spindler) and the more or less explicit onstage presentation. One extreme of the latter case is the story of Capsoni. It is depicted in a realistic manner onstage, and completely detached from the rest of the performance. The other extreme is fixed by the lyrical mime in which the procession of actors accompanies the final moments of the Iceman. Set in the high mountains, five thousand years before the story of Virgil, the mime is verbally delineated by the offstage recorded voice of the protagonist. The Iceman is represented by a puppet constructed out of a broken chair and operated by a chorus consisting of the entire company. Divergent as they are in terms of both technical solutions and spatio-temporal imagery, the majority of these—and other—introduced stories operate within the frame of the phone conversation between Virgil and Alice. This is possible because of the Chinese box convention that structures certain aspects of the narrative. Multiplied levels of quotations within quotations (Konrad Spindler's account of the Iceman) and narratives within narratives (the case of Capsoni) appear.

Notwithstanding the dispersed construction and fragmentariness of the storyline, Complicite uses various theatrical means of sustaining isomorphism (equivalence) even between the most detached episodes. Equivalence may be set by all available means. Such is, for example, the role of the repetition of individual words, phrases or longer passages, motifs, themes and broad fields of association, intonation, the sound of the voice, gestures, tableaux and other audiovisual devices.

SIMON MCBURNEY'S BODY

Yet, it is chiefly the physical onstage presence of Simon McBurney that integrates various planes of the narrative and elements of the construction in the most potent way. His domination over the world of the stage is strongly pronounced in the introductory fragment of the performance. He is not only the first—and for several minutes the only—actor who appears onstage, but also the one who introduces various characters (Simon, Director, Virgil) and endows them with a number of roles (actor, listener, spectator). He also sets various points of spatial reference (e.g. the theatre, the fictional audience, the foyer, Virgil's London flat), and underlines elementary aspects of theatrical communication (e.g. stage-audience *semiosis*, aural and visual channels, internal monologue and phone conversations).

McBurney's presence is stressed verbally and visually. He speaks to the audience using a microphone, listens to his own recorded voice, is engrossed in his own thoughts and then talks on the phone. Being visually present onstage throughout the entire performance, McBurney (Simon/Director/Virgil) either actively stimulates the development of the action or takes the role of a passive observer who contemplates what is going on around him.

The physicality of McBurney is also endowed with a very prominent role in a more explicit way. For a substantial part of the performance the naked actor reveals his muscular body.[8] His nakedness turns into a very potent theatrical signal. His naked body enhances the performative immediacy of the contact between the stage and the audience (i.e. 'liveness'). It fulfils also a significant role in establishing another sequence of compositional segments (dressed → naked → half-dressed → naked → dressed). Naked McBurney takes the roles of both Virgil and the body of the Iceman, and thus strengthens the internal coherence of the world of the stage. Different as they are, the narratives are linked by the image of the naked body of the leading actor. Furthermore, one of the refrain-like questions asked by Alice concerns the meaning of a naked body, which in a verbal way stresses the prominence of the theme for the ongoing universalising generalisation. The naked body of the Iceman and the naked body of Virgil are incorporated in the play by the single naked body of Simon McBurney.[9] In the world of the stage there emerges a strong equivalence between these three dimensions of artistic arrangement. The story of the Iceman is endowed with the role of the story of Everyman. What is known about his life sets the pattern for structuring fictional characters (especially Alice's father and Virgil) but is also presented as reflecting the internal experience of the leading actor. In *Mnemonic*, the naked body turns into the artistic signature of Simon McBurney that turns into the most prominent element of the stage language.[10]

There is none of the physical immediacy of the naked body in the text of the play, the radio play or even the video recording. By changing the medium, nakedness shifts from the sphere of sensory experience to the sphere of semiotic relations. There is no immediacy of 'liveness'. This is the core discrepancy between theatrical performativity and other forms of art. The former a priori assumes the material presence of another human being; the latter assumes the existence of signal material that refers to another human being.

Notably, the semiotic shift which occurs here is the best illustration of the meaning of 'complicity' between the stage and the audience. Complicite catches this semiotic discrepancy:

- The sensory experience has a material immediacy: individual emotions are experienced when being confronted with the naked body of another human being.

- The naked body of an actor onstage is additionally endowed with meanings created by a range of semiotic mechanisms; this means McBurney's body may be made equivalent to the body of the Iceman and simultaneously foster highly personal emotions (e.g. fascination, shame, excitement, embarrassment); both types of experience are equally prominent for the onstage *semiosis*.
- The meanings ascribed to the naked body are multiplied by its involvement in a variety of relations with other constructional and compositional elements (e.g. the other naked body of Alice, verbal discussion on the meaning of nakedness, meanings detected from the naked body of Icemen by scientists, projection of Alice's face on his chest); notably, in *Mnemonic* this is one of the central themes.
- In other media, such as printed and radio plays, the physicality of a naked body (its functioning as the signal material) turns into an abstract semiotic construct that is to be reconstructed from its verbal description.

A DEAD BODY

It is most intriguing that *Mnemonic* makes use of the juxtaposition between the theatrical presence of a living naked body and the archaeological investigation motivated by the finding of the ancient dead, if naked, body of the Iceman. The isomorphic equivalence between these two types of nakedness is most explicit when Simon McBurney's naked body incarnates the dead body of the Iceman. Arguably, this isomorphy develops into a figure that conveys the crucial paradox of the aesthetics of Complicite, namely the mutual complementariness of contradictory notions such as:

(**McBurney**: the naked live body/the sensory experience of presence)

vs.

(**the Iceman**: the naked dead body/the absence experienced through random traces)

Diagram 7.2

The paradox turns into two divergent models of communication: that which is epitomised by the semiotics of theatrical performativity and that which is embodied by the semiotics of archaeological investigation. Whereas the former revolves around such notions as physical presence, unavoidable transience and material immediacy of signals, the latter is grounded on scrupulous reconstruction, long-lasting investigation and formulation of hypothetical models based on random and fragmented objects of scrutiny. In *Mnemonic* the isomorphic figure of the naked body is additionally related to the paradoxical confrontation of the mechanisms of memory (duration of a textual recording) and those of oblivion (transience of a singular experience).

The dichotomy has further auto-referential implications because the paradox of communicative processes envisaged by Complicite is grounded on parallel principles. The physical immediacy of an individual encounter between the interlocutors of theatrical communication that is the feature of each performance would be epitomised in this model by the live body of an actor. The long-lasting reconstruction of more general artistic mechanisms that characterise the entire *oeuvre*, achieved from the whole spectrum of available materials, traces which are left—intentionally or not—by the company, would be analogous to the procedures used in archaeology. Indeed, this book has been an account of an 'archaeological' reconstruction of the aesthetics of Complicite from random 'scraps of leather' such as audiovisual recordings, printed plays, unpublished scripts, notes, research and development sources and other archival materials.

ARCHAEOLOGY

It is important that the mechanisms and metaphors I have been discussing emerge directly from those employed by Complicite. The auto-referential dimension of the company's aesthetics is key to the line of interpretation offered in this book. By adapting the metaphor of archaeological scrutiny and that of scraps of leather, I have attempted to pursue meanings emerging from an exploration of the potential of various aspects of artistic communication. The confrontation of its transient 'liveness' with random traces left behind by a theatre production is one of the central issues shaping the aesthetics of the company. Indeed, Simon McBurney makes extensive use of the paradoxical intermingling of the mechanisms of memory with those of oblivion, and when doing so alludes to metaphors we know from *Mnemonic*.

Significantly, when explaining the reasons for producing *A Disappearing Number* in the 2010 programme, McBurney states:

> I am ... obsessed with what I do not know. ... Piecing together [Hardy and Ramanujan's] story in rehearsal it became clear that our re-telling of their relationship should be exactly that. A piecing together. A kind of

archaeology into what we do not really know. Just as coming to terms with
the death of a loved one also involves a kind of **archaeology**. We have to
console ourselves with piecing together something from the fragments that
remain. (3, emphasis added)

A similar artistic strategy operates in *The Noise of Time*, where the introductory collage of biographical quotes, photographs, radio recordings,
diaries and memoirs prepares the ground for the final delivery of Dmitri
Shostakovich's *15th String Quartet*. In this case, the musical coda functions in opposition to the biographical story recreated from kaleidoscopic
fragments that survived. Finally, *The Vertical Line*, with its exploration of
the elementary paintings discovered in the darkness of the Chauvet cave,
testifies to the legacy of McBurney's father's profession of archaeologist.
Thinking about the past is something that shapes him as a human being
as much as an artist.

Notes

1. *A Disappearing Number* toured to: Plymouth, Warwick, Germany, Vienna,
   Holland, London (2007), Barcelona, Michigan, Paris, London, Australia
   (2008), the Lincoln Center in New York, Mumbai, Hyderabad, London's
   West End (2010) (www.complicite.org).
2. Unlike documentary audiovisual recordings of the performance, these are
   complete artistic versions of *A Disappearing Number*.
3. Their involvement in determining both the textual materiality and the
   compositional division is reflected in the precise way the photographs are
   described in the table of contents: 'An eight-page plate section of rehearsal
   photographs from the 2007 production of *A Disappearing Number* can be
   found between pages 32 and 33. All photographs are by Sarah Ainslie'
   (2008: 5). Typically of Complicite, the name of the photographer is important, as are the numbers in their different roles—the year of the production
   (2007), the page length of the unnumbered 'plate section' (8) and the
   page numbers of pages embedding the visual essay (32, 33). The page
   numbers framing the 'hiatus' between scenes '3' and '4' stunningly revolve
   around the number three.
4. The poetic quality of the language is prominent for McBurney. When
   interviewed by Morris, he uses phrases like 'layers of the single story', 'the
   poetry of words', 'poetic resonance of words' and 'poetic action' in reference to *Mnemonic* (16:50–17:45).
5. One other similar example occurs in *A Dog's Heart* where the operatic
   conventions clash with the insistent implications derived from popular cul-

ture: the figure of Sharikov seems to echo the iconic punk hero 'Johnny Rotten' of the Sex Pistols.

6. Rozik somehow surprisingly states that '*whereas the affinity between theatre and cinema is intrinsic, the similarity between theatre and other performative arts, based on bodily experience, is marginal*' (2008: 88). I see the issue the other way round.

7. The frozen body found in the Alps was initially associated with the disappearance of Capsoni (Spindler 1994: 12, 23).

8. For a comprehensive interpretation of *Mnemonic* in general and the meanings of nakedness in particular see Freshwater 2001. Nakedness has been more frequent on the British stage since its unrestricted exploitation by the 'in-yer-face theatre' of the 1990s. For more details on this, see Sierz 2001, for example: 8–9, 21–35 and 74–80. For a contextual interpretation of *Mnemonic*, see Malinowska 2014: 59–77.

9. This may be, perhaps, the situation in which Rozik's postulate of the material incorporation works in the most straightforward way. For his discussion on 'the materiality of a nude body on stage', see 2008: 184–6.

10. In *Mnemonic* the dynamics of the fictional ('deflection of reference') and the self-referential participates in the creation of meanings. On the one hand, the introductory monologue of Simon/Director explores the personality of the actor and thus seems to infringe its signal character (personal connotations dominate) and, on the other, the nakedness of Virgil explicates 'the unmediated' contact 'between the live actors and the live spectators' and simultaneously redirects the semantics of the stage from self-referential connotations to fictional ones. In the latter case the intensity of the performative aspect of the theatrical *semiosis* (stage → audience) is paired with increasing concretisation of the fictional world. We are dealing here with the profound experience of the process of communication and rapid deictic shifts that multiply layers of the construction of the fictional world and complicate internal relations within the world of the stage. Thus, the principle of unexpected fluctuations operates here at its best.

CHAPTER 8

The Ongoing Narrative

THE EXPERIENCE OF OTHERNESS

In *The Singularity of Literature* Derek Attridge writes about 'ethical risks' undertaken when approaching the 'singular staging of otherness' (2004: 124) in a 'creative response' to a work of art. By this he hints at the paradox characterising studies in aesthetics: any attempt to accommodate the original to a given culture ('to convert the other into the same') is accompanied by the simultaneous exploration of what eludes any straightforward interpretation ('to register its resistance and irreducibility' [125]). In his view,

> Responding responsively to a work of art means attempting to do justice to it as a singular other; it involves a judgement that is not simply ethical or aesthetic, and that does not attempt to pigeonhole it or place it on a scale of values, but that operates as an affirmation of the work's inventiveness. (128)

The word 'invention' is of special importance for Attridge as 'the act [of] a mental feat, a step into the unknown', and 'originality of the fullest kind' (42) that is always oriented towards the addressee. By definition 'inventiveness' is the quality that fosters a pivotal 'shift in shared understanding and expectations' (48).

Despite important discrepancies between his and Lotman's models, these remarks by Attridge come very close to the suggestions concerning the mutual infiltration of various semiospheres explored in this book.

© The Author(s) 2016
T. Wiśniewski, *Complicite, Theatre and Aesthetics*,
DOI 10.1007/978-3-319-33443-1_8

It is significant that the two scholars refuse to determine analytical and interpretative processes by mechanical procedures, institutional require-ments and/or dogmatic theoretical premises. Instead, they postulate a creative—or inventive—openness to the external/other. For both of them this type of reception is understood as a voluntary disposition towards the world of signs rather than as an institutional obligation.

Such an approach to the world of signs is an intrinsic element of the world vision that emerges from the aesthetics of Complicite. Not only is the company attentive to a variety of experiences, voices and texts that come from 'outside', but also endeavours to impose a similar attitude on the audience. 'Otherness' is formative for individual performances/plays/pieces, and audiences are, simultaneously, exposed to the 'experience of otherness' created during a performance. Thus, the hermeneutic process employed by the company is ostentatiously elaborate and, in the initial stage, involves an innovative accommodation of external signs/structures/systems by the theatre ensemble. Their response to the internalised mate-rial is, subsequently, meant to provoke creative responses on the part of an audience. Hence, through improvised episodes, fluctuating structures, and strongly pronounced liveness, Complicite disperses univocal meanings and induces analytical and interpretative responsibilities in an audience. We have again trespassed into George Steiner's concept of 're-iteration'.

THE QUESTION OF ORIGINALITY

When compared with much British theatre and drama of the last three decades, Simon McBurney's company seems to explore 'openness to oth-erness' in particularly innovative ways. This, perhaps, explains the equivo-cal status of their work among critics and scholars. Popular among young audiences (Morris interview)[1] and theatre-makers—as David Gothard puts it: 'They changed everything in British theatre. I mean EVERYTHING' (in conversation)—the company seems not to generate abundant criticism or scholarship. The role of Complicite is frequently sidelined in studies on contemporary British drama and theatre and this results in a habitual reduction of their artistic originality. This tendency is well illustrated by the critical response to *Mnemonic*—journalists notoriously abridged the complexity of the piece to the cliché of two interwoven detective storylines (e.g. Kingston 1999, PT 1999, Gross 1999, Jones 2001). Interestingly, a much more comprehensive response dominates French reviews of the com-pany's work (e.g. Héliot 2002 and 2008, Bouteillet 2008, Tanneur 2002 and 2004, Il 2001, Salino 2010, H. 2002, Darge 2004). In scholarship, the singularity of Complicite is frequently reduced to labels such as 'physical', 'post-dramatic' or 'post-modern' theatre. Attractive as they are, such categorisations tend to mystify the peculiarities of the company and leave the most prominent features of its aesthetics untouched.

Attempts to accommodate the *oeuvre* of Complicite to the paradigm of text-centred dramatic theatre seem similarly inadequate. Because the position of the playwright prevailed in much British theatre till—at least—the turn of the millennium (Rebellato 1999), scholarship established evaluative norms that were antagonistic to more radically pronounced influences of continental experimentation.[2] This is, perhaps, best illustrated by Peter Brook's assertion that 'The English have a fine, long and wonderful tradition. Simon McBurney and Complicite are not part of it' (quoted by McBurney in Chia 2013). In the initial stages of the company's development, this tendency increased the awkwardness of Complicite's ambitions of achieving autonomy in the medium of theatre. We may contemplate their contribution to the ongoing shift in theatre practice in Britain, but even this commonly accepted observation has not, as yet, attracted sufficient scholarly attention.

In the late twentieth century, the conventions and devices employed by Complicite were common—or mandatory—in continental and global experimental theatre influenced by Craig, Meyerhold, Reinhardt, Artaud, Brecht, Suzuki, Kantor, Grotowski, Barbra, Staniewski and others,[3] and yet they were considered awkward in the context of British text-centred dramatic theatre. In this sense the London-based company with international aspirations promoted a 'semiotic explosion' that attempted to blend continental avant-garde experimentation with more traditional aspects of British drama. The explosion was strengthened by the assimilation of conventions emerging from non-institutional theatre forms such as *commedia dell'arte*, improvisation, clowning and street performance. Such accommodation of external elements prompted reciprocity. This astonishing fusion has been decisive for the singularity of Complicite's aesthetics. For example, the explicit meta-theatrical orientation that emerges from continental experimentation merges with a typically British mastery when it comes to depicting a well-made storyline.

THE ENCOUNTER, OR COMPLICITE IN SEPTEMBER 2015

As with any study of a 'living organism', questions arise concerning its most recent state. Complicite has continued to work in a number of fields. The creative education programme included events ranging from teaching workshops held in schools, through open workshops involving theatre-makers, to more specific projects such as *Embodying Maths, The Intensive Cancer University* and *Like Mother, Like Daughter*.[4] Intensive creative teaching is nothing new for the company and dates back to the early workshops on mime, mask, *commedia dell'arte* and other similar forms of theatre offered in the 1980s. Throughout the years, however, their educational activities have changed in nature and the company has developed a network of associates and collaborators who conduct a wide range of training. Education, now under the leadership of Poppy Keeling, involves cooperation with institutions such as Why Not Theatre (Toronto), the Battersea Arts Centre (London), John Lyon's Charity, Sheffield Hallam University and schools from London and elsewhere.

Since early 2015 Complicite's website has been in the process of renewal. This involves a general rearrangement of layout, provides a thorough update of written and audiovisual documentation and vastly expands available online resources such as photographs, resource packs, research and development materials, rehearsal notes, interviews and film documentaries. Although the website renewal is not yet complete, it will certainly be a major online source for any future study of the company's work.

In April 2015 Complicite published the second edition of Simon McBurney's collection of essays, *Who You Hear It from*, which includes two additional narratives. Part One now finishes with 'The real art underground' where McBurney's impressions of Werner Herzog and his 3D film on the Chauvet cave are mixed with memories of his parents, recollections from childhood and hints at collaboration with John Berger on *The Vertical Line*. The other new essay is called 'Mystery and revelation in Moscow' and is placed last in Part Two. The narrative focuses on key moments in McBurney's recent visit to the capital of Russia, suggested by his brother, Gerald, when he heard of the plans to produce Bulgakov's *The Master and Margarita*. Apart from these essays, there are some minor editorial changes in what is now a 133-page book. These include graphic underscoring of the title and author on the front cover, a new lead quote on page 46, an update in 'A Note on the Author' and one additional name in the final acknowledgements (Dina Mousawi). In spite of the shifts all these changes introduce, they do not alter the overall implications of *Who You Hear It from* discussed in Chap. 2. On the contrary, the decision to publish a revised edition of this concise volume proves the prominence given to this volume by the company and the readership.

McBurney's Artistic Signature

More importantly, *The Encounter*—a new production credited to Complicite/Simon McBurney and inspired by Petru Popescu's book *Amazon Beaming*—had its world premiere on 8 August 2015 at the Edinburgh International Festival.[5] It then toured to Théâtre Vidy-Lausanne in Switzerland (8–12 September), and the Bristol Old Vic (18–20 September), and will be staged at the Warwick Arts Centre (10–11 October), the Barbican in London (12 February—6 March 2016), HOME in Manchester (16–19 March 2016) and the Onassis Cultural Centre in Athens (1–3 April 2016). Enthusiastic reactions of audiences and critics mean that *The Encounter* will certainly continue its tour. The production is in the early stages of its emerging 'artistic life' and as such cannot be fully grasped: it may develop in a number of ways.

The Encounter marks a radical shift after *Lionboy* and other recent productions. McBurney's artistic signature is clearly evident in this two-hour one-man show where sonic tissue dominates over the visual. The performance involves an ensemble consisting of himself in the role of actor/director, and the 'invisible' team of technicians, producers and creatives. During the performance McBurney creates many characters and performs numerous actions, which include speaking, listening, dancing, walking, running, sitting at the table, drinking mineral water, talking on the phone, taking pictures, producing sounds by clasping hands, chest and other parts of the body, shaking a bottle of mineral water, delivering recorded interviews from his phone, modulating, looping and editing sounds, destroying the stage design, reading aloud a passage from *Amazon Beaming*, eating crisps, controlling the audience and removing his top. Simple as his actions are, they establish the basis for the stage language. They stress the materiality of the stage world and simultaneously contribute to the creation of the fictional/presented reality. It is clear from the very beginning that all those gathered in the theatre are involved in an act of communication happening on stage here and now and at the same time are participating in the creative interpretation of Loren McIntyre's adventures presented in *Amazon Beaming*. Under these circumstances one gesture of the performer may transform a bamboo stick into the cockpit of a plane landing on the Amazon river, and in a later episode the same stick may represent a well-crafted arrow delivered by a tribesman as a gift. The language of the stage creates its own rules and they do not depend on the principles of similarity or representation.

OUTSIDER

There are numerous echoes of the poetics of *Who You Hear from* in *The Encounter*. The main storyline is narrated from the perspective of Loren McIntyre—an American photographer—who in 1969 wished to publish in the *National Geographic* the first photographic documentation of the Mayoruna people, an indigenous tribe that was believed to live in total isolation from the outer world. After his voluntary landing in the wilderness of the Amazonian jungle (the remote Javari Valley), McIntyre soon finds the tribe. While pursuing them, he becomes disconnected from all traces of modern civilisation. He joins the tribe and lives with them. Little by little he gets used to their rudimentary lifestyle and its vulnerable, unsettled character. One day the few remains of his previous life—such as shoes and a watch—are burnt in a symbolic gesture by the natives. Moreover, his camera—the main motivation for his eccentric adventure—is destroyed by a monkey, together with rolls of film. This means, there will be no photographic record of his exploration for the *National Geographic*.

McIntyre's position as a total outsider is explicit. There is no way to overcome the clash of modern and ancient visions of the world. At the beginning, the visitor is unable to communicate with the inhabitants of the jungle in any language. The Mayoruna people know none of the European languages, just as McIntyre knows none of their dialects. At one point, however, with some disbelief, McIntyre realises that he is able to exchange basic thoughts with one of the members of the tribe (Barnacle) in 'the other'/ancient/non-verbal language. Communication is made even more efficient after meeting Cambio, an interpreter who has learned some of the basics of Portuguese while working as a kidnapped servant to a white radio operator.

The Encounter uses the phrase 'some of us are friends' as one of its refrains. This is the first telepathic message that McIntyre receives from Barnacle. The phrase is later repeated several times, and it closes the main part of the performance. In a sense, the meaning of the phrase echoes the title of McBurney's collection of essays. Both 'some of us are friends [and some of us are enemies]' and '[it is important] who you hear it from' focus our attention on the relationships between human beings. They depend on our decisions about whom to rely on. Proper choices may help overcome even the most extreme estrangement. For this reason, the meeting between McIntyre and Barnacle parallels the one described in the essay 'To kill a caribou (and feast on its guts)' when the 18-year-old Simon McBurney meets his Inuit peer named Roger. In both cases the recollection of an individual acquires the status of an archetypal generalisation. In the world of McBurney there is a chance to commune with the other.

FAMILY BONDS

The story of Loren McIntyre is embedded in several compositional frames. The one which structures the narrative situation is the most intriguing as it confirms the prominence of family bonds. It is a night when McBurney/performer/father is left alone with his six-year-old daughter, who is represented by a recorded voice. She has problems with sleeping and interrupts her working father by pointed and appropriate questions concerning incessant phone calls and the presence of a strange head in his room (i.e. the microphone). She also asks him why he is speaking to himself or wearing his shoes at home 'when mummy says you mustn't'. The daughter also asks for something to eat, and for a story to be read so as to send her to sleep. Indeed, she finally falls asleep when McBurney/father reads her a fairy-tale-like passage from *Amazon Beaming*.

The theme of family bonds opens the entire show. In what seems to be a casual introduction ('prologue') that is meant to fill time while spectators who are late are given the chance to take their seats, McBurney comments on the numerous photographs of his kids that are on his mobile. The ironic comment that the number of pictures taken within the last two weeks exceeds that of all the photographs taken during his own childhood leads him to the discussion of how much these photographs participate in shaping ('editing') the narrative of his kid's childhood. He then briefly alludes to the sparse pictures taken during the childhood of his parents and takes a 'selfie' that is meant to prove to his daughter that he really works in the evenings. As with each well-crafted '*lazzi*', this generates an overall outburst of laughter.

THEATRE-MAKER

The role of a father is thus paired with that of a theatre-maker. *The Encounter* explores the specificity of ongoing theatre *semiosis* in a radical way. By modelling the communication via microphones and headphones, Complicite/McBurney not only stresses the dominance of sonic—not visual—tissue but also reshapes the usual relations between members of the audience. The paradox of being alone (isolated from others by headphones) and the communal sense of forming the collective known as an audience (individual spectators are well aware that others are following the same story) is made even stronger when McBurney introduces a degree of intimacy between himself and each spectator. He achieves this by the simple means of 'breathing the air' into spectators' right ears through headphones. Just as he has said a moment earlier, the sound of this exhalation tricks the audience into believing that it makes our right ears a bit warmer. Each member of the audience is meant to experience the feeling that their nervous system habitually reacts to sound rather than to physical stimuli. All this strengthens the impression of the singularity of theatre communication.

In the work of Complicite, the prologue frequently fulfils the role of a 'curtain' that demarcates the boundaries of 'normal life' and 'an act of theatre communication'. In *The Encounter*, McBurney begins the performance with no unnecessary delay (or, as in Bristol, even a couple of minutes early). He disregards the illusion of the fourth wall by delivering his introductory monologue directly to the audience and alluding to some generally known biographical information (his kids, his profession, his being a Londoner). The auto-referentiality of the prologue is strengthened when he gets involved in the dialogue with the recorded voices of other people, including his daughter and Professor Marcus du Sautoy, a mathematician from Oxford who collaborated with Complicite on *A Disappearing Number*.

This dimension of the performance is particularly noticeable when McBurney is arguing with the recorded voice of his past self. He moves around the binaural head/microphone situated in the middle of the stage as if to preserve the circular proxemics between his two selves. It is now clear that the central position of the head/microphone is not accidental—it is endowed with the totemic prominence of a device that is capable of linking individuals, cultures and merging modern and ancient times. The meanings created onstage are intertwined with those gathered in the Amazonian jungle. The binaural head/microphone/totem accompanied the ensemble in their expedition to the Amazonian jungle where many of the sounds used in the play were recorded (see McBurney's 'Amazon Diaries' and Fry 2015).

THE NOMAD LIFE

In *The Encounter* the notion of a nomadic life is more than a convenient metaphor: the lifestyle of the Mayoruna people may indeed be best described as 'nomadic'. Their permanent escape from the annihilating dangers brought by the civilisation of white people—the names of Hernando Cortez and Francisco Pizarro are mentioned at one point—have determined most of their habits and customs. In constant motion through the jungle, they skilfully build transient villages in the woods, then leave them behind shortly afterwards and move to another location. This is most puzzling for McIntyre, especially when, after some time, their motion is paired with the obsession of a mythical 'return'. For the Mayoruna people the idea of a 'return' develops into the urgency of the total annihilation of all their material belongings. Joyful as it is, the ritual of 'burning it all' in the fire is understood by them as a most exciting occasion: freeing them from the burden of the past.

At this point of the performance, McBurney intermingles various aspects of communication by posing the question as to what would happen if modern man followed their example. By juxtaposing the tribal worldview of the Mayoruna people with metropolitan desires of challenging the primacy of material consumerism, he incorporates an act of violent destruction into the world of the stage. When shouting slogans encouraging the burning of cosmopolitan centres such as Washington and San Francisco, McBurney rapidly builds a savage aggression that suddenly dominates the performance. His destruction of the stage design (breaking a green glass bottle, kicking the loudspeaker, hammering the table and so on) resembles the performative act of destroying instruments by The Who, Jimi Hendrix, Nirvana and the like. There is, however, much irony in this onstage act of destruction. In spite of his ferocious idea of finishing with the destruction of his Iphone, McBurney/performer immediately changes his mind once the phone rings. Modern man cannot help it; he suspends the destruction and answers the phone. So much for the nomadic ethos of twenty-first-century man.

CONFRONTATIONS

As elsewhere in Complicite, the model of the world that emerges from *The Encounter* abounds in juxtapositions and confrontations. This is already explicit in the title. The meeting between Loren McIntyre and the Mayoruna people not only enables McBurney to juxtapose an ancient culture rooted in 'long-gone' beliefs with the 'virtues' of modern Western civilisation, but also to depict the ambiguities underlying this juxtaposition. When confronted with the tribe's natural symbiosis with the Amazonian jungle, our exhausting pursuit of material goods—epitomised by the gold of the conquistadors—turns into a mere, if destructive, trifle. Innovations such as shoes, cameras and Iphones may be precious to us but they in no way make us better human beings. Indigenous as it is, the system of values of the Mayoruna people surprisingly echoes many of the dreams, desires and fears of humankind in the twenty-first century. The encounter between an ancient axiology of tribesmen with that of modern man poses many similar questions.

Juxtapositions are equally strong when we consider spatio-temporal imagery. The interface between McIntyre's narrated story and the meta-theatrical plane where McBurney/performer directs his words to the audience through the fourth wall makes us immediately aware of a number of them:

- the story of McIntyre (1969) vs the here and now of the performance (2015),
- the Amazonian jungle vs the Western world,
- America of McIntyre vs the stage world of McBurney,
- ancient beliefs vs myths of the present,
- narrated story vs theatre communication,
- the world of the stage vs the perspective of the audience.

In addition to this, a number of devices used by Complicite/McBurney strengthen the discrepancy between the visual and sonic channels of communication. These, in turn, lay emphasis on the conventionality of theatre communication and simultaneously on its exceptional quality of liveness. The frictions between these two principles—i.e. conventionality and liveness—unavoidably lead to internal contradictions, strengthen the semantics of paradox and increase the fluctuating character of all the employed structures.

THE MULTIPLICATION OF VARIANTS

Even at this early stage in the evolution of the performance it is clear that it leaves space for multiplying variants. A brief comparison between the archival material gathered during the research and development phase of work, workshops and scripts documenting presentations in Berlin (workshop), Edinburgh (world premiere), Switzerland and Bristol indicates the direction in the creative process taken so far. This seems to reflect the general method the company has developed and which was discussed in earlier chapters of this book. The main difference is that, for the first time, a substantial part of the archival material is available to the general public on Complicite's website. Thus, in the case of *The Encounter*, theatre *semiosis* is embedded in a more general framework that provides extra-theatrical information for a more comprehensive understanding of the performance.

As usual, the prologue serves well to illustrate the direction of some of these changes. In the version of the script dated 18 April 2015,[6] Simon McBurney greets the audience, introduces himself and explains why he has decided to present a workshop version of a new piece to the public in Berlin. This is because Thomas Ostermeier—the director of 'this festival' (i.e. Festival of International New Drama)—has invited him for what is described as a public rehearsal. By providing an anecdotal description of his reaction to Ostermeier's invitation, McBurney not only underscores the unfinished character of his show but also defines relations between the stage and the audience. There appears to be a degree of familiarity, exceptionality (it is a rare occasion to see Complicite's work in progress) and unexpectedness as to what might happen (these are still unfinished fragments, so who knows if it will work well). At one moment, McBurney takes a photo of a spectator for posterity and comments on the linguistic difference between the German phrase 'ein Bild machen' (making a portrait) and the English 'take a photograph', by which he juxtaposes the stage and the audience in a humorous way.

Situational as it is, the prologue makes extensive use of an improvisation-like style that creates the impression of an exceptional one-time theatre experience in which everybody gathered in the Schaubuehne Berlin participates. As we might expect, these fluctuating elements are well structured and intermingled with others that recur in later variants of the performance. Examples of this abound: the photographs of children on the phone, the *lazzi* of destroying the only VHS with childhood memories, the motif of telling a story, the memory of the reading of bedtime stories by his father, the intimacy provided by headphones, the transmission of voice, the trickery of the brain, altering the pitch of the voice, the audience's closing their eyes, breathing in the right ear, the bottle of water, scissors, the mosquito, speaking to his past self, and many others. Thus, in spite of the unfinished nature of the Berlin workshop, the 'prologue' is structured in a very similar way to the 'prologue' of *A Minute Too Late*: it stresses the liveness of theatre communication and simultaneously probes invariant elements of the production.

The other Schaubuehne script (undated) does not mention the name of Ostermeier, and shortens the opening part to establish the here and now of the presentation. After naming the show a public rehearsal, there are a few announcements concerning the headphones, the live speech, the reasons for speaking in English, the suggestion that tomorrow's show will have subtitles. Interestingly, the subsequent part of the prologue echoes in a more or less precise way most of the passages from the 18 April 2015 script. But its fluctuating character is stressed by some textual uncertainties. They are presented as questions or options that are yet to be developed.

In this version, the conversation between the live (2015) and recorded (2011) selves of McBurney is far more personal. The autobiographic dimension develops so much that the live self of 'Simon' decides to conclude it by formulating the question of whether the audience should know so much about his private life. Another passage which is more developed is that described by the recorded voice of Simon [McBurney] and Judith [Dimant]. It is set in 2011 and concerns McBurney's journey to Paris to meet Petru Popescu. A short description of the author of *Amazon Beaming* and some details on McBurney's reading of his book over the years are provided. Towards the end of the 'Opening', the 2014 self of McBurney appears and describes himself as trying to work at home, while being disturbed by the internet and the phone. In the two Bristol performances of 20 September 2015 (matinee and evening) this passage was transformed into a more sketchily depicted narrative situation.

When compared with the Berlin version, the script of the workshop presentation at Shoreditch Town Hall (named as 'WIP showing 11 April 2013') is more self-referential and concerned mainly with phatic experiments with the sonic transmission of the voice from microphone to headphones. The actual communicative situation is referred to by mentioning the names of Marcus du Sautoy and Martin Crimp as listeners, and Simon McBurney seems to be more engrossed in the improvised expression of his thoughts and emotions when performing in front of the audience. Although there are some elements that reappear in later versions (e.g. putting on headphones, closing eyes, drinking water, scissors, breathing in the right ear, the conversation of the selves), the major part of the monologue is not reflected in later versions.

The script dated '10 August 2015' is of particular significance because it reflects the shape of *The Encounter* in the world premiere. Generally speaking, the prologue is structured in accordance with the overall arrangement of its Berlin version. There are obvious alterations that reflect the here and now of the communication: rather than mentioning Thomas Ostermeier's invitation, McBurney explores the fictional (abstract) character of notions such as the United Kingdom, Europe, a pope, Pope Francis, God, 7:30 pm (i.e. the time the performance begins) or money. And yet, he stresses that these abstract and conventionally made-up notions are decisive for the collective imagination since the stories they create are crucial for shaping the world we live in. He then explains to the audience how responsible he feels for the stories he tells his children (by analogy the stories he tells his audiences). Apparently, marginal comment on the kind of responsibility we owe to forthcoming generations tells us a lot about McBurney's attitude towards notions such as truth, fiction and illusion.

Some details added in the Edinburgh version of *The Encounter* are striking. First, there is the comment on the Mickey Mouse quality of the voice after altering its pitch from the 'Loren McIntyre' microphone to the 'normal' voice of McBurney. Second, the direction of the binaural microphone/head/totem is changed at one point from the initial position in which it faces the audience (i.e. the perspective of actors) to one reflecting the perspective of spectators. This changes the proxemics of the soundscape and overlaps the visual and aural dimensions of communication. The right ear of the binaural reflects the right ear/headphone, and the left is left. The same is true now of the forward and backward noises. Through this simple gesture of replacing the microphone, the visual and aural aspects of communication cease to be contradictory. Third, the speaker takes us to his London home/office and opens the window (created by a horizontal bamboo stick) to let us hear the noise of the street. For those who remember the associations of similar noise in the essay 'All in the mind', this action has some added significance (the noise of the street = the traces of the dead). Finally, we can hear the voices of his daughter, Noma, Marcus [du Sautoy], and witness the phone conversation with Rebecca [Spooner] and others.

Later presentations of *The Encounter*—even though there have not yet been that many—involved some minor changes in the prologue. When presented at Théâtre Vidy-Lausanne in Switzerland, McBurney did the introduction in French (Claire Gilbert in conversation). In Bristol, he was more attentive to dispersing the opening delineation of the performance and stressed at the beginning that we were still waiting for the latecomers to take their seats. He told the audience to switch off their mobile phones, warning us that in the previous show the person whose phone rang was recognised. Finally, he introduced the moment of breathing the air in the right ear by saying it should make us feel the warmth. This is perhaps more persuasive than the reverse order of the earlier versions (including the Edinburgh one).

THE AESTHETICS OF COMPLICITE

Even such a provisional analysis of *The Encounter* seems to confirm that there is some value in the proposed vision of the aesthetics of Complicite, even when dealing with productions that have not been part of my study. When discussing the artistic signature, the logic of the plot, the world of the stage, the textual tissue, the overall aesthetics and kaleidoscopic fragmentariness, *The Encounter* could not be taken into detailed consideration for the simple reason that the main part of the book was completed before its world premiere. And yet, I feel, the discussion provides a set of features (whatever we name them: fields of association, methods of theatre-making, artistic mechanisms, aesthetic strategies, semiotic principles or otherwise), and an exploration of the way in which these function in particular productions, which may be applied—albeit with substantial modifications at times—when experiencing various levels of communication in our singular ways and for varied purposes. The vision of the company's aesthetics—I would maintain—is as useful for individual performances as it is for the entire *oeuvre*.

The Encounter proves that a discussion of the aesthetics of Complicite is a work in progress. Artistic and aesthetic objectives developed by the company since 1983 find new and innovative ways of expression and create, as ever, original meanings. The Mayoruna people clearly echo the Iceman from *Mnemonic*, but when juxtaposing their worlds with the worldview of a modern man, many analogies arise as differences. This book, perhaps, provides material that may encourage some of us to watch, think and interpret performances by Complicite/Simon McBurney in the light of the earlier achievements of the company. Theatre communication is a singular experience that leads to the appreciation—or denunciation—of artistic and aesthetic values and hopefully some observations provided in *Complicite, Theatre and Aesthetics: from Scraps of Leather* may contribute to this process.

But the only way to validate a theatre study is by confronting its assumptions and conclusions with the real thing—a live performance. In September 2015 Complicite made plans for the future, which means that confrontation is still possible.

Sopot, February 2016

NOTES

1. The case of *Lionboy* is special as it is conceived for young audiences.

2. McBurney approaches the issue in the following way: 'Why are we on the outside of British theatre? For me, what you see is as important as what you hear. In the majority of English theatre, what you see is a sort of vague window dressing, in relation to the rest of it. And our critics are by and large visually and theatrically illiterate. They might know their text, but what they see—they have absolutely no idea' (Chia 2013).

3. In Complicite, we may observe, for example, the whole spectrum of devices that were listed by Hans-Thies Lehmann as typical features of contemporary theatre in his seminal, if disappointingly schematic, *Post-dramatic Theatre*.

4. Poppy Keeling provides the following summary of Complicite's creative education programme: '*Like Mother, Like Daughter* involved 24 women from London and ran at the Battersea Arts Centre from 26 May to 6 June. *Embodying Maths* is conducted in 4 primary schools from London with approximately 60 children at each school this year. The company plans to add 10 more schools next year. There are 15 participants in the 2015 programme of *The Intensive Cancer University* which covers 9 meetings that took place at theatres/cinemas and in the Complicite office. In 2014/15 Complicite worked with more than 2,500 people in the teaching workshops in schools, colleges, clubs and other institutions across the UK and internationally' (email correspondence).

5. As the programme of the festival announces, the performance was presented 13 times between 8 and 23 August, including the preview on 7 August (Edinburgh programme: 19-20).

6. In the version dated 17 April 2015, the text of 'THE INTRODUCTION' is not provided. The text is marked by a hyphen and immediately precedes the scene '2. OVER THE OCEAN FOREST'. In the festival programme the show is named as 'Amazon Beaming: Work in Progress'.

BIBLIOGRAPHY

PRIMARY SOURCES

Published Plays, Books, Resource Packs and Essays

Alexander, Catherine. 1997a. *The Caucasian Chalk Circle Background Pack.* London: Theatre de Complicite.

Alexander, Catherine. 1997b. *The Chairs: The Story of a Play.* Resource Pack. London: Theatre de Complicite.

Alexander, Catherine. 2001. *Complicite: Teachers Notes—Devising.* Resource Pack. London: Complicite.

Alexander, Catherine, Natasha Freedman and Victoria Gould. [No date.] *A Disappearing Number Information Pack.* London: Complicite.

Complicite. 2000. *Light.* London: Oberon Books.

Complicite. 2001. *Mnemonic.* London: Methuen.

Complicite. 2003. *Plays 1: The Street of Crocodiles, The Three Lives of Lucie Cabrol, Mnemonic.* London: Methuen.

Complicite. 2004. *Complicite. Twenty One Years 1983–2004.* London: Complicite.

Complicite. 2008. *A Disappearing Number.* London: Oberon Books.

Complicite. 2010. *Rehearsal Notes: A Visual Essay of the Unique Working Methods of the Company.* London: Complicite.

Complicite. 2014. *Lionboy.* Adaptation by Marcello Dos Santos. London: Nick Hern Books.

McBurney, Simon. 2012. *Who You Hear It from.* 1st edition. London: Complicite.

McBurney, Simon. 2015. *Who You Hear It from.* 2nd revised edition. London: Complicite.

Rintoul, Douglas and Natasha Freedman. [No date.] *Measure for Measure Background Pack.* London: Complicite and the National Theatre.

© The Author(s) 2016

223

T. Wiśniewski, *Complicite, Theatre and Aesthetics,*

DOI 10.1007/978-3-319-33443-1

Sparshatt, Kate [ed.]. [No date.] *The Street of Crocodiles Information Pack*, London: Theatre de Complicite.

Theatre de Complicite. 1995a. *The Three Lives of Lucie Cabrol*. London: Methuen Drama.

Theatre de Complicite. 1995b. *The Three Lives of Lucie Cabrol. A Body of Work*. Resource Pack. London: Theatre de Complicite.

Theatre de Complicite. 1999a. *Mnemonic*. London: Methuen.

Theatre de Complicite. 1999b. *The Street of Crocodiles*. London: Methuen.

Uncollected Essays and Notes by Simon McBurney (Selected)

McBurney, Simon. [Untitled note] in *Out of the House* programme.

McBurney, Simon. 'Let it happen' in *Brick*: 147–50.

McBurney, Simon. 'Touching history: Private Ryan and the filming of war' in *Brick*, No 62: 24–32.

McBurney, Simon. 1997. 'Watching your back'. In *The Caucasian Chalk Circle* programme.

McBurney, Simon. 2002. 'On directing'.

McBurney, Simon. 2003. 'Prologue'. In *Complicite: Plays 1*: ix–xii.

McBurney, Simon. 2004. [Untitled introduction.] In *Complicite. Twenty One Years 1983–2004*: 3–4.

McBurney, Simon. 2009. 'Here'. In *Endgame* programme.

McBurney, Simon. 2009a. 'I'm going to die'. *Guardian*, 18 November.

McBurney, Simon. 2009b. 'My week: Simon McBurney'. *Guardian*, 27 September.

McBurney, Simon. 2010a. 'Note from the director'. In *A Disappearing Number* programme: 3.

McBurney, Simon. 2010b. 'Preface'. In *Rehearsal Notes*: 9–12.

McBurney, Simon. 2012. 'Mystery and revelation in Moscow'. In *The Master and Margarita* programme: 7–8.

McBurney, Simon. 2013. 'Silent approval'. In *The Magic Flute* programme: 9–13.

McBurney, Simon. 2015. 'We see only what we want to see'. In *The Encounter* programme (inside).

McBurney, Simon and Mark Wheatley. 2003. 'Note on the script'. In *Complicite: Plays 1*: 4–5.

Notes and Essays by Other Company Associates (Selected)

Alexander, Catherine. 2010. 'Complicite—*The Elephant Vanishes (2003/4)*—The elephant and keeper have vanished completely… They will never be coming back'. In *Making Contemporary Theatre: International Rehearsal Processes*,

Jen Harvie and Andy Lavender (eds): 59–80. Manchester: Manchester University Press.

Bell, Clive. 2010. 'Beyond all endurance'. In *Shun-kin* programme: 12–13.

Berger, John. 1995. 'John Berger on Theatre de Complicite'. In *The Three Lives of Lucie Cabrol*: 5 (unnumbered).

Canny, Steven. 2000. 'Rehearsing *Light*'. In *Light*: 85–103.

Dimant, Judith. 2010. 'Foreword'. In *Rehearsal Notes*: 7.

Dodd, Stephen. 2010. 'An outstanding storyteller'. In *Shun-kin* programme: 10–11.

Houben, Josef. [Untitled poster.] In *Out of the House* programme.

Margolies, Eleanor. 2010. 'The street of animation'. In *Shun-kin* programme: 6–7.

McBurney, Gerald. [Untitled note.] In *Out of the House* programme.

McBurney, Gerald. 1997. 'Mountain music'. In *The Caucasian Chalk Circle* programme.

Noda, Manabu. 2010. 'A moment of truth or why the West misunderstands Japanese culture'. In *Shun-kin* programme: 8–9.

Ratcliffe, Michael. 1995. 'Collusion between celebrants'. In *The Three Lives of Lucie Cabrol*: 6–9 (unnumbered).

Sautoy, Marcus du. 'Mozart and maths'. In *The Magic Flute* programme: 22–4.

Wigmore, Richard. 'A heterogeneous opera'. In *The Magic Flute* programme: 18–21.

INTERVIEWS, SPEECHES AND PUBLIC EVENTS (SELECTED)

Chia, Adeline. 2013. 'Interview: Simon McBurney on origins of Complicite'. 29 August. Online recording.

Dickson, Andrew. 2010. 'Simon McBurney: Complicite is a nomadic family'. *Guardian* Interview. Online recording.

Frizzell, Nell. 2013. 'Judith Dimant: producing Complicite'. 2 July. Online recording.

Fry, Gareth. 2015. 'Capturing sound for Complicite's *The Encounter*'. *The Stage*. 29 September.

Houben, Jos. 2013. 'Theatre is something very simple, very simple'. Interview by Tomasz Wiśniewski. In *A Between Almanach for the Year 2013*: 99–109.

Jacques, Adam. 2011. 'How we met: Simon McBurney and Kathryn Hunter'. *Independent*. 3 September.

Jeffreys, Louise. 2013. 'Complicite at 30: Simon McBurney and Judith Dimant in conversation'. National Theatre Discover. Online recording.

Kelting, Lily. 2015. 'Simon McBurney: "It's all there, isn't it?"' Exberliner. 16 December.

Knapper, Stephen. 2010. 'Simon McBurney: shifting under/soaring over the boundaries of Europe'. In Maria M. Delgado and Dan Rebellato (eds), *Contemporary European Theatre Directors*. London: Routledge, pp. 233–48.

Lecoq, Fay. 2013. 'Beautiful masks, or "That's what I know I'm goot at"'. Interview by Tomasz Wiśniewski. In *A Between Almanach for the Year 2013*: 90–8.

Levine, Michael. 2011. 'The legend library'. Interview by R.H. Thompson. Theatre Museum Canada. Online recording.

Magni, Marcello. 2013. 'The instinctiveness and liveness of a child'. Interview by Tomasz Wiśniewski. In *A Between Almanach for the Year 2013*: 110–16.

Magni, Marcello. 2015. 'From the physical theatre to the theatre of the word'. Interview by Tomasz Wiśniewski. In *Stories for the Future. A Between Almanach for the Year 2015*: 137–41.

McBurney, Simon. 2011. 'French passions: Simon McBurney on Rabelais'. In conversation with Boyd Tomkin. Culturetheque IFRU. 1:02:24. Online recording.

McBurney, Simon. 2013. 'Illusion'. A lecture at the University of Michigan: Ann Arbor. Recording.

McBurney, Simon. 2014. 'Pensamento em processo'. A meeting with the audience at MITsp—Mostra Internacional de Teatro de São Paulo, Brasil. 8 March. Recording.

Mendus, Clive. 2006. '"Competitive co-operation": playing with Theatre de Complicite'. In conversation with Maria Shevtsova. *New Theatre Quarterly*, 22:3 (August): 257–67.

Morris, Tim. 'Tim Morris interviews Simon McBurney'. Audio recording. Royal National Theatre Platform.

Pengilley, Teri. 2009. 'Simon McBurney: "It's chaos. You start with a bomb…"' In *The Big Interview*, 23 January.

Rintoul, Douglas. 2013. 'Work in transition'. Interview by Tomasz Wiśniewski. In *A Between Almanach for the Year 2013*: 120–3.

Sebba, Anne. 2008. 'In praise of diasporas. Simon McBurney and Adam Thirlwell discuss place, memory, imagination of the work of Bruno Schulz with Anne Sebba at Jewish Book Week, March 2nd'. *Jewish Quarterly*, Spring, No 209: 34–7.

Trueman, Matt. 2013. 'Interview: the founders of Complicité'. *Financial Times*. 24 May.

Williams, David. 2005. 'Simon McBurney (1957–)'. Entry in *Fifty Key Theatre Directors*, Shomit Mitter and Maria Shevtsova (eds). London and New York: Routledge, pp. 252–6.

Gould Victoria. 2010. 'Nothing is off limits apart from not turning up'. Interview by Sanjna Kapoor and Sameera Iyengar. In *A Disappearing Number* programme: 13–14.

AUDIOVISUAL RECORDINGS (SELECTED)

Complicite. *To the Wedding.* Radio play.

Complicite. 2002. *Mnemonic.* Radio play. Released in 2002.

Complicite. 2008. *A Disappearing Number.* Radio play. First broadcast BBC Radio 3 on 21 September 2008.

Laillias, Jean-Claude (directeur de la collection). 2006. *Les deux voyages do Jacques Lecoq.* DVD. Entrer en Théâtre. On Line Productions.

Miklaszewski, Krzysztof. 1992. *Street of Crocodiles in Thames.*

A Disappearing Number. 3 October 2011. *National Theatre Live.*

A Disappearing Number. 19 September 2007. Barbican Centre, National Archive of Performance.

A Minute Too Late. 18 February 2005. National Theatre Archive.

The Caucasian Chalk Circle. 14 June 1997. National Theatre (Olivier).

The Chairs. 9 December 1997. Evening performance. Royal Court Downstairs (Duke of York's). National Video Archive.

Endgame. 25 November 2009. Matinée. Theatre Museum.

Foe (fragment). Date unknown. Copenhagen.

Light. 2000. Theatre Museum Archive.

McBurney, Simon. 2015. 'Amazon diaries'. Film documentary. http://www.complicite.org/encounterresource/. Viewed on 30 September 2015.

Measure for Measure. 16 March 2006. National Theatre (Lyttleton). Evening performance. Theatre Museum Archive.

Mnemonic. 3 February 2001. National Theatre Archive.

Mnemonic. January 2000. Riverside Studios. Theatre Museum.

The Caucasian Chalk Circle. 14 June 1997. Theatre Museum.

Please, Please, Please. Date unknown. Video recording.

The Street of Crocodiles. 4 November 1994. Evening performance. Whitehall Theatre. Theatre Museum.

The Elephant Vanishes. 17 September 2004. Evening performance. Theatre Museum.

The Master and Margarita. 4 April 2012. 2 DVDs. Theatre Museum.

The Noise of Time. 2001. BBC broadcast. Recording dated 2001. Copyrights 2000.

The Visit. 1991. A set of five DVDs. The National Theatre (The Lyttleton).

PROGRAMMES, NOTES AND POSTERS (SELECTED)

A Minute Too Late. 2005. NT January–April. Programme details book.

A Disappearing Number. 2010. Programme. Complicite.

A Dog's Heart. 2010. Programme. Complicite and ENO.

Lionboy. 2015. Programme. Complicite.

Shun-kin. 2011. Programme. Complicite/Simon McBurney (Barbican).
The Magic Flute. 2013. Programme. ENO and Complicite.
The Master and Margarita. 2012. Programme. Complicite/Simon McBurney (Barbican).
The Noise of Time. 2002. Programme. Complicite with the Brodsky Quartet. Performances at Theatre Royal Bath.
Out of a House Walked a Man. 1994. Programme.
Put It On Your Head. [No date.] Note on the show.
The Encounter. 2015. Programme to the 2015–16 tour.

REVIEWS AND ARTICLES OTHER SOURCES

Allain, Paul. 2013. 'Ways of hearing'. In *A Between Almanach for the Year 2013*: 145–58.
Allfree, Claire. 2012. 'A devilishly difficult plot'. Review of *The Master and Margarita*. *Metro*, 20 March.
Allfree, Claire. 2009. 'Keeping it real with Beckett'. Review of *Endgame*. *Metro*, 13 October: 37.
Babbage, Frances. Forthcoming. 'How books matter: theatre, adaptation and the life of texts'. In Tomasz Wiśniewski and Martin Blaszk (eds), *Between Page and Stage*. Gdańsk: WUG.
Barnett, Laura. 2007. 'Portrait of the artist: Annabel Arden, director'. *Guardian*, 4 December.
Billington, Michael. 1992. '*The Street of Crocodiles*'. Review. *Guardian*, 13 August.
Billington, Michael. 1999. 'Limitless possibilities'. Review of *Mnemonic*. *Guardian*, 26 November.
Billington, Michael. 2005. '*A Minute Too Late*'. Review. *Guardian*, 28 January.
Billington, Michael. 2013. 'Margaret Thatcher casts a long shadow over theatre and the arts'. *Guardian*, 8 April.
Bouteillet, Maïa. 2008. 'L'insoluble equation de McBurney'. Review of *A Disappearing Number. Liberation*, 1 October.
Bredin, Henrietta. 2009. 'Ready for anything'. *The Spectator*, 17 October: 52.
Burney [sic!], Simon. 2000. 'A juggling act'. *Independent*, 7 February: 12.
Calder, John. 2009. '*Endgame*: Beckett for a beginner?' Review. thecnj.co.uk, 13 November.
Campbell, Julie. 2010. '*Endgame* at the Duchess Theatre, London'. Review of *Endgame. The Beckett Circle. Le Circle de Beckett*, Spring 2010, vol. 33, no 1: 1–3.
Campos, Liliane. 2014. 'This is not a chair: Complicite's *Master and Margarita*'. *New Theatre Quarterly*, 30: 175–82.
Carter, Miranda. 1994. 'Out of the body experiences: The actress Kathryn Hunter is a master practitioner of the theatre of physical contortion, despite serious, permanent injury'. *Independent*, 11 May.

Costa, Maddy. 2004. 'Silent classic given soundtrack for today'. Review of *Pet Shop Boys Meet Eisenstein. Guardian*, 13 September.

Darge, Fabienne. 2004. 'Voyage hypnotique au coeur de la solitude des foules modernes'. *Le Monde*, 5 October.

De, Aditi. 2012. 'Theatre: Simon McBurney and Complicite—*Measure for Measure*'. Blog entry: Mulled Ink, 12 April, http://mulledink.blogspot.com/2012/04/theatre-simon-mcburney-and-complicite.html. Accessed on 22 December 2014.

Edwardes, Jane. 1999. '*Mnemonic*'. Review. *Time Out*, 30 November.

Freshwater, Helen. 2001. 'The ethics of indeterminacy: Theatre de Complicite's *Mnemonic*'. *New Theatre Quarterly*, 17 (3): 212–19.

Freud, Emma. 2011. 'Introduction to *A Disappearing Number—NT Live*'. Recording.

Il., A. 2001. 'L'imagination de McBurney'. Review of *Mnemonic. Le Figaro*, 22 February.

Jones, Oliver. 2001. '*Mnemonic*'. Review. *What's On*, 7 February: 61.

Gardner, Lyn. 2002. 'Why I go to the theatre'. Online.

Gardner, Lyn. 2003. '*Mnemonic*'. Review. *Guardian*, 8 January.

Gardner, Lyn. '*The Elephant Vanishes*'. Review. *Guardian*.

Giannachi, Gabriela and Mary Luckhurst (eds). 1999. *On Directing. Interviews with Directors*. London: Faber and Faber.

Gross, John. 1999. 'How to put the tragic into tragedy. *The Oresteia, Mnemonic, Jane Eyre*'. Review. *Sunday Telegraph*, 9 December.

H., A. 2002. 'Mémorable *Mnemonic*'. Review. *Le Figaro*, 16 December.

Héliot, Armelle. 2002. 'McBurney, la traverse des apparences'. Review of *Mnemonic. Le Figaro*, 11 December.

Héliot, Armelle. 2008. 'La fascinant voyage de Simon McBurney'. Review of *A Disappearing Number. Le Figaro*, 29 September.

Hitchings, Henry. 2012. 'Devilishly difficult, wonderfully nuts'. *Evening Standard*, 22 March: 33.

Isherwood, Charles. 2015. 'A valiant cub goes on the hunt: *Lionboy*, a fairy tale set in a dystopian future'. Review of *Lionboy. New York Times*, 25 January.

Kingston, Jeremy. 1999. '*Mnemonic*'. Review. *Times*, 26 November.

Knapper, Stephen. 2004. 'Complicite's Comintern: internationalism and *The Noise of Time*'. In *Contemporary Theatre Review*, vol. 14 (1): 61–73.

Lane, Harriet. 2005. 'Send in the clowns'. *Guardian*, 2 January.

Malinowska, Aneta Marta. 2014. *Staging the Scientist: The Representation of Science and Its Processes in American and British Drama*. Unpublished MA dissertation. Universidade Nova de Lisboa.

Marmion, Patrick. 1999. 'Wizardry on a wild-goose chase'. Review of *Mnemonic. Standard*, 26 November.

Martorell, Jordi. 2004. 'Pet Shop Boys meet Battleship Potemkin—Revolution in Trafalgar Square'. *In Defence of Marxism*. Blog entry. 14 September 2004, http://www.marxist.com/pet-shop-boys-meet-battleship-potemkin-revolution-in-trafalgar-square.htm. Accessed on 10 September 2014.

McCabe, Eamonn. 2005. 'Anarchy in the UK'. *Guardian*, 1 January: 16–20.

McKenna, Jon. 2013. 'How I met Simon McBurney'. In *A Between Almanach for the Year 2013*: 117–19.

Miklaszewski, Krzysztof. 2009. 'Bruno z Drohobycza nad Tamizą, czyli... rewelacja'. In Krzysztof Miklaszewski, *Zatracenie się w Schulzu. Historia pewnej fascynacji*. Warszawa: PWN, pp. 79–88.

Miklaszewski, Krzysztof. 2014. 'Schulz w Complicite, czyli brytyjska lekcja Kantorowskiego seansu'. Review of *The Street of Crocodiles*. *Topos*, 3: 35–9.

Murphy, Siobhan. 2009. 'Tragedy in the trash can'. Review of *Endgame*. *Metro*, 20 October: 27.

Murray, Simon. 2013. 'Jacques Lecoq and the Paris School, 1983–2013'. In *A Between Almanach for the Year 2013*: 85–9.

Nathan, John. 2008. 'Judith Dimant: the woman who puts brilliance on the stage'. *Jewish Chronicle*, 17 October.

Nightingale, Benedict. 'Dedicated Inconstancy'. In *Barbican News*: 8–9.

Nightingale, Benedict. 2009. 'Simon McBurney turns Japanese as Complicite mount *Shun-Kin* at the Barbican'. Review of *Shun-kin*. *The Times*, 24 January.

Ojrzyńska, Katarzyna. 2012a. 'Teatr współtworzony według Complicite'. *Tekstualia*, 1: 41–54.

Ojrzyńska, Katarzyna. 2012b. 'Teatralny kalejdoskop Complicite'. *Topos*, 3: 39–45.

Overton, Tom. 2012. 'The British Library's John Berger Archive: From Page to Stage and Back Again.' Conference paper delivered at 'Between Page and Stage Conference'. 18 May.

PT. 1999. 'Memories are made of this'. Review of *Mnemonic*. *Independent*, 1 December.

Reinelt, Janelle. 2001. 'Performing Europe: Identity Formation for a "New" Europe'. In Helka Mäkinen, S.E. Wilmer and W.B. Worthen (eds), *Theatre, History and National Identities*. Helsinki: HUP, pp. 227–56.

Salino, Brigitte. 2010. 'Le theatre cruel et sublime de Simon McBurney'. Review of *Shun-kin*. *Le Monde*, 20 November.

Shenton, Mark. 2005. '*A Minute Too Late*'. Review. *What's on Stage*. January.

Shevtsova, Maria and Christopher Innes. 2009. *Directors/Directing: Conversations on Theatre*. Cambridge: Cambridge University Press.

Smyth, David. 2004. 'The Pet Shop Protest'. Review of *Pet Shop Boys Meet Eisenstein*. *Evening Standard*, 13 September.

Spencer, Charles. 1992. '*The Street of Crocodiles*'. Review. *Daily Telegraph*, 17 August.

Spencer, Charles. 1999. '*Mnemonic*: Miraculous, moving and mysterious'. Review. *Daily Telegraph*, 29 November.

Tanneur, Huques Le. 2002. '*Mnemonic*, prodigieux spectacle du Britannique Simon McBurney'. Review. *Ade*, 23 November, pp. 11–17.

Tanneur, Huques Le. 2004. 'Tokyo: Images d'un monde flottant'. Review of *The Elephant Vanishes*. *Aden (Scéne)*, 29 September, p. 29.

Taylor, Paul. 1996. 'Silence is powerful, especially on the stage'. Review of *Foe*. *Independent*, 9 March.

Taylor, Paul. 2005. '*A Minute Too Late*, Lyttelton, National Theatre, London'. Review. *Independent*, 1 February.

Wiśniewski, Tomasz. 2012a. 'Poezja sceny w teatrze Complicite: przykład *Ulicy Krokodyli* według Brunona Schulza' (Poetry of the stage in *The Street of Crocodiles* by Complicite). *Tekstualia*, 1: 55–66.

Wiśniewski, Tomasz. 2012b. 'The Textual Tissue of *Mnemonic* by Complicite'. In Katarzyna Pisarska and Andrzej Sławomir Kowalczyk (eds), *The Lives of Texts: Exploring the Metaphor*. Cambridge Scholars Publishing: Newcastle upon Tyne, pp. 129–40.

Wiśniewski, Tomasz. 2013a. 'Kształtowanie czasoprzestrzeni symbolicznej we współczesnym dramacie angielskim' (Symbolic potential of time-space imagery in contemporary English drama). In *Tekstualia: symbolizm czy symbolizmy* (*Symbolism or Symbolisms*). Electronic publication. 36 pages.

Wiśniewski, Tomasz. 2013b. 'Świat dźwięków w teatrze Complicite, czyli *Mnemoniczny* jako słuchowisko' (Soundscape in Complicite, or *Mnemonic* as a radio-play). *Tekstualia*, 1; 85–95.

Wiśniewski, Tomasz. 2013c. 'The Mathematics in a Dramatic Text—*A Disappearing Number* by Complicite'. In Joanna Kazik and Paulina Mirowska (eds), *Reading Subversion and Transgression*. Łódź: University of Łódź Press, pp. 105–14.

Wiśniewski, Tomasz. 2015. 'Intermingling Literary and Theatrical Conventions'. In Magda Romańska (ed.), *The Routledge Companion to Dramaturgy*. New York and London: Routledge, pp. 300–3.

Yeni, Naz. Forthcoming. 'Multiplicity in Complicite's *The Master and Margarita*'. In Tomasz Wiśniewski and Martin Blaszk (eds), *Between Page and Stage*. Gdańsk: WUG.

OTHER SOURCES

Abbott, H. Porter. 1996. *Beckett Writing Beckett. The Author in the Autograph*. Ithaca and London: Cornell University Press.

Abbott, H. Porter. 2013. *Real Mysteries: Narrative and the Unknowable*. Columbus: Ohio State UP.

Allain, Paul and Jen Harvie. 2006. *The Routledge Companion to Theatre and Performance*. London and New York: Routledge.

Aston, Elaine and George Savona. 2005. *Theatre as Sign-System: A Semiotics of Text and Performance*. London and New York: Routledge.

Attridge, Derek. 2004. *The Singularity of Literature*. London and New York: Routledge.

Bakhtin, Mikhail. 1984a. *Problems of Dostoevsky's Poetics*. Trans. by Caryl Emerson. Manchester: Manchester UP.

Bakhtin, Mikhail. 1984b. *Rabelais and His World*. Trans. by Hélène Iswolsky. Bloomington: Indiana UP.

Balcerzan, Edward. 1982. *Kręgi wtajemniczenia. Czytelnik. Badacz. Tłumacz. Pisarz*. Kraków: Wydawnictwo Literackie.

Banham, Martin (ed.). 1995. *The Cambridge Guide to Theatre*. Cambridge: Cambridge University Press.

Berger, John. 2005. *Here Is Where We Meet*. London: Bloomsbury.

Berger, John. 2008. *The Ways of Seeing*. London: Penguin.

Brater, Enoch. 2011. *Ten Ways of Thinking About Samuel Beckett*. London: Methuen Drama.

Carlson, Marvin. 1996. *Performance: A Critical Introduction*. London: Routledge.

Cuddon, J.A. (ed.). 1991. *The Penguin Dictionary of Literary Terms and Literary Theory*. London: Penguin.

Czermińska, Małgorzata. 1987. *Autobiografia powieść czyli pisarz i jego postacie*. Gdańsk: Wydawnictwo Morskie.

Czermińska, Małgorzata. 2000. *Autobiograficzny trójkąt: świadectwo, wyznanie i wyzwanie*, Kraków: Universitas.

Czermińska, Małgorzata. 2015. 'On Autobiography and the Autobiographical'. Trans. by Sebastian Zmysłowski. In *Stories for the Future. A Between Almanach for the Year 2015*: 262–9.

Degler, Janusz (ed.). 2003. *Problemy teorii dramatu i teatru*. Wrocław: Wydawnictwo Uniwersytetu Wrocławskiego.

Eco, Umberto. 1984. *Role of the Reader: Explorations in the Semiotics of Texts*. Bloomington: Indiana UP.

Eco, Umberto. 1989. *The Open Work*. Trans. by Carla Concogni. Cambridge, MA: Harvard UP.

Elam, Keir. 1980. *The Semiotics of Theatre and Drama*. London: Methuen.

Frost, Anthony and Ralph Yarrow. 2007. *Improvisation in Drama*. Basingstoke and New York: Palgrave Macmillan.

Giesekam, Greg. 2007. *Staging the Screen: The Use of Film and Video in Theatre*. Basingstoke: Palgrave Macmillan.

Głowiński, Michał. 1973. *Gry powieściowe*. Warszawa: PWN.

Hardy, G.H. 2001 [1940]. *A Mathematician's Apology*. Cambridge: Cambridge University Press.

Harvie, Jen. 2005. *Staging the UK*. Manchester: Manchester University Press.

Fischer-Lichte, Erika. 1997. *The Show and the Gaze of Theatre: A European Perspective*. Iowa City: UIP.

Hertel, Ralf and David Malcolm (eds). 2015. *On John Berger: Telling Stories*. Leiden, Boston: Brill Rodopi.

Hilton, Julian (ed.). 1993. *New Directions in Theatre*. Basingstoke: Palgrave Macmillan.

Iser, Wolfgang. 1978. *The Act of Reading: A Theory of Aesthetic Response*. Lud and Henley: Routledge and Kegan Paul.

Iser, Wolfgang. 2000. *The Range of Interpretation*. New York: Columbia UP.

Iser, Wolfgang. 2006. *How to Do Theory*. Oxford: Blackwell.

Jackson, Shannon. 2004. *Professing Performance: Theatre in the Academy from Philology to Performativity*. Cambridge: Cambridge University Press.

Jarzębski, Jerzy. 1998. 'Wstęp'. In Bruno Schulz, *Opowiadania; Wybór esejów i listów*. Wrocław: Zakład Narodowy im. Ossolińskich.

Kennedy, Dennis (ed.). 2011. *Oxford Companion to Theatre and Performance*. Oxford: Oxford University Press.

Kerrigan, Christine. 'The symbolic qualities. Different varieties of Trees'. Online.

Knowles, Ric. 2004. *Reading the Material Theatre*. Cambridge: Cambridge University Press.

Knowlson, James. 2003. *Images of Beckett*. Cambridge: Cambridge University Press.

Krafft, John M. 2012. 'Biographical Note'. In Inger H. Dalsgaard, Herman Luc and Brian McHale, *The Cambridge Companion to Thomas Pynchon*. Cambridge and New York: Cambridge University Press, pp. 9–16

Lecoq, Jacques. 2006. *Theatre of Movement and Gesture*. Ed. David Bradby. London: Methuen.

Lecoq, Jacques. 2009. *The Moving Body: Teaching Creative Theatre*. Trans. by David Bradby. London: Methuen Drama.

Lehmann, Hans-Thies. 2006. *Post-dramatic Theatre*. Trans. by Karen Jürs-Munby. London and New York: Routledge.

Lotman, Yury. 1976. *Analysis of the Poetic Text*. Ed. and trans. by D. Barton Johnson. Ann Arbor: Ardis.

Łotman, Jurij. 1999. *Kultura i eksplozja*. [*Culture and Exlosion*.] Trans. by Bogusław Żyłko. Warszawa: PIW.

Lotman, Yuri. 2001. *Universe of the Mind: A Semiotic Theory of Culture*. by Trans. Ann Shukman. Bloomington: Indiana University Press.

Lotman, Juri. 2005. 'On the semiosphere'. Trans. by Wilma Clark. *Sign Systems Studies*, 33.1: 205–29.

Limon, Jerzy. 2002. *Między niebem a sceną. Przestrzeń i czas w teatrze*. Gdańsk: słowo/obraz terytoria.

Limon, Jerzy. 2005. 'The Play-Within-The-Play: A Theoretical Perspective'. In Dariusz Pestka and Jerzy Sobieraj (eds), *Enjoying the Spectacle: Word, Image,*

Gesture. Essays in Honour of Professor Marta Wiszniowska. Toruń: UMK Press, pp. 17–32.

Limon, Jerzy. 2010. *The Chemistry of Theatre: Performativity of Time.* Basingstoke: Palgrave Macmillan.

Limon, Jerzy and Agnieszka Żukowska (eds). 2010. *Theatrical Blends. Art in the Theatre/Theatre in the Arts.* Gdańsk: słowo/obraz terytoria.

Malcolm, David. 2000. *That Impossible Thing: The British Novel 1978–1992.* Gdańsk: WUG.

Maziarczyk, Grzegorz. 2005. *The Narrative in Contemporary British Fiction. A Typological Study.* Lublin: Towarzystwo Naukowe KUL.

Mukařovský, Jan. 1970. *Wśród znaków i struktur.* Warszawa: PWN.

Murray, Simon. 2003. *Jacques Lecoq.* London: Routledge.

Ossowski, Stanisław. 1958. *U podstaw estetyki.* Warszawa: PWN.

Pavis, Patrice. 1992. *Theatre at the Crossroads of Culture.* London: Routledge.

Pavis, Patrice (ed.). 1996. *The Intercultural Performance Reader.* London: Routledge.

Pavis, Patrice. 2013. *Contemporary Mise en Scène.* Trans. by Joel Anderson. London: Routledge.

Pfister, Manfred. 1991. *The Theory and Analysis of Drama.* Trans. by John Halliday. Cambridge: Cambridge University Press.

Pickering, Kenneth. 2010. *Key Concepts in Drama and Performance.* Basingstoke: Palgrave Macmillan.

Ratajczakowa, Dobrochna. 2006. *W krysztale i w płomieniu. Studia i szkice o dramacie i teatrze.* Wrocław: WUW.

Ratajczakowa, Dobrochna. 2015. *Galeria gatunków widowiskowych, teatralnych i dramatycznych.* Poznań: Wydawnictwo Naukowe UAM.

Rebellato, Dan. 1999. *1956 and All That. The Making of Modern British Drama.* London, New York: Routledge.

Rebellato, Dan. 2009. *Theatre and Globalization.* Basingstoke: Palgrave Macmillan.

Rozik, Eli. 2008. *Generating Theatre Meaning: A Theory and Methodology of Theatre Analysis.* Brighton, Portland, Toronto: Sussex Academic Press.

Rudlin, John. 1994. *Commedia dell'Arte: An Actor's Handbook.* New York: Routledge.

Ruta-Rutkowska, Krystyna. 1999. 'Dramatyczne gry w podmiot'. *Teksty Drugie.* 1/2: 31–48.

Shank, Theodore (ed.). 1994. *Contemporary British Theatre.* Basingstoke: Macmillan.

Serpieri, Alessandro. 1989. *On the Language of Drama.* Pretoria: University of South Africa.

Sierz, Aleks. 2001. *In-Yer-Face Theatre: British Drama Today.* London: Faber and Faber.

Sinko, Grzegorz. 1982. *Opis przedstawienia teatralnego. Problem semiotyczny.* Wrocław: Ossolineum.

Skwarczyska, Stefania. 1970. *Wokół teatru i literatury. Studia i szkice.* Warszawa: PAX.

Sławińska, Irena. 1990. *Teatr w myśli współczesnej. Ku antropologii teatru.* Warszawa: PWN.

Sławińska, Irena. 2014. *Filozofia teatru. Wykłady uniwersyteckie.* Lublin: Wydawnictwo KUL.

Spindler, Konrad. 1995. *The Man in the Ice.* Trans. by Ewald Osers. London: Phoenix.

Steiner, George. 1970. *Language and Silence.* New York: Atheneum.

Steiner, George. 2002. *Grammars of Creation.* New Haven and London: Yale Nota Bene.

Steiner, George. 2003. *Lessons of the Masters.* Cambridge, MA: Harvard University Press.

Steiner, George. 2008. 'Translation as *conditio humana*'. In Harald Kittel et al. (eds), *Übersetzung Translation Traduction*, vol. 1, Berlin and New York: Walter de Gruyter.

Sugiera, Małgorzata. 2005. 'Pytania o dramat'. *Teksty Drugie.* 1/2: 60–71.

Świontek, Sławomir. 1999. *Dialog—dramat—metateatr. Z problemów teorii tekstu dramatycznego.* Warszawa: Errata.

Tynianow, Jurij. 1978. *Fakt literacki.* Warszawa: PIW.

Uspienski, Boris. 1997. *Poetyka kompozycji. Struktura tekstu artystycznego i typologia form kompozycji.* Trans. by Piotr Fast. Katowice: Śląsk.

Wiśniewski, Tomasz, David Malcolm, Monika Szuba and Żaneta Nalewajk. 2013. *The Between Almanach for the Year 2013.* Gdańsk: Maski.

Wiśniewski, Tomasz, David Malcolm, Monika Szuba and Żaneta Nalewajk. *Stories for the Future. A Between Almanach for the Year 2015.* Gdańsk: Maski.

Worthen, W.B. 2009. *Print and Poetics of Modern Drama.* Cambridge: Cambridge University Press.

Zgorzelski, Andrzej. 1999. *System i funkcja.* Gdańsk: Wydawnictwo Gdańskie.

Żyłko, Bogusław. 2009. *Semiotyka kultury.* Gdańsk: słowo/obraz terytoria.

Żyłko, Bogusław. 2011. *Kultura i znaki. Semiotyka stosowana w szkole tartusko-moskiewskiej.* Gdańsk: WUG.

INDEX[1]

---

[1] Note: Page numbers with "n" denote notes.

© The Author(s) 2016

T. Wiśniewski, *Complicite, Theatre and Aesthetics*,
DOI 10.1007/978-3-319-33443-1

Printed by Printforce, the Netherlands